Sailers and Strawbridges in America

Family History of Joseph Sailer and Mary Lowber Strawbridge

Sailers and Strawbridges in America

Family History of Joseph Sailer and Mary Lowber Strawbridge

Alexander S. White

WHITE KNIGHT PRESS
HENRICO, VIRGINIA

Published by
White Knight Press
9704 Old Club Trace
Henrico, Virginia 23238
www.whiteknightpress.com
contact@whiteknightpress.com

ISBN: 978-1-937986-80-3 (hardback)
        978-1-937986-81-0 (ebook)

To my Sailer and Strawbridge relatives, past, present, and future.

Contents

INTRODUCTION

I have had an interest in family history for most of my life, and I have gone through a few periods of digging through old documents and photos in the boxes of materials we had at home, including many items that were passed down through the family over a few generations.

The materials in those boxes were so fascinating that I felt a need to share them with other interested persons. For a few years in the 1990s, I produced the Strawbridge Family Newsletter, which included some of the more interesting photos and transcriptions of some of the old documents, especially letters.

In addition, I have maintained a family history website since 1999 (its latest address is https:// strawbridgefamily.net), and through that site and other forms of communication I have accumulated a growing collection of documents and photographs relating to my ancestors and other family members. I still feel a strong need to share some of the more interesting items with relatives and others who may be interested, and so, in order to preserve those items in a format more permanent than web pages or newsletters, I decided to produce this book.

One of the problems I faced in starting this project was to determine its scope. The documents and photos I have accumulated include materials that relate to several family lines, most notably the Whites, Sailers, and Strawbridges, along with some relatives from other family trees, such as Doughten, Lowber, Maffitt, Welsh, and West.

After consulting several resources that explain how to write a family history book, I settled on an approach that I believe will let me share as much of the information I have accumulated as possible.

I decided to discuss the family history starting with two couples from several generations past, one from the Sailer family and one from the Strawbridge family. I do not attempt to discuss all of the descendants of these two couples. Instead, I discuss those descendants of these two couples who also are ancestors of the grandchildren of Joseph Sailer and Mary Lowber Strawbridge. That group of grandchildren, which had a total of sixteen members over the years, makes up the "Sailer cousins." I am a member of that group. In this book, I mention the names of the cousins, but, with a few exceptions, I do not provide birth dates or other details about those who are living as I write the book. I provide some information about those who have died. The individuals in this group are discussed in the last section of Part A, on the Sailers.

As I discuss the members of the generations of Sailers and Strawbridges I cover, there are considerable differences in the amount of detail I include for any given person. Those differences should not be taken as indicative of how interesting or important a person was; they merely reflect the amount of information I had available for that person. My goal in this book is largely to make available the family history materials that have come into my possession, not to conduct original research for every individual in the family tree. In some cases I have done basic research to improve my understanding of a person's life, but by and large I have limited the book to presenting the information that I found in the boxes of old documents and photographs that I have received over the years.

The book is divided into two main parts, part A for the Sailers and part B for the Strawbridges. In each part, I start with the earliest ancestor who lived in America and descend through the generations from that couple. I discuss the siblings of each main person (ancestor), but not the children of those siblings. For example, Joseph Sailer, the newspaper editor who lived from 1809 to 1883, had seven children: Louisa, Randolph, Morris, Sarah ("Sallie"), John, Isaac, and Franklin. Several of those children had children of their own. However, I do not discuss, or even mention, those children, except in passing in one or two instances. Instead, from that group, I discuss only on the children of John Sailer (1840–1913), who was the father of my grandfather, Joseph.

I have used a numbering system to help identify each person within the proper generation. Each person within each of the two sections of the book has a unique identifying number, from 1 to 50 for the Sailers and 1 to 30 for the Strawbridges. When a person who is in the ancestral line I am following has children, each of those children is assigned a lower-case Roman numeral, ranging from i to xii, as needed. Those numbers indicate the birth order of the children in that family.

When a person has a plus sign (+) to the left of his or her name, that means that that person's full information is included in the next chapter, because that person had children or otherwise needs to be discussed in more detail. For a person with no plus sign to the left of the name, all information I have is included with the discussion in which that person first appears. In most cases, the individuals with plus signs by their names are those who had children, although there are a few exceptions to that rule.

The superscript number after a person's first or middle name, such as John^2 Strawbridge, indicates which generation that person is from, with the first generation being that of the first ancestor included in this book. Those numbers should not be confused with the footnote reference numbers, which are generally placed in the text after statements of fact, and not after people's names. In the list of children of a couple, only the first child has the generation number; all other children in the list have the same number, but it is not shown.

The names in italics and parentheses after a person's name indicate the lineage of that person, descending from the first-generation ancestor. Note that, if a name in parentheses is not in italics, that name is a nickname, alternate name, or married name, not part of an ancestral line.

For example, the following portion of an entry in the Sailer section of the book illustrates a few of the principles mentioned above:

39. WILLIAM WILSON^6 WHITE JR. (*Mary White^5, Joseph^4, John^3, Joseph^2, Wilhelm^1*) was born in Philadelphia on 18 April 1934.

The number 39 is William's unique identifying number, and the names in italics, with superscript generation numbers, indicate his Sailer ancestry: the first-generation ancestor was Wilhelm Sailer, followed by Joseph Sailer of the second generation, John of the third, and so forth. His immediate Sailer ancestor was his mother, born Mary Lowber Sailer but shown as Mary White. The superscript 6 after his middle name indicates that he was from the sixth generation of Sailers discussed in this book.

Although my general practice is to cite both the city and state, and sometimes also the county, for a location, because so many of the people in this book are associated with Philadelphia, Pennsylvania, I have omitted the name of the state, and just listed the location as Philadelphia wherever it applies.

The chart below is intended to provide an overview of the Sailer and Strawbridge lines of descent that are discussed in this book. It includes information about some individuals who are not discussed in the book. That information has not been verified or documented, but it is believed to be generally accurate.

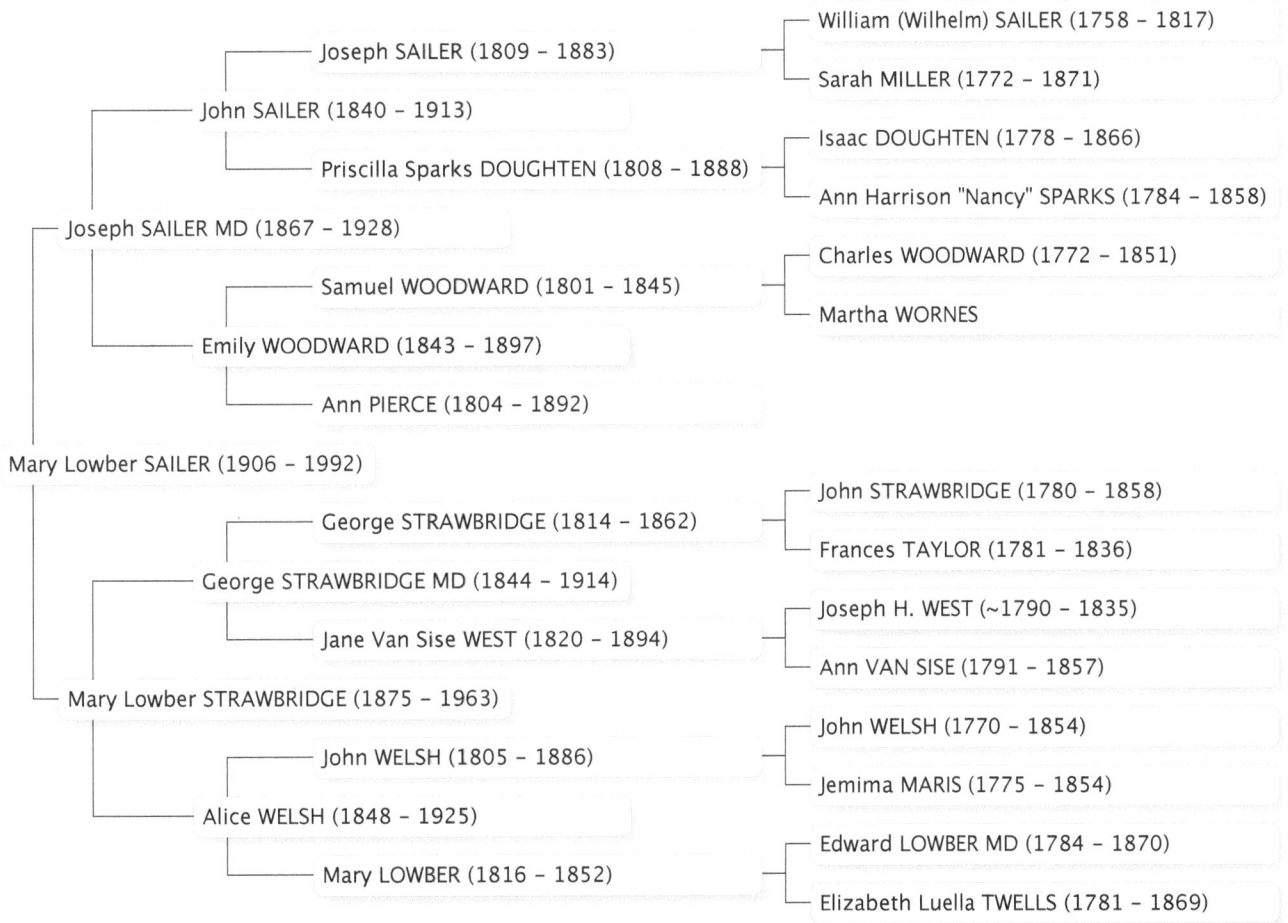

```
                                                                          ┌── William (Wilhelm) SAILER (1758 – 1817)
                         ┌────── Joseph SAILER (1809 – 1883) ──┤
                         │                                      └── Sarah MILLER (1772 – 1871)
              John SAILER (1840 – 1913) ──┤
              │                           │                                ┌── Isaac DOUGHTEN (1778 – 1866)
              │                           └──── Priscilla Sparks DOUGHTEN (1808 – 1888) ──┤
              │                                                            └── Ann Harrison "Nancy" SPARKS (1784 – 1858)
   Joseph SAILER MD (1867 – 1928) ──┤
   │                                │                                      ┌── Charles WOODWARD (1772 – 1851)
   │                                │      ┌───── Samuel WOODWARD (1801 – 1845) ──┤
   │                                │      │                               └── Martha WORNES
   │                    Emily WOODWARD (1843 – 1897) ──┤
   │                                       │
   │                                       └───── Ann PIERCE (1804 – 1892)
Mary Lowber SAILER (1906 – 1992) ──┤
   │                                                                       ┌── John STRAWBRIDGE (1780 – 1858)
   │                       ┌────── George STRAWBRIDGE (1814 – 1862) ──┤
   │                       │                                          └── Frances TAYLOR (1781 – 1836)
   │          George STRAWBRIDGE MD (1844 – 1914) ──┤
   │          │                           │                                ┌── Joseph H. WEST (~1790 – 1835)
   │          │                           └───── Jane Van Sise WEST (1820 – 1894) ──┤
   │          │                                                           └── Ann VAN SISE (1791 – 1857)
   └── Mary Lowber STRAWBRIDGE (1875 – 1963) ──┤
              │                                                            ┌── John WELSH (1770 – 1854)
              │               ┌────── John WELSH (1805 – 1886) ──┤
              │               │                                  └── Jemima MARIS (1775 – 1854)
              └── Alice WELSH (1848 – 1925) ──┤
                              │                                            ┌── Edward LOWBER MD (1784 – 1870)
                              └───── Mary LOWBER (1816 – 1852) ──┤
                                                                          └── Elizabeth Luella TWELLS (1781 – 1869)
```

Sailer and Strawbridge Ancestors of Mary Lowber Sailer (White) (Knight)

PART A: THE SAILERS

The First Generation

1. WILHELM[1] (WILLIAM) SAILER was born on 6 August 1758, possibly in Cumberland, New Jersey. His father may have been born in Germany.[1] Wilhelm died on or about 28 September 1817 at Clarksboro, Gloucester County, New Jersey.[2] He married, first, in about 1784, JANE, last name possibly REMSON, born possibly 9 May 1756 in New York and died before 1797 in New Jersey.

WILHELM married, second, on 20 April 1797[3], SARAH MILLER, who was born 22 November 1772 and died 27 March 1871 in Clarksboro, Gloucester County, New Jersey.[4]

> Mrs. Sarah M. Sailer, widow of William Sailer, died at Clarksboro, Gloucester county, N.J., on the 27th inst., in the 100th year of her age. Mrs. S. was married at 26, was twenty years a wife and fifty-four years a widow. She was the mother of ten children, the first seven of whom were sons. The seventh, Mr. Joseph Sailer, has been for over thirty-four years connected with journalism in this city.
>
> But five of her children (four sons and one daughter) survive her. Besides these, she leaves thirty-seven grandchildren, sixty great-grandchildren, and three great-great-grandchildren, aggregating one hundred and five descendants living at the time of her death. Until within a few years all her mental faculties were unimpaired. Mrs. Sailer was a woman of industrious habits, great energy of character, and devotedly attached to her children.[5]

---

1   *New Jersey, Births and Christenings Index, 1660–1931*, online database at ancestry.com, citing Family History Library (FHL) film no. 820016. This index entry shows Wilhelm Seiler, born 6 Aug 1758, Christening date 24 June 1759, father Zacharius Seiler, mother Maria. Wilhelm's father probably came from Germany, possibly the area of Wurttemberg. Some unverified records at ancestry.com show Wilhelm's parents as Zacariah Sailor, born in Wurttemberg, living 1729–1810, and Anna Maria Waggoner, born in New Jersey, living 1732-1813.

2   *New Jersey, Abstract of Wills, 1670–1817, Vol. XLII, Abstract of Wills, 1814–1817*, online database at ancestry.com. A record from 29 Sep 1817 shows the inventory of the estate of William Sailor of Greenwich Township, Gloucester County, New Jersey. Inventory amounted to $3,468.00; inventory made by Joseph V. Clark and Matthew Gill, Jr., and sworn to by Sarah M. Sailor and William Sailer, Administrators, on 3 October 1817.

3   Craig, H. Stanley, *Gloucester County, New Jersey, Marriage Records* (Merchantville, New Jersey, 1930), 250. In section headed Marriage Register of Jeffrey Clark, Esq., J.P., record shows Sailor, Wm., and Sarah Miller, 4-20-1797.

4   *Cemeteries*, online database at gchsnj.org, Gloucester County Historical Society, viewed on 26 March 2019. Data shows Sarah M. Sailer, born 22 Nov 1772, died 27 Mar 1871, buried at Mickleton Friend's Burial Ground, Upper Greenwich, New Jersey, citing *Misc. Gloucester County Cemeteries*, vol. 1.

5   "Aged Lady Deceased," *The Philadelphia Inquirer*, 30 March 1871, p. 2.

William and Sarah at various times managed the "Death-of-the-Fox" inn or tavern, located at 217 Kings Highway, in Mount Royal, New Jersey. Figure 1 shows this building on the left as it appeared in a photo on Google Maps in 2014; on the right it is shown as it appeared when photographed in a historic American buildings survey in the 1930s.[6] (It is now a private residence, no longer an inn.) The building was first used as a tavern in about 1727. William Sailer was the proprietor from about 1811 to 1813, then operated a different tavern for a while. He reopened the Death-of-the-Fox Inn in about 1817, but died later that year. Within a few years after his death, his widow, Sarah Sailer, was granted a license to operate the inn, which she apparently did until at least 1832.[7]

Figure 1. Death-of-the-Fox-Tavern. Left, as it Appeared in 2014; Right, as it Appeared in the 1930s

Children of Wilhelm[1] Sailer and Jane (Remson?) Sailer:

2. i. WILLIAM[2] SAILER JR. was born about 1785 and died at Woodbury, Gloucester County, New Jersey, on 19 October 1822.[8] He married, at Gloucester County, New Jersey, on 10 January 1811,[9] ACHSAH HARKER, who was born about 1789 and died in Woodbury, Gloucester County, New Jersey, on 27 July 1865.[10]

3. ii. JOHN SAILER was born about 1789.[11]

Children of Wilhelm[1] Sailer and Sarah (Miller) Sailer:

4. iii. JOHN MILLER SAILER was born on 18 Jan 1798[12] and died on 5 March 1864.[13] He married, first, at Gloucester County, New Jersey, on 10 June 1819, SUSANNA T. WOOD, who was born possibly 7 March 1800 in Gloucester County and died possibly 14 February 1826.[14] He married, second, at Clarksboro,

---

6   Left image: Copyright © 2019 Google; right image: downloaded from Library of Congress at https://www.loc.gov/resource/hhh. nj0518.photos. Photograph from Historic American Buildings Survey number HABS NJ-231.
7   "History of 'Death of Ye Fox Inn' Death of the Fox Tavern," online article at nj.searchroots.com/EG/deathoffox.htm.
8   New Jersey Deaths and Burials Index, 1798–1971, online database viewed at ancestry.com, citing FHL film number 543522, shows William Sailer, date of death 20 October 1822, at Woodbury, New Jersey.
9   New Jersey, Marriage Records, 1670–1965, online database viewed at ancestry.com, citing FHL film number 1001862, shows Ackey Harker married William Sailor, Jr., at Gloucester, New Jersey, on 10 January 1811.
10   New Jersey Deaths and Burials Index, citing FHL film number 584565, shows Achsah Sailer, born about 1789, died 27 July 1865 in Woodbury, Gloucester County, New Jersey.
11   No documentary information has been found to support his birth date and nothing is known about his death date. The birth information has been reported on several family trees submitted to ancestry.com, without source information.
12   1850 U.S. Federal Census, Spring Garden Ward 3 Precinct 2, Philadelphia, roll M432_818, p. 43A, line 16, viewed at ancestry.com, image 85; 1860 U.S. Federal Census, Philadelphia Ward 19, Philadelphia, roll M653_1170, page 648, line 30, viewed at ancestry.com, image 650.
13   Pennsylvania and New Jersey, Church and Town Records, 1669–2013, Pennsylvania, Philadelphia, Episcopal, Church of the Messiah, online database viewed at ancestry.com. Church burial register, page 463, shows John M. Sailer died 5 March 1864, age 67, buried in Lafayette Cemetery.
14   Certificates of Gloucester County, online database at gchsnj.org, viewed on 5 April 2019. Certificate shows Susannah T. Wood married John M. Sailer on 10 June 1819. Birth and death dates of Susannah T. Wood are unverified.

Gloucester County, New Jersey, on 28 August 1828,[15] ANN C. ALBERTUS, who was born about 1805 in Burlington County, New Jersey,[16] and died 17 April 1889 in Deptford Township, Gloucester County, New Jersey[17].

5. iv. JAMES SAILER was born in 1799 and died on 6 April 1889.[18] He married, first, at Gloucester County, New Jersey, on 17 November 1824,[19] FRANCES B. WARE, who was born 12 December 1803 and died 7 November 1833[20]. He married, second, at Gloucester County, New Jersey, on 30 August 1837,[21] CHARLOTTE GABR, who was born in about 1809[22] and died 6 September 1862 at Philadelphia.[23]

6. v. SAMUEL SAILER was born on 2 January 1802 and died on or about 13 February 1849.[24] He married, at Gloucester County, New Jersey, on 6 February 1834,[25] MARY ANN PAUL, who was born 10 December 1810,[26] and died 17 May 1893 at Philadelphia.[27]

7. vi. BOWMAN SAILER was born on 20 May 1804 and died on 6 December 1885 in Washington, D.C. He married, in New Jersey about 1826, ANNIE C. COX, who was born on 29 December 1804 in New Jersey and died on 6 December 1885 in Washington, D.C.[28]

As noted above, both Bowman Sailer and his wife, Annie, died on 6 December 1885. A contemporary newspaper article explained the reason:

---

15   New Jersey Marriage Records, 1670–1965, online database viewed at ancestry.com, citing FHL film no. 1543466. Record shows Ann Albertus married John M. Sailer on 28 August 1828 at Clarksboro.
16   1860 U.S. Federal Census, Ward 19, Philadelphia, Roll M653_1170, Page 648, viewed at ancestry.com. This census sheet shows John Sailer, age 60, with Ann Sailer, age 55, and others.
17   New Jersey Deaths and Burials Index, citing FHL film no. 589315. This record shows Ann C. Sailer, born about 1808, died 17 April 1889 at Deptford, widowed.
18   Pennsylvania and New Jersey Church and Town Records, Philadelphia, Family History, D.H. Brown and Sons. Funeral home register shows James Sailer, in 90th year of age, residence 1128 S. 10th St., buried in Lafayette Cemetery. Date given as 6 April 1889; not specified as death or burial date. In same database, Burials register of Church of St. John the Evangelist (Episcopal), page 220, shows death of James Sailer, age 90 years, on 6 April 1889, burial 9 April.
19   New Jersey Marriage Records, citing FHL film number 1543528, showing marriage of Frances Ware and James Sailor on 17 November 1824.
20   Online image at findagrave.com/memorial/128081274; photo of gravestone shows Frances B. Sailer, born 12 December 1803, died 7 November 1833; Pennsylvania and New Jersey Church and Town Records, Woolwich, New Jersey, Trinity Episcopal Church, Baptisms register shows baptism 8 January 1809 of Francis B. Ware, child of Mary and John Ware, born 12 December 1803.
21   New Jersey Marriage Records, citing FHL film number 1543471, showing Charlotte Gabr married James Sailer at Gloucester, New Jersey, on 30 August 1837.
22   1850 U.S. Federal Census, Southwark Ward 5, Philadelphia, Roll M432_362, Page 362, showing James Sailor, age 50, Charlotte Sailor, age 40, and others.
23   Online image of death certificate for Charlotte Sailer, viewed at ancestry.com on 8 April 2019; uploaded to a family tree by username cburton45c1. Certificate shows Charlotte Sailer, age 52, born in New Jersey, died 6 September 1862 at Philadelphia. Burial in Lafayette Cemetery.
24   Online memorial, with no images, at findagrave.com/memorial/142944844. Information at site says Samuel Sailer was born 2 January 1802 at Gloucester County, New Jersey, and died 8 February 1849 at Clarksboro; New Jersey Deaths and Burials Index, citing FHL film number 1543564. Record shows Samuel Sailer, born about 1802, died 13 February 1849.
25   New Jersey Marriage Records, citing FHL film number 1001862, showing Samuel Sailer married Mary Ann Paul in Gloucester County, New Jersey, on 6 February 1834.
26   U.S., Quaker Meeting Records, 1681–1935, New Jersey, Gloucester, Woodbury Monthly Meeting, Minutes, 1884–1935, database online, citing Swarthmore College, Swarthmore, Pennsylvania, Collection: Quaker Meeting Records, call number RG2/Ph/W6/3.2, viewed at ancestry.com on 29 March 2019. Register shows birth of Mary Ann Paul to Delia Paul on 10 Dec 1810.
27   New Jersey Deaths and Burials Index, citing FHL film number 1001894. Record shows Mary Ann Sailer, born about 1811, death date 17 May 1893; Cemeteries, online database at gchsnj.org, citing Misc. Gloucester Cemeteries, vol. 4, viewed on 29 March 2019, shows Mary Ann Sailer, died 17 May 1893, aged 83 years, 3 months, 7 days, buried in Mickleton Friends Burying Ground, Mickleton, New Jersey.
28   1850 U.S. Federal Census, Township of Deptford, Gloucester County, New Jersey, Roll M432_451, Page 79B, showing Bowman Sailer, age 46, Surrogate, born in New Jersey, and others; online image at findagrave.com/memorial/86715144; photo of gravestone shows Bowman Sailer, born 20 May 1804, died 4 Dec 1885, and Ann Sailer, born 29 December 1804, died 4 December 1885.

THEY DIED TOGETHER

An Aged Couple, Formerly Philadelphians,

Die from Suffocation

The death is announced of Mr. and Mrs. Bowman Sailer, formerly of this city, in Georgetown, D.C., where they have resided for some years. Mr. Sailer was in the eighty-second year of his age, and his wife, to whom he had been united for many years, was over seventy. The aged couple were found dead in bed yesterday morning, and investigation showed that their unexpected death was due to suffocation. Whether from coal or burning gas had not transpired at last accounts. They had retired the evening before in their usual health.

Mr. Sailer was a brother of the late Joseph Sailer, of this city, and consequently uncle to Isaac D. Sailer, and to the late Randolph Sailer, formerly with Powers & Weightman's Chemical Works. The deceased was formerly in business in this city as a coal merchant, his office being at Fifth and Willow Streets. He was a member of the Society of Friends, as are many of the Sailer family, who are still settled in the vicinity of Gloucester, N.J., where years ago quite a number of families of the name resided.[29]

8. vii. THOMAS SAILER was born on 7 June 1806 and died on 8 June 1885.[30] He married, at Gloucester County, New Jersey, on 1 November 1832,[31] HANNAH MOORE, who was born 3 October 1810 and died 12 December 1888.[32]

9. viii. GEORGE SAILER was born in or about 1808 and died soon afterward in infancy.[33]

+ 10. ix. JOSEPH SAILER was born on 23 April 1809 and died on 15 January 1883. He married PRISCILLA SPARKS DOUGHTEN.

---

29   *The Philadelphia Inquirer*, 7 December 1885, p. 2.

30   Philadelphia, Death Certificates Index, online database at ancestry.com, citing Death Records housed at Philadelphia City Archives, FHL Film Number 2070483. Record shows Thomas Sailer, birth date about 1806 in New Jersey, died 8 June 1885 in Philadelphia, age 79, burial date 10 June; occupation physician, married; U.S. Quaker Meeting Records, Records of Deaths of the Monthly Meeting, showing Thomas Sailer, M.D., born 6 mo. 7 1806, died 6 mo. 8 1885, age 79 years, 1 day.

31   New Jersey, Marriage Records, 1670–1965, database online viewed at ancestry.com, citing FHL film number 1001862.

32   U.S. Quaker Meeting Records, Records of Deaths of the Monthly Meeting, showing Hannah Sailer, widow of Dr. Thomas Sailer, born 10 mo. 3 1810, died 12 mo. 12 1888, aged 78 years, 2 mos., 9 days.

33   No documentary information has been found to support his birth or death date. The information has been reported on several family trees submitted to ancestry.com, without source information.

11. x. SARAH W. SAILER was born on 9 October 1811[34] and died on 1 January 1894.[35] She married, between 1856 and 1860,[36] JAMES TAGGART, who was born about 1805 and died on 30 July 1886 in East Greenwich, Gloucester, New Jersey[37].

12. xi. JOSHUA SAILER was born in 1812 and died in infancy that year.[38]

13. xii. MARY SAILER was born about 1817 and died on 23 April 1856.[39] She married, at Gloucester County, New Jersey, on 20 November 1842,[40] JAMES TAGGART, who was born about 1805 and died on 30 July 1886 in East Greenwich, Gloucester County, New Jersey.

---

34   1850 U.S. Federal Census, Greenwich Township, Gloucester County, New Jersey, Roll M432_451, Page 103, shows Sarah Sailer, age 38, with James Taggart, age 41, and others; 1880 U.S. Federal Census, Greenwich Township, Gloucester County, New Jersey, Roll T9_781, FHL Film Number 1254781, page 341.1000, shows Sarah Taggart, age 69.

35   Online image at findagrave.com/memorial/168684130; photo of gravestone shows Sarah Taggart, wife of James Taggart, born 9 October 1811, died 1 January 1894; New Jersey Deaths and Burials Index, citing FHL Film Number 589796, shows Sarah Taggart, born about 1812, died 1 January 1894, in Woodbury, Gloucester County, New Jersey; says her father was born in Germany, mother born in United States.

36   I have not found an official record of this marriage, but it appears to have taken place between 1856 and 1860. James Taggart was first married to Mary Sailer, a younger sister of Sarah, as is discussed below. Mary died in April 1856. In the next census, James Taggart, age 55, was living with Sallie Taggart, age 48, along with his children by Mary. 1860 U.S. Federal Census, Greenwich Township, Gloucester County, New Jersey, Roll M653_691, Page 110. Also, as noted above, Sarah's last name is shown as Taggart on her gravestone and in the New Jersey Deaths and Burials index.

37   New Jersey Deaths and Burials Index, citing FHL film number 589308, shows Jas Taggart, born about 1805, died 30 July 1886 at East Greenwich, Gloucester County, New Jersey, at age 81 years 5 months; occupation farmer; married; Deaths, online database at gchsnj.org, viewed on 11 Apr 2019, shows last name Taggart, age 82 years, died 30 July 1886 at Clarksboro, New Jersey, citing Woodbury Constitution newspaper of 4 August 1886.

38   No documentary information has been found to support his birth or death date. The information has been reported on several family trees submitted to ancestry.com, without source information.

39   1850 U.S. Federal Census, Greenwich Township, Gloucester County, New Jersey, Roll M432_451, Page 103, shows Mary Taggart, age 34, in household with James Taggart and others; New Jersey Deaths and Burials Index, citing FHL film number 584565, shows Mary Taggart (Mary Sailer), born about 1817 in Clarksboro, died 23 April 1856 in Clarksboro.

40   New Jersey Marriage Records, citing FHL film number 864905, shows James Taggart married Mary M. Sailor on 20 November, 1842. This is the same James Taggart who later married Mary's older sister, Sarah, in the late 1850s, as discussed above.

The Second Generation

10. JOSEPH[2] SAILER (*Wilhelm*[1]) was born on 23 April 1809 in Clarksboro, Gloucester County, New Jersey, and died in Philadelphia on 15 January 1883. He was buried in Woodlands Cemetery, Philadelphia.[41] He married, at Gloucester County, New Jersey, on 1 April 1830,[42] PRISCILLA SPARKS DOUGHTEN, who was born in New Jersey on 3 November 1808 and died in Philadelphia on 22 January 1888,[43] daughter of Isaac Doughten and Ann Harrison "Nancy" Sparks.

Not much appears to be known about Joseph's early life in Gloucester County, New Jersey. He is said to have trained as a printer, and in the 1830s was publisher and owner of a newspaper in Woodbury. In 1839, he moved to Philadelphia.[44] There, he started a newspaper called the *Spirit of the Times*. In July 1840, he began working as financial editor of the *Public Ledger* newspaper in Philadelphia. He remained in that position for about forty-two years; it was reported that every issue of the paper during that time included material written by Joseph Sailer.[45]

In a detailed profile written not long before his death, he was called "the pioneer of the 'money article' feature in journalism." The profile said:

> His intimacy with J. Edgar Thomson, Colonel Scott, John Tucker, Asa Packer, Jay Cooke, Franklin B. Gowen and other noted financiers and railroad kings is accepted as a strong proof of the weight which his judgment in money affairs had, and it is said that no great financial enterprise was ever carried out by those men without first taking Mr. Sailer into their confidence, getting his opinion on the subject and through him communicating so much of the scheme as was advisable to the public. His judgment on investments was regarded as next to infallible, and a comfortable fortune, acquired through a common-sense use of his money, bears evidence of the correctness of this estimate of his financial shrewdness.[46]

Children of Joseph[2] Sailer and Priscilla Sparks (Doughten) Sailer:

---

41   1850 U.S. Federal Census, Southwark Ward 4, Philadelphia, Roll M432_822, Page 268, showing Joseph Sailer, age 41, Editor, with wife Priscilla and children; Philadelphia Death Certificates Index, citing FHL film number 1003709, shows Joseph Sailer, newspaper editor born about 1810 in New Jersey, died 15 January 1883 in Philadelphia; "Death of a Veteran Editor," *Monmouth [N.J.] Democrat*, 25 January 1883, p. 2, viewed at newspapers.com, reporting death of Joseph Sailer in Philadelphia on 15 January; online image at findagrave.com/memorial/88476282; photo of gravestone shows Joseph Sailer, born 23 April 1809, died 15 January 1883.

42   Marriages, online database at gchsnj.org, viewed on 11 April 2019, shows marriage of Joseph Sailer and Priscilla L. [sic] Doughten in Gloucester County on 1 April 1830, with certificate recorded and filed on 2 April 1830.

43   Online image at findagrave.com/memorial/88476282; photo of gravestone shows Priscilla S., wife of Joseph Sailer, born 3 November 1808, died 22 January 1888; 1850 U.S. Federal Census, Southwark Ward 4, Philadelphia, Roll M432_822, Page 268, shows Joseph Sailer with wife Priscilla, age 41. "Mrs. Joseph Sailer Dead," *The Times* (Philadelphia), 24 January 1888, p. 2.

44   Bower, Henry, *A Memoir of Randolph Sailer* (Second Ed., Philadelphia: Smith, English & Co. 1871) 1.

45   "Death of a Veteran Editor," *Monmouth (New Jersey) Democrat*, 25 January 1883, p. 5.

46   "A Veteran Editor," *Philadelphia Times*, 27 August 1882, p. 5.

14. i. LOUISA[3] SAILER was born in New Jersey on 16 January 1831 and died in Philadelphia on 31 December 1916.[47] She married, in Gloucester County, New Jersey, on 12 January 1852,[48] DANIEL NEHR MALSEED, who was born on 2 April 1829 in Philadelphia, and died on 3 February 1891 in Philadelphia,[49] son of John Malseed and Mary McDonald.

15. ii. RANDOLPH SAILER was born in Gloucester County, New Jersey, on 24 May 1833 and died in Philadelphia, on 22 January 1869.[50] He married, in Philadelphia, on 1 May 1866,[51] JOSEPHINE PILE, who was born on 14 August 1841 and died on 6 March 1929,[52] daughter of Wilson H. Pile and Jeanette F. Schultz.

Although Randolph died in 1869 at the age of thirty-five, he made a great impression on people he associated with. One of them published a memoir of Randolph's life that was reissued in 1871 in a second edition.[53] This book, about 144 pages long, provides a glowing portrait of a man who was a brilliant student with great warmth and strength of character. It includes a portrait of Randolph, shown below.

47   1860 U.S. Federal Census, Ward 3, Philadelphia, Roll M653_1153, page 142, FHL film number 805153, shows Daniel Malseed, age 31, with Louisa Malseed, age 29, and others; 1880 U.S. Federal Census, District 43, Philadelphia, Roll 1167, page 179B, shows Daniel Malseed, age 51, with Louisa Malseed, age 49, and others; Pennsylvania, Death Certificates, 1906–1966, online database at ancestry.com, certificate no. 132901 shows Louisa Sailer Malseed, born in New Jersey on 16 January 1831, father's name Joseph Sailer, mother's maiden name Priscilla Doughten, died 31 December 1916, burial 4 January 1917 at Woodlands Cemetery.

48   New Jersey Marriage Records, citing FHL film number 1001859.

49   1860 U.S. Federal Census, Ward 3, Philadelphia, Roll M653_1153, Page 142, FHL film number 805153, shows Daniel Malseed, age 31, and others; 1880 U.S. Federal Census, District 43, Philadelphia, Roll 1167, Page 179B, NARA Pub. T9, shows Daniel Malseed, age 51; online image at findagrave.com/memorial/88211048; photo of gravestone shows Daniel L. Malseed, 2 April 1829–3 February 1891; "Death Notices," The Philadelphia Times, 7 February 1891, p. 5, reporting sudden death of Daniel Malseed.

50   1850 U.S. Federal Census, Southwark Ward 4, Philadelphia, Roll M432_822, Page 268, showing Randolph Sailer, age 17, in household of Joseph Sailer; online image at findagrave.com/memorial/98809093; photo of gravestone shows Randolph Sailer, 24 May 1833–22 January 1869; Philadelphia Death Certificates Index, citing FHL film number 1994246, shows Randolph Sailer, born about 1834 in Woodbury, New Jersey, died 22 January 1869 in Philadelphia, buried in Woodlands Cemetery; Pennsylvania and New Jersey, Church and Town Records, 1669–2013, online database at ancestry.com, Woodlands Cemetery Register of Internments, shows interment of Randolph Sailer, age 35, on 25 January 1869.

51   U.S., Presbyterian Church Records, 1701–1970, online database at ancestry.com, citing Presbyterian Historical Society, Philadelphia, Third Presbyterian Church Philadelphia_Register_Baptisms, Marriages, Deaths_1794–1955, accession number V M146 P54rg; image of church register shows marriage of Randolph Sailer and Josephine Pile on 1 May 1866.

52   U.S. Passport Applications, 1795–1925, online database at ancestry.com, citing Roll 263, 1 Apr 1884–30 Apr 1884. Application by Josephine Sailer dated 4 April 1884 says she was born in Philadelphia on 14 August 1842; 1860 U.S. Federal Census, Ward 3, Philadelphia, Roll M653, Page 240, shows Josephine Pile, age 19, in household of Wilson H. Pile; online image at findagrave.com/memorial/98809093; photo of gravestone shows Josephine Sailer, 14 August 1841–6 March 1929.

53   Bower, Henry, A Memoir of Randolph Sailer (Philadelphia: Smith, English & Co., 2d ed 1871), available through Google Books at https://books.google.com/books?id=kH5BAAAAYAAJ&pg=PP1#v=onepage&q&f=false.

Figure 2. Randolph Sailer

Randolph Sailer grew up in Philadelphia, did well in school, and graduated with honors from the University of Pennsylvania in July 1857. He then enrolled in the Union Theological Seminary in New York, having developed a strong interest in religion. He did well in his studies, but he developed serious eye problems, which made it difficult to read, and he had to drop out of the seminary in 1859.

Randolph eventually returned to Philadelphia and worked as a traveling representative for Powers & Weightman, a major chemical manufacturing company. One of the founders of that company was Thomas H. Powers, who had employed Randolph when Randolph was younger, and after whom Randolph and his wife named their only child, Thomas Henry Powers Sailer.

In January 1869, Randolph walked to a prayer meeting on a rainy evening and afterwards was stricken with pneumonia. He died after about ten days, on January 22.

16. iii. MORRIS C. SAILER was born on 28 June 1835 and died in Camden, New Jersey, on 7 February 1873.[54] He married, in Gloucester County, New Jersey, on 23 September 1859,[55] MARY C. LEE, who was born about 1839 in Pennsylvania and died after 1879, daughter of Ralph Lee and Rachael.[56]

17. iv. SARAH ANN "SALLIE" SAILER was born in Philadelphia on 22 November 1837 and died in Philadelphia on 7 September, 1917.[57] She did not marry, but lived close to some of her relatives, who visited her often.

---

54   1860 U.S. Federal Census, Camden North Ward, Camden, New Jersey, Roll M653_686, Page 538, shows Morris C. Sailor living in household of Ralph Lee and working as clerk in railroad office, the household of the parents of his new wife, Mary Cecelia Lee. Census form says Morris was born in Pennsylvania. 1870 U.S. Federal Census, Camden North Ward, Camden, New Jersey, Roll M593 _856, Page 725A, shows Morris Sailer, age 34, as head of household, with Mary C. Sailer as his wife. This form says he was born in New Jersey. Online image at findagrave.com/memorial/98909048; photo of gravestone shows Morris C. Sailer, 28 June 1835–7 Feb 1873. New Jersey Deaths and Burials Index, citing FHL film number 584594, shows Morris C. Sailer, born about 1835 at Philadelphia, died 7 February 1873 at Camden County, New Jersey; clerk; married.

55   New Jersey Marriage Records, citing FHL film number 846905, shows Morris C. Sailer, bookkeeper, of Philadelphia, PA, married Mary C. Lee of Camden, NJ, in Gloucester County, New Jersey, on 23 September 1859.

56   1860 U.S. Federal Census, Camden North Ward, Camden, New Jersey, Roll M653_686, Page 538, shows Morris C. Sailor living in household with his wife, Mary Cecelia Sailor, age 21. 1870 U.S. Federal Census, Camden North Ward, Camden, New Jersey, Roll M593 _856, Page 725A, shows Morris Sailer, age 34, as head of household, with Mary C. Sailer, age 32, as his wife.

57   1850 U.S. Federal Census, Southwark Ward 4, Philadelphia, Roll M432_822, Page 268, shows Sarah Ann Sailer, age 13, in household of Joseph Sailer. 1910 U.S. Federal Census, 907 Pine Street, Ward 7, District 89, Philadelphia, Roll T624_1389, Page 38, shows Sarah A. Sailer, head of household, age 72, with Sarah Sailer, cousin, age 73. Online image at findagrave.com/memorial/88476282; photo of gravestone shows Sarah A. Sailer, 22 November 1837–7 September 1917. Pennsylvania, Death Certificates, 1906–1966, database online, ancestry.com, certificate number range: 104501–107800. Certificate number 104764 records death of Sarah Ann Sailer, birth date 22

There are a few references to visits to "Aunt Sallie" in the discussions of the family of Joseph Sailer, M.D., later in this book.

+ 18. v. JOHN SAILER was born in Philadelphia on 6 September 1840 and died in Scarborough, Cumberland County, Maine, on 13 July 1913. He married EMILY WOODWARD.

19. vi. ISAAC DOUGHTEN SAILER was born in Philadelphia on 4 April 1843 and died in Orlando, Florida, on 6 March 1917.[58] He married, first, in Washington, D.C., on 27 September 1866,[59] LUCIA R. CROSBY, who was born about 1845, probably in Delaware County, Pennsylvania, and died in Philadelphia about 3 June 1931, daughter of Edward Crosby and Amanda Berry.[60] Isaac and Lucia were divorced in about 1883.[61] He married, second, in Philadelphia in 1886,[62] HANNAH BLANCHE LEIBMAN, who was born in Pennsylvania on 6 November 1864 and died in Philadelphia on 1 December 1925, daughter of Leon Leibman and Marie Bechtel.[63]

20. vii. FRANKLIN DOUGHTEN SAILER was born in Philadelphia on 24 September 1845 and died in Philadelphia on 22 March 1923.[64] He married, in Philadelphia on 6 October 1870,[65] ANNA REISKY, who was born in Philadelphia on 28 December 1847 and died in Philadelphia on 19 April 1892, daughter of James and Isabella Reisky.[66]

November 1837, date of death 7 September 1917. Certificate signed by Joseph Sailer, M.D., her nephew. She was buried in Woodlands Cemetery.

58   1880 U.S. Federal Census, District 16, Philadelphia, Roll 1170, Page 33D, shows Isaac D. Sailer, age 36, in household of Joseph Sailer, occupation clerk. Letter, Isaac Doughten Sailer to Adjutant General, U.S. Army, Washington, D.C., 20 June 1861, accepting army commission and stating that he was born in Philadelphia on 4 April 1843; viewed online at fold3.com in collection, Letters Received by the Adjutant General, 1861–1870. Online image at findagrave.com/memorial/98807729; photo of gravestone shows Isaac D. Sailer, 4 April 1843–6 March 1917. "Died," *The Philadelphia Inquirer*, 10 March 1917, p. 7, brief notice of the death of Isaac D. Sailer, age 73, in Orlando, Florida, on 6 March.

59   District of Columbia, Marriage Records, 1810–1953, online database at ancestry.com, citing FHL film number 2079252, shows Lucia R. Crosby married Isaac D. Sailer on 27 September 1866.

60   1850 U.S. Federal Census, Township of Chester, Delaware County, Pennsylvania, Roll M432_776, Page 84B, shows Lucia Crosby, age 5, born in Pennsylvania, in household of Edward and Amanda Crosby. "Mrs. Lucia C. Sailer" [death notice], Delaware County Times, 10 June 1931, p. 8, reporting funeral held in St. Paul's Protestant Episcopal Church for Mrs. Lucia Crosby Sailer, age 86, who died in hospital in Philadelphia. Item says she was "a member of the Old Crosby family, which occupied the same house in Irvington, on the outskirts of the city, for five generations."

61   "Legal Notices," *The Philadelphia Inquirer*, 10 October 1883, p. 6, giving notice to Lucia R. Sailer, Respondent, of action taking place in divorce case filed by Isaac D. Sailer.

62   Philadelphia, Marriage Index, 1885–1951, online database at ancestry.com, citing digital GSU number 4141875, shows Hannah Blanche Liebman married Isaac D. Sailer at Philadelphia in 1886, with marriage license number 5275.

63   1900 U.S. Federal Census, Ward 7, Philadelphia, Roll T623 1454, Page 94a, shows Isaac D. Sailor, Head, and Blanche, Wife; her birth date shown as 6 November 1864; says she and her mother were born in Pennsylvania, her father was born in Germany; no children living. "Died," *The Philadelphia Inquirer*, 2 December 1925, p. 30, says Blanche Sailer, widow of Isaac D. Sailer, died 1 December 1925. "Woman Killed by Gas," *The Philadelphia Inquirer*, 2 December 1925, p. 2, news article reports death of Mrs. Blanche Sailer, 40, of 1410 Pine Street, who died in the Polyclinic Hospital on 1 December after being exposed to gas from a leaky tube in her apartment. The age is far from correct for the widow of Isaac Sailer, but the other facts fit her situation, so it is probable that the age was reported incorrectly in the article. Pennsylvania, Death Certificates, 1906–1966, online database at ancestry.com; certificate no. 11600 shows death of Blanche L. Sailer on 1 Dec 1925 of acute nephritis after gas poison; died in Polyclinic Hospital. Father Leon Leibman, born in Germany; mother Marie Bechtel, born in United States.

64   1850 U.S. Federal Census, Southwark Ward 4, Philadelphia, Roll M432_822, Page 268, shows Franklin Sailer, age 4, in household of Joseph Sailer. Online image at findagrave.com/memorial/98801335; photo of gravestone shows Frank Sailer, 24 September 1845–22 March 1923. "Died," *The Philadelphia Inquirer*, 24 March 1923, p. 27, reports death on 22 March of Frank Sailer in his home at 207 Pelham Road, Germantown.

65   "Married," *The Daily Evening Telegraph* (Philadelphia), 7 October 1870, brief notice of wedding on October 6 of Frank Sailer to Anna Reisky, daughter of James Reisky, Esq., at residence of bride's parents.

66   Online image at findagrave.com/memorial/98801335; photo of gravestone shows Anna R., Wife of Frank Sailer, 28 December 1847–19 April 1892. Philadelphia Death Certificates Index, 1803–1915, online database at ancestry.com, citing FHL film number 1901683, shows Anna R. Sailer, born about 1848 in Philadelphia, died 19 April 1892 in Philadelphia, buried 22 April 1892 at Woodlands Cemetery,

The Third Generation

18. JOHN[3] SAILER (*Joseph,*[2] *Wilhelm*[1]) was born in Philadelphia on 6 September 1840 and died in Scarborough, Cumberland County, Maine, on 13 July 1913. He was buried in Woodlands Cemetery, Philadelphia.[67] He married, in Philadelphia on 20 December 1866,[68] EMILY WOODWARD, who was born in Philadelphia on 18 May 1843 and died in Philadelphia on 31 October 1897, daughter of Samuel Woodward and Ann Pierce.[69]

John Sailer served with distinction in the Civil War, starting as a lieutenant with the Keystone Battery, later known as Battery A, of the United States Army. In 1912, men associated with that unit published a history of the organization, which they dedicated to Colonel John Sailer, "[f]ormerly Second Lieutenant of Keystone Battery A and the only surviving officer who served with our organization in the Civil War."

Figure 3. Portrait of John Sailer Taken in 1912

Philadelphia. 1850 U.S. Federal Census, South Mulberry Ward, Philadelphia, Roll M432_815, Page 237B, shows James Reisky, age 45, Isabella Reisky, age 40, wife, and Anna Reisky, age 3, and others.

67   1850 U.S. Federal Census, Southwark Ward 4, Philadelphia, Roll M432_822, Page 268, shows John Sailer, age 10, in household of Joseph Sailer. Online image at findagrave.com/memorial/98769327; photo of gravestone shows John Sailer, 6 September 1840 – 13 July 1913. "John Sailer Dies at Prout's Neck," *The Philadelphia Inquirer*, 15 July 1913, p. 7. Philadelphia Death Certificates Index, online database at ancestry.com, citing FHL film number 1421394, shows John Sailer, born about 1841, died in Scarborough, Cumberland County, Maine, on 13 July 1913, burial at Woodlands Cemetery.

68   "Married," *The Philadelphia Inquirer*, 22 December 1866, p. 2.

69   Online image at findagrave.com/memorial/98769718; photo of gravestone shows Emily Woodward, wife of John Sailer, 18 May 1843–31 October 1897, Woodlands Cemetery. Philadelphia Death Certificates Index, online database at ancestry.com, shows Emily W. Sailer, born about 1845, died 31 October 1897 at Philadelphia, buried at Woodlands Cemetery.

The first chapter of the book is headed "Reminiscence of Civil War Service," by John Sailer. That chapter includes the following details, with some material omitted:

> [I]n the month of August, 1862, the Battery left Philadelphia for Washington. . . . The officers when we left the city were Captain Matthew Hastings, Lieutenants Creely, Poulterer, Roberts and Sailer. We were encamped near Washington, employing our time in constantly drilling our men and horses, and our battery soon became one of the best drilled in the service. [In the early summer of 1863, while they were encamped at Union Mills, near Warrenton, Virginia,] I was appointed as an aide-de-camp on the staff of General Hays. During my staff duty the Adjutant General on the staff was ordered to another position and I, although the youngest member, was ordered to take his place . . . . While at Union Mills the entire Army of the Potomac passed through our camp on the way to Gettysburg. It required several days' time and was a sight never to be forgotten. Shortly afterwards our encampment broke up and we were ordered to Gettysburg. Our guns were placed on cars and reached the vicinity of Gettysburg during the battle, where we were held in reserve. [After the battle ended, General Meade was pursuing General Lee, who was waiting to cross a river.] As soon as Lee crossed Meade followed, and so close was the pursuit that, in order to gain time for the main part of his army, Lee spread a division in a place called Snicker's Gap. Here was our first experience in real service. Our battery was placed in position for firing and we were all prepared for action, but the battle was confined to the skirmishers and infantry. After the attack had been made on the Confederate position by Sickles' Division the enemy retired, their object of delaying Meade's army for twenty-four hours having been accomplished. We continued with Meade until August, 1863, when, our term of enlistment having expired, we were ordered to Philadelphia and mustered out.[70]

In June 1866, not long after the war, John Sailer and George Stevenson organized the banking firm of Sailer & Stevenson in downtown Philadelphia. They remained in business there for more than forty years, when they both retired on the first day of 1911, and turned management of the firm over to their sons, John Morris Sailer and George Stevenson, with a third associate.[71]

When he died at his summer home in Prouts Neck, Maine, in 1913, he was described as "one of the best known of the 'old guard' of bankers in this city."[72]

In 1900, John wrote a letter to his son, Joseph, discussing family events. The reference to "Powers" evidently is John's nephew, Thomas Henry Powers Sailer, the son of Randolph Sailer, who died in 1869. Thomas, who lived from 1868 to 1962,[73] was often called "Powers." The reference to the "Wambeck" apparently refers to the Wambeck House, a resort at Jefferson, New Hampshire (also called the Waumbek), near the White Mountains. The text of the letter is below:

---

70   Howard-Smith, Logan and J.F. Reynold Scott, *The History of Battery A (Formerly Known as the Keystone Battery) and Troop A, N.G.P.* (Philadelphia: The John C. Winston Co. 1912) 13–17.

71   "Sons Succeed to Banking Business," *The Philadelphia Inquirer*, 14 December 1910, p.15.

72   "John Sailer Dies at Prout's Neck," *The Philadelphia Inquirer*, 15 July 1913, p. 7.

73   U.S., Presbyterian Church Records, 1701–1970, online database at ancestry.com, citing Presbyterian Historical Society, Philadelphia, *Session. Minutes & Records, 1867–1891*; Accession Number Vault BX 9211.P49147 G71 v.1; original record is page from baptisms register of Greenwich Street Presbyterian Church, Philadelphia, showing birth of Thomas Henry Powers Sailer on 23 May 1868 and baptism on 8 November 1868. "Dr. T. Sailer, Was Mission Executive," *The Jersey Journal* (Jersey City, New Jersey), 2 August 1962, p. 7, reporting death of T.H.P. Sailer, age 94, on 31 July 1962 in Englewood Hospital.

Bryn Mawr 9/15/00
Dear Joe

I received to-day letters from Powers and yourself. This being Saturday I was not at the office, but they telephoned me. Tell Powers they sent the money to Bill and himself as directed, only the Telegraph Co would not receive it for Jamestown so I had to send it by Express. I also sent $100 by Express to the Wambeck.

I am very sorry Powers is not well, and am very glad you were there to take him to the White Mountains. I don't think there is any necessity for you to hurry home and if you can be of any service to Powers I would stay, it will also do you good. We have had some very hot weather since you left, last Tuesday being one of the most oppressive days this summer. It is cooler to-day with prospects of a storm. It is a fine day for Tennis however, cool and no sun. Daisy, Jack and I have been at [it?] all the morning. Jack says he is almost rid of his cold, and has certainly had very little trouble with it this time. Anna is still away with the Stoddards and is over at Winnipeg. We received a letter this morning, saying she was having a fine time. They expect to come home next week. We go to the City next Wednesday week but go to Atlantic City for a week, while the house is being put in order. Lucy Holland spends next week with us. The Bryn Mawr Horse Show is also next week. We are all well and getting along nicely. Give my kind regards to Powers.

Affectionately
Father[74]

In the summers, like many wealthy Philadelphians, John Sailer and his family took the train to Maine. He had a beautiful coastal property at Prouts Neck, an exclusive peninsula in the town of Scarborough, within Cumberland County.

Figure 4. Overview of Prouts Neck in About 1900

Figure 5. John Sailer's House at Prouts Neck in About 1900

---

74   Letter from John Sailer to Joseph Sailer, 15 September 1900, available online at https://strawbridgefamily.net/documents/john-sailers-letter-to-his-son-joseph-in-1900/, original in possession of the author.

Figure 6. John Sailer in Maine with Grandchild Alice

Figure 7. John Sailer, at Right, with Family and Others in Maine

Children of John[3] Sailer and Emily (Woodward) Sailer:

+ 21.   i. JOSEPH[4] SAILER was born in Philadelphia on 1 October 1867 and died in Philadelphia on 31 Dec 1928.

  22.   ii. ANNA PRISCILLA SAILER was born in Philadelphia on 9 April 1875, baptized on 16 January 1876, and died in Radnor, Delaware County, Pennsylvania, on 5 May 1945.[75] She married, in Philadelphia on 9 June 1904,[76] ALBIN GARRETT PENINGTON, who was born in Philadelphia on 27 April 1874 and died in Radnor on 20 February 1942, son of Morris Penington and Mary Frances Fox.[77]

Anna was known as "Aunt Nancy" in the Sailer family. She had considerable interaction with the family of Joseph Sailer, M.D., over the years.

---

75   U.S. Presbyterian Church Records, 1701–1970, online database at ancestry.com, citing Presbyterian Historical Society, Philadelphia; Accession Number: 11–0520 63J Box 1; church register shows Annie, child of John and Emily Sailer, born on 9 April 1875, baptized on 16 Jan 1876, Arch Street Presbyterian Church, Philadelphia. 1880 U.S. Federal Census, District 182, Philadelphia, Roll 1172, Page 347D, shows Anna, age 5, in household of John Sailor. Pennsylvania, Death Certificates, 1906–1966, online database at ancestry.com; certificate no. 41504 shows death of Anna P. S. Pennington at Radnor, Pennsylvania, on 5 May 1945.
76   "Pennington–Sailer," The Philadelphia Inquirer, 10 June 1904, p. 6, reporting wedding on 9 June of Anna Priscilla Sailer and Albin G. Pennington [sic], at residence of bride, 2039 Spruce Street.
77   U.S. World War I Draft Registration Cards, 1917–1918, online database at ancestry.com, citing National Archives and Records Administration, M1509, 4,582 rolls. Image of his draft card shows he reported his birth date as 27 April 1874. "Albin G. Penington, Broker, Dies at 67," The Philadelphia Inquirer, 21 February 1942, p. 7, reporting his death on 20 February at his home in Radnor, Pennsylvania. Burial to be in West Laurel Hill Cemetery.

Figure 8. Anna Priscilla Sailer in February 1887, Age 11

Figure 9. Anna Priscilla Sailer Penington

23. iii. EMILY WOODWARD SAILER was born in Philadelphia on 15 November 1877 and died in Philadelphia on 11 August 1959.[78]

Emily was nicknamed "Daisy," which was the only name many of her relatives knew her by. (She was called "Aunt Daisy" or "Dais" (sometimes spelled "Daise") in the Sailer family. She never married. In her youth, and at least into her thirties, she was an accomplished competitor in the sport of fencing. A newspaper article featuring a large photo of Daisy and her two teammates began as follows:

> Bearing the proud title of "Inter-city Champions," the Philadelphia fencing team returned to this city yesterday, after their bloodless victory over the New York foilswomen. The bouts were fought in the club house of the rival team, at the Windsor Arcade, Fifth avenue and Forty-eighth street and with New York judges on the stand. Added to this, there was, according to the Philadelphians, "blood in the eyes" of the New Yorkers, and the duels were "A l'outrance," [meaning to the limit, or unsparing in their ferocity] despite the buttons on the foils.

> It was the first bout fought under the new championship rules recently passed by the fencers of this country, and the results proved the efficiency of the ruling as well as the power of thrust and parry of the three young Philadelphians.

> Charles Latham acted as master of ceremonies and announced each match, the first one being between Miss Emily Sailer, of the Philadelphia team, and Miss Stimson, of New York.

---

78   U.S. Presbyterian Church Records, 1701–1970, online database at ancestry.com, citing Presbyterian Historical Society, Philadelphia; Accession Number: 11–0520 63J Box 1; church register shows Emily Woodward Sailer, child of John and Emily Sailer, born on 15 November 1877, baptized on 27 October 1878, Arch Street Presbyterian Church, Philadelphia. 1880 U.S. Federal Census, District 182, Philadelphia, Roll 1172, Page 347D, shows Emily, age 2, in household of John Sailor. Death Notice, *The Philadelphia Inquirer*, 13 August 1959, p. 29, announcing death of Emily W. Sailer, daughter of the late John Sailer and Emily W. Sailer, on 11 August.

The New Yorkers were anxious to wipe out the stigma of their defeat in this city several weeks ago, and for the first minute or two of the opening bout neither side could claim any advantage. Miss Sailer attacked with great vim, however, and soon was able to penetrate Miss Stimson's guard.[79]

She was still competing at least as late as 1912, at the age of 34, when she won at least one match in the national championship, though she did not become the champion.[80]

In later years, she lived in an apartment in downtown Philadelphia, at 13 S. 18th Street, and led an active social life. Each year, she held a Christmas party for family members. She was known as a warm and loving aunt to her many nieces, nephews, and their children. She also was known for the royal treatment bestowed on her cats, who received elegant meals of steak that was specially cooked and hand-fed to the cats by one of Daisy's two live-in servants. She also continued the tradition established by her father of spending summers in Prouts Neck. In her youth she had taken walks on the beach there with Winslow Homer, but she never bought any of his paintings; they were not her style.[81] In her heyday at Prouts Neck, she was the "queen" of the local social set, holding court on the beach under a large umbrella, and exchanging local news with her many friends and neighbors.[82]

Figure 10. Emily Woodward "Daisy" Sailer in February 1887, Age 10

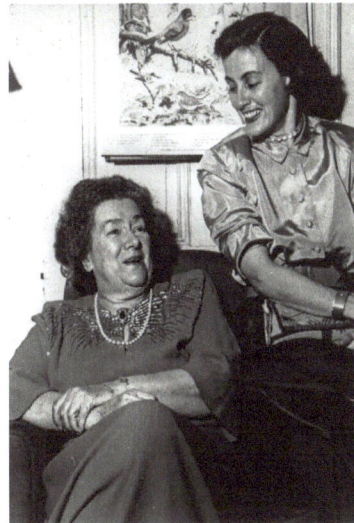

Figure 11. Emily Woodward "Daisy" Sailer with Her Niece, Elizabeth Twells Churchman, in the 1940s or 1950s

24. iv. JOHN MORRIS SAILER was born in Philadelphia on 9 April 1884 and died in Philadelphia on 29 September 1943.[83]

---

79   "Quaker Fencing Girls Victorious," *The Philadelphia Inquirer*, 29 April 1908, p. 14.

80   "Fencing Girl Wins Foil Honors," *The New York Times*, 27 April 1912, p. 9.

81   Email from Emily Starr to Alexander White and others, May 11, 2019.

82   Letter from Priscilla Deaver to Mary L. White, 9 July 1945, original in possession of the author.

83   U.S., Presbyterian Church Records, 1701–1970, online database at ancestry.com, citing Presbyterian Historical Society, Philadelphia, *Baptismal Certificates and Stubs 1881–1891*; Accession Number: V M146 P533r v5a. Image of stub from baptismal register of Second Presbyterian Church shows John Morris Sailer, born 9 April 1884, son of John and Emily W. Sailer, baptized 1 January 1888. U.S. Passport Applications, 1795–1925, online database at ancestry.com, citing NARA Roll 238, Certificates 51581–52400. Certificate no. 51091, is an application dated 2 March 1915, handwritten and signed by John M. Sailer, saying he was born on 9 April 1884 in Philadelphia, and is traveling to the Bahamas on pleasure. Pennsylvania, Death Certificates, 1906–1966, online database at ancestry.com; certificate no. 85738

John Morris, known to his nieces and nephews as "Uncle Jack," who never married, followed his father into the world of banking. When he was 26, his father, John, and his father's partner, George Stevenson, turned over control of their banking firm, Sailer & Stevenson, to John Morris and Stevenson's son, George, along with a third partner.[84]

In 1929, John Morris purchased a Duesenberg Model J automobile, which has been described as the "fastest, most expensive, most luxurious, and most prestigious" automobile of its time, "owned by only the very top of society." The purchase price for this model in 1929 was about $15,000, which would have purchased thirty new Ford automobiles at that time. The car was returned to the factory in 1932, perhaps a casualty of the Depression.[85]

Figure 12. John Morris Sailer as a Child

Figure 13. John Morris Sailer Passport Photo, Age 30

---

shows death of John M. Sailer in Philadelphia, on 29 September 1943. He is listed as Single.

84   "Sons Succeed to Banking Business," *The Philadelphia Inquirer*, 14 December 1910, p. 15.

85   Email to Alexander S. White from Chris Summers, Auburn-Cord-Duesenberg Club Member, 24 May 2008, stating that he researches purchases of the cars, and found the record of this purchase by John Morris Sailer.

The Fourth Generation

21. JOSEPH[4] SAILER (*John*[3], *Joseph*[2], *Wilhelm*[1]) was born in Philadelphia on 1 October 1867 and died there on 31 December 1928.[86] He married, at Philadelphia on 5 February 1901,[87] MARY LOWBER STRAWBRIDGE, who was born in Philadelphia on 4 July 1875 and died in Philadelphia on 26 July 1963, daughter of George Strawbridge, M.D., and Alice Welsh.[88]

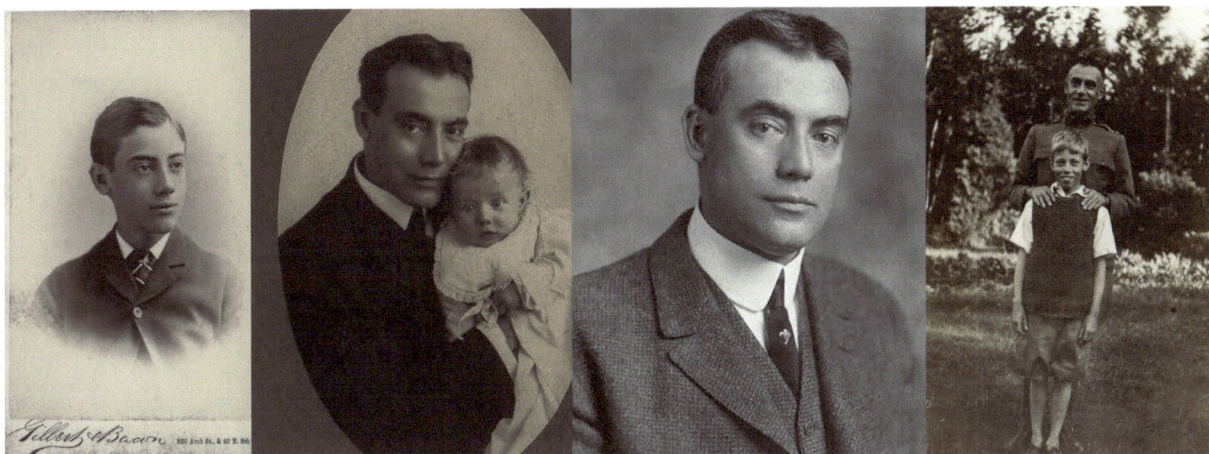

Figure 14. Joseph Sailer, M.D., in Two Images Shown with Joseph Sailer Jr.

As discussed above, Joseph Sailer's father, John, was a prominent banker in Philadelphia, and John's father, in turn, was the prominent financial editor of a major newspaper.[89] Joseph's father expected his son to follow in the family tradition of banking and finance, but Joseph, having already graduated from the University of Pennsylvania at the age of eighteen, was determined to study medicine instead. His father, though disappointed, did not stand in his way.

---

86   1880 U.S. Federal Census, District 182, Philadelphia, Roll 1172, Page 347D, showing household of John Sailor, including Joseph, age 12. Pennsylvania Death Certificates, 1906–1966, online database at ancestry.com; certificate no. 123058 shows birth of Joseph Sailer on 1 October 1867 in Philadelphia and death on 31 December 1928 in Philadelphia. U.S. Passport Applications, 1795–1925, online database at ancestry.com, NARA Roll No. 286, 1 October 1886–30 November 1886; application no. 8369, dated 8 November 1886, says Joseph Sailer was 19 years old, born 1 October 1867 in Philadelphia.

87   Pennsylvania and New Jersey, Church and Town Records, 1669–2013, online database at ancestry.com, citing Historical Society of Pennsylvania, Philadelphia, Historic Pennsylvania Church and Town Records, Reel 196; register of St. Luke's Episcopal Church, shows wedding of Joseph Sailer, M.D., and Mary Lowber Strawbridge on 5 February 1901.

88   1880 U.S. Federal Census, District 149, Philadelphia, Roll 1171, Page 470A, showing George W. Strawbridge, age 35, Alice, age 30, Mary, age 4, and others; 1900 U.S. Federal Census, Ward 22, Philadelphia, shows George Strawbridge, age 55, Alice, age 51, Mary, age 24, and others; Pennsylvania, Death Certificates, 1906–1966, online database at ancestry.com, citing Pennsylvania Historic and Museum Commission, Pennsylvania Death Certificates, 1906–1965, certificate number range 71551–74400, certificate no. 74374 shows death of Mary Lowber Sailer in Philadelphia on 26 July 1963; shows her birth date as 4 July 1875.

89   This summary of the life of Joseph Sailer is drawn from several sources, which are all cited in this footnote, in order to avoid cluttering the text with multiple footnotes. Truman G. Schnabel, M.D., "Memoir of Joseph Sailer, M.D.," *Transactions of the College of Physicians of Philadelphia* 1929; David Riesman, M.D., Sc. D., "Joseph Sailer," unpublished manuscript in family papers; "Dr. J. Sailer Dies in Philadelphia," *The New York Times*, 2 January 1929, p. 27; email to the author from Emily Starr, 22 April 2019.

When he was about nineteen years old, he travelled to Darmstadt, Germany, to study the German language, then returned to the University of Pennsylvania, where he graduated from the medical school in 1891. He had internships at the Presbyterian and Philadelphia hospitals, then eighteen months of study in Europe, followed by several years of clinical and laboratory work in Philadelphia.

In 1902 he obtained a position as professor of diseases of the stomach and intestines at the Philadelphia Polyclinic, and he began to concentrate on gastroenterology. He was elected president of the American Gastro-Enterological Association in 1921. During the Spanish-American War of 1898, he served as an assistant surgeon in the Naval Reserve battalion. In World War I he served in the Army Medical Corps, including some time overseas. When he returned along with some of his colleagues, the event was recorded in a local newspaper:

> Many Pennsylvania surgeons and medical men who did heroic work in the hospitals on the battlefields of France came in today on board the big troopship President Grant, which carried 4700 officers and enlisted men. Her voyage across the Atlantic from Brest, France, was marked by a succession of gales and the answering a call for help from a distressed ship, which sent her off course and delayed her arrival for at least five days.

> Notable among the arrivals were Lieutenant Colonel Joseph Sailer, 1718 Spruce Street; Major A.P. Francine, 264 South Twenty-first Street; Major B.F Baer, Jr., 2039 Chestnut Street, and major Charles F. Nassau, 1515 Wallace Street, all of Philadelphia.

> For the last six months of the war Colonel Sailer was the medical consultant at the combined hospitals in and around Vichy, France, which were known as Base Hospital No. 1. The hotels at the world-famed resort were turned over to the Americans and at Vichy alone there were 18,000 beds and the total number of beds in the surrounding towns swelled the grand total to 30,000 beds. Five towns were in the assemblage of hospital units. Most of the time these beds were occupied by American wounded and there was a staff of 200 surgeons to care for them.

> Lieutenant Colonel Sailer offered his services to the Government as a member of the Medical Reserve Corps soon after the United States entered the war. He was commissioned major in November, 1917, and sent to Camp Wheeler, Macon, Ga., where he was made medical chief of the base hospital. One of Colonel Sailer's first duties at Camp Wheeler was to aid in combating an outbreak of pneumonia cases.

> In August, 1918, he was transferred from Camp Wheeler to overseas duty, and sailed for France August 23. There he was assigned to Vichy. In all of these hospitals were physicians from Philadelphia and various parts of the United States who knew Colonel Sailer's high standing in the profession as a consultant, and it was in this capacity that he rendered distinguished service in restoring to health thousands of sick and wounded soldiers.

> Colonel Sailer is professor of clinical medicine in the University of Pennsylvania, and a member of the medical staffs of the Presbyterian, University and Philadelphia General Hospitals.

> He was born in Philadelphia, October 1, 1867, the son of John and Emily Woodward Sailer. His father was the founder of Sailer & Stevenson, an old firm of Philadelphia bankers. His grandfather, Joseph Sailer, preceded Joel Cook as financial editor of the "Public Ledger."

The degree of M.D. was conferred on Colonel Sailer by the University of Pennsylvania in 1891 and he pursued post-graduate studies in Paris, Zurich, and Vienna. From 1902 till 1909 he was professor of diseases of the stomach and intestines in the Philadelphia Pilyclinic [sic; Polyclinic]. In the University of Pennsylvania he was made demonstrator of pathology in 1899, and later instructor, assistant professor and professor of clinical medicine. Colonel Sailer is a director of the Philadelphia Society for Organizing Charity, fellow of the College of Physicians, and a member of various medical associations. In February, 1901, he was married to Miss Mary Lowber Strawbridge, daughter of Dr. George Strawbridge, an eminent Philadelphia physician.[90]

After his military service ended in 1919, Sailer shifted his main interest to cardiology. He organized the Philadelphia Association for the Prevention and Treatment of Heart Disease and spurred the creation of a new Children's Heart Hospital, which opened its doors shortly before his death. He also spent a considerable amount of time in teaching medicine.

Beyond the world of medicine, he was devoted to his large family, and he had deep interests in modern literature, particularly writings about exploration and travel.

Figure 15. Children of Joseph and Mary Lowber Sailer, About 1920. From Left: Alice, Mary, Joseph Jr., John, Priscilla, Elizabeth, Albin Penington

In 1923, he took some of the family members on a trip to the western United States. He sent postcards to those who remained behind, in Camden, Maine. His card to the youngest boy, Albin Penington, called Pen, described an incident in which the mule carrying Mary, age 17, fell off the trail with no ill effects to anyone.

---

90   "Lieut. Col. Sailer and Three Phila. Physicians Back After Service with Army in France," *Philadelphia Press*, 26 February 1919, copy in possession of the author.

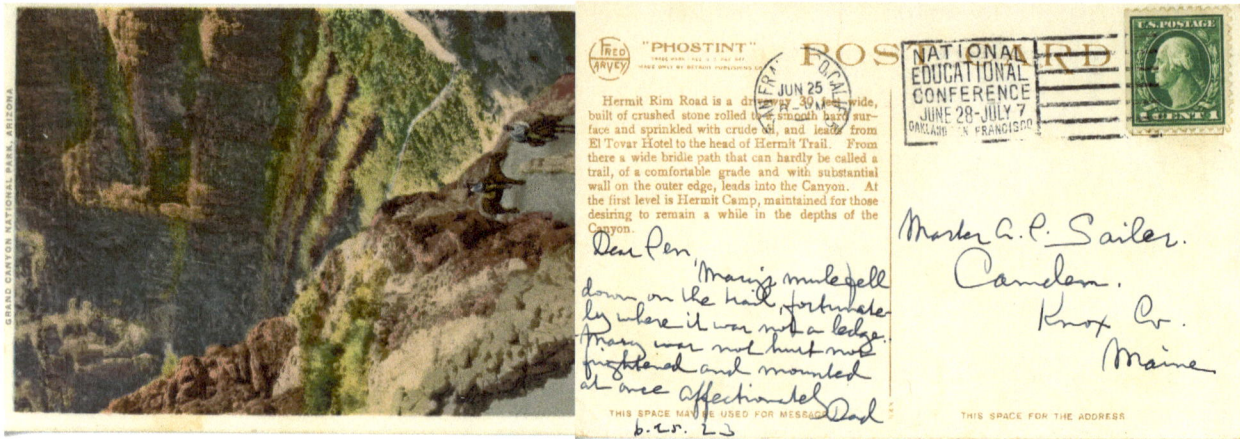

Figure 16. Postcard from Dr. Joseph Sailer to his Son, A. Penington Sailer, 25 June 1923

Sailer loved art and was well known as an authority on etchings, which he collected with great expertise. He died of heart disease on the last day of 1928.

Children of Joseph[4] Sailer and Mary Lowber (Strawbridge) Sailer:

25. i. EMILY WOODWARD[5] SAILER was born in Philadelphia on 4 March 1902, baptized on 18 May 1902, and died in Philadelphia on 25 March 1906.[91]

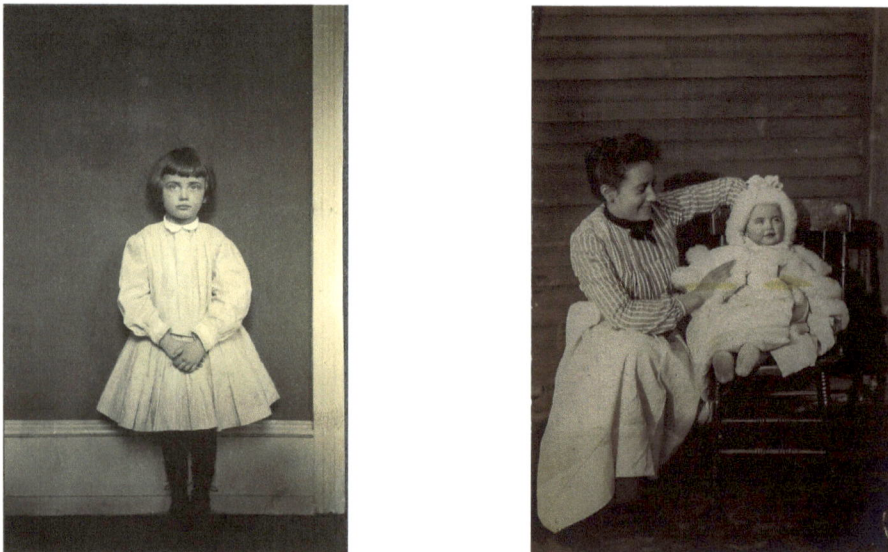

Figure 17. Emily Woodward Sailer, 1902–1906; at Right, with Nurse

As might be expected, Joseph and Mary Sailer were devastated when their first-born child died of pneumonia shortly after her fourth birthday. They both wrote journals for several months after her death, in which they

---

91 U.S., Presbyterian Church Records, 1701–1970, online database at ancestry.com, citing Presbyterian Historic Society, Philadelphia, Accession Number 12 0421 61J 2 Box 2; First Presbyterian Church baptisms register shows Emily Woodward Sailer, child of Joseph and Mary Lowber Sailer, born 4 March 1902, baptized 18 May 1902. Pennsylvania, Death Certificates, 1906–1966, online database at ancestry.com, citing Pennsylvania Historic and Museum Commission, Pennsylvania, Death Certificates, 1906–1966, certificate number range 24390–27869, certificate no. 26096 shows death of Emily Woodward Sailer in Philadelphia on 25 March 1906; shows her birth date as 4 March 1902.

recorded their memories of Emily's brief life. Those journals were later edited for consistency and clarity and compiled into a privately printed booklet titled "Emily."[92]

Mary Sailer's journal begins as follows:

> Emily was born on the fourth of March, 1902, at about nine o'clock in the morning. I did not see her until about two hours later and I shall never forget what a dark little baby she seemed to me at first, and how much like Joe. Miss Russel was her nurse for the first few weeks, and for the next five, Miss Roe. She had a great deal of colic and Joe worried about her a great deal so, of course, I did too. She slept for the first few weeks on the couch with the nurse, and then Mother sent her little brass crib; since then she has always slept in it when we were at 248 South 21st Street.
>
> As she was the first grandchild on both sides of the family, she received a great many presents, about two hundred I think, and a great many people wrote to us. She did seem like a very wonderful baby and Joe and I were so proud of her. Before she came we had decided what her name would be if she were a girl. So she was named before she was many minutes old.

One of her last entries is the following:

> I remember the last time we were there [at the house of Aunt Sally Sailer, Joseph Sailer's aunt], her little chair [a small chair that was brought into the room when Emily came to visit] was in front of the bureau, and as Emily rocked with little Sally [a doll] on her lap, she would turn her head to see how it looked in the long, low glass. Last winter, she was old enough to know that Aunt Sally was deaf and she was very good about talking loud enough for her to hear. A day or two after her little fur and muff came home that Gran gave her, we went down to Aunt Sally's and Emily was very much pleased with how fine Aunt Sally thought she was.

One of the passages by Emily's father, Joseph, discussed Emily's love of popular songs:

> She had many favorite tunes: perhaps the one she liked best of all, at least for a time, was "Mr. Dooley," which she could sing, at least the chorus. "Dixie," "Old Black Joe," "Mary Brown," on her music box were great favorites, and at Dr. Strawbridge's she liked best "Bedelia," "Dixieland," "Funiculi, Funicula," to all of which she would dance. At Mr. Sailer's, she liked best "Rigoletto," "The Mocking Bird," and, particularly, "Everybody Works But Father." She always enjoyed the Faust waltz and always danced to it, recognizing the dancing rhythm.

Another of Joseph's recollections touched upon Emily's final hours:

> I did not see her again before she was taken ill, indeed, not until Tuesday at two o'clock, when she was barely conscious. When I first saw her then, she said, "Daddy, is there a sick lady in your office?" I said "no." "Then you won't go, will you Daddy. I'm sick." She never was wholly conscious again. When I first saw her I kissed her cheek and she looked at me with one of her old smiles, which I believe was her last."

---

92   Undated pamphlet titled *Emily* in Sailer-Strawbridge family papers. The pamphlet has no page numbers, so no further citations are made in this book for the passages set forth here in the text.

+ 26. ii. Aʟɪᴄᴇ Wᴇʟsʜ Sᴀɪʟᴇʀ was born in Philadelphia on 20 April 1904 and died in Philadelphia on 16 April 2002.

+ 27. iii. Mᴀʀʏ Lᴏᴡʙᴇʀ Sᴀɪʟᴇʀ was born in Philadelphia on 19 January 1906, and died in Philadelphia on 15 November 1992.

28. iv. Jᴏsᴇᴘʜ Sᴀɪʟᴇʀ Jʀ. was born in Jamestown, Rhode Island, on 14 August 1907, and died in combat in the Solomon Islands on 7 December 1942.[93]

Joe Sailer enjoyed summers in Camden, Maine, along with his siblings and parents. After attending school in Philadelphia, Joe enrolled in Princeton University, where he majored in mechanical engineering and graduated with honors in 1930. In June 1930, he began flight training with the U.S. Naval Reserve. During this period, he kept a record of his many social activities, which shows he was constantly going to dinner or the movies, or having or attending parties, with a wide range of relatives and friends.

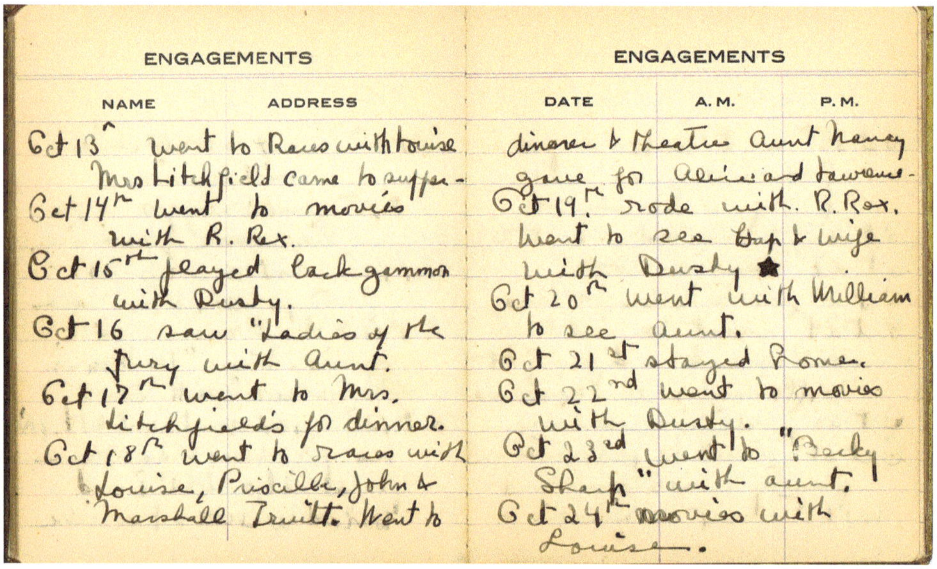

Figure 18. Joseph Sailer's Engagements Book Entries for Part of October 1930

One story passed down through the family illustrates Joe's love of social life. In August 1933, the local social set was buzzing because a cousin of the Sailers, Robert Frazer Welsh, had announced his engagement to a much younger woman who worked in a restaurant.[94] Joe and his brother John wanted to throw an engagement party for the couple, which was problematic because of Prohibition and the fact that their mother did not allow liquor in the house. Regardless of these obstacles, Joe and John apparently manufactured "bathtub gin" and hosted a very lively party, while their mother went to a restaurant.[95] According to family lore, a Philadelphia newspaper reported the next day that Mrs. Joseph Sailer hosted a party at her house the night before, in honor of the engagement of Robert Welsh.[96]

---

93   1910 U.S. Federal Census, Ward 7, Philadelphia, Roll T624_1389, Page 4B, showing household of Joseph Sailer with Joseph Jr, age 2, born in Rhode Island, and others. 1940 U.S. Federal Census, Dayton, Montgomery, Ohio, District 94-6, Roll m-t0627–03251, Page 82B, showing Joseph Sailer Jr., age 32, born in Rhode Island, occupation service engineer in airplane industry, income $1,840.00. Typed resume of Joseph Sailer Jr. in Sailer-Strawbridge family papers showing birth date of 14 August 1907 in Jamestown, Rhode Island. Date of death from multiple sources, including web page with official list of World War II Marine Corps casualties, at http://www.naval-history.net/WW2UScasaaDB-USMCbyDate4212.htm, viewed on 27 May 2019.

94   "Banker, 59, and Waitress, 20, Secure License to Wed," *The Philadelphia Inquirer*, 4 August 1933, p. 2.

95   Email from Emily Starr to Alexander White, 23 April 2019.

96   Email from Emily Starr to Alexander White, 22 June 2019. I have not been able to locate this newspaper article.

In 1932, after his training had ended, he pursued civilian jobs and further education, then landed a job with United Air Lines as a ground agent in 1935. He went back on active duty with the military for a while, then went to work for the Sperry Gyroscope Company in Brooklyn, New York, in 1938.

Figure 19. Left: Joseph Sailer Jr. as a Child at Rockledge, Maine, Home of Strawbridges; Center: With his Aunt Anne West Strawbridge; Right, in the U.S. Marine Corps in World War II

In October 1940, Joe and Frederic Vose traveled to England on a secret mission to deliver a new Sperry bomb sight for use by the Royal Air Force. That trip was memorialized in a film produced by Sperry, including footage from the trip to England and the events that took place in that country.[97]

In 1941, Sailer was back on active duty with the U.S. Marine Corps, eventually assuming command of a squadron of dive-bombing planes. His squadron was sent to Guadalcanal, where they arrived on November 1, 1942. Sailer led several dive-bombing missions against Japanese warships. On December 7, 1942, he was shot down while attacking a destroyer. For his actions in combat, he was posthumously awarded the Navy Cross.[98] A Marine Corps after-action report summarized his contribution to the war effort:

> In the death of Major Sailer, the flying forces of this country have lost one of their most outstanding, courageous, able and industrious officers. As CO of VMSB-132 he has participated in 25 missions from Henderson Field since November 1st; 19 of these were attack missions and on the twelve of these whereon contact was made with the enemy, Major Sailer scored 6 direct hits and 3 close misses. During the period from November 13–15, Major Sailer first contacted the Jap BB of the Kongo Class early on the morning of the 13th off Savo Island, scored a direct hit on it later in the day, and another in a solo attack at dusk on a CL acting as part of its screening force. Early on the morning of the 14th he scored a direct hit on a CA of the Nachi class off New Georgia which later sank, and made 3 hits out of 4 attacks on the APs approaching Cactus on the 14th and 15th. The intangible effect of his leadership and personality upon both officers and men in this period is incalculable.[99]

In February 1945, Joe Sailer's mother and three of his siblings traveled to a new Sperry facility in Great Neck, Long Island, where Sperry officials showed the completed film depicting Joe's trip to England with Fred Vose to provide the bomb sight to the RAF. (A photograph of the group visiting Sperry is at Figure 64, later in this book.)

---

97   As of 26 May 2019, this video is available for viewing on YouTube, where it was posted by the author. The Internet address for the video is https://youtu.be/n4_4FHABGtY.

98   This account of Joseph Sailer Jr.'s life is taken from White, Alexander S., *Dauntless Marine* (Pacifica Press 1996).

99   Marine Air Group 14 war diary, quoted in *Dauntless Marine* 107–108.

Much later, in the 1990s, two of Joe Sailer's nephews met with Howard Stanley, the Marine Corps gunner who had accompanied Sailer on all of his flights at Guadalcanal except the final one.

Figure 20. Left to Right: Alexander White, Mrs. Stanley, Howard Stanley, John Churchman

+ 29. v. JOHN SAILER was born in Philadelphia on 3 June 1909 and died in Philadelphia on 7 November 1981.

+ 30. vi. PRISCILLA SPARKS SAILER was born in Philadelphia on 13 November 1910 and died in Camden, Maine, on 20 August 1994.

+ 31. vii. ELIZABETH TWELLS SAILER was born in Philadelphia on 27 January 1912 and died in Lafayette Hill, Montgomery County, Pennsylvania, on 19 March 1988.

  32. viii. ALBIN PENINGTON SAILER was born in Philadelphia on 8 December 1913 and died in Tinicum Township, Bucks County, Pennsylvania, on 11 February 2003.[100] He married CHRISTINE L. TAUB, who was born on 4 March 1919 and died on 1 January 2013.[101]

The Albin Penington Sailers had no children and lived a quiet life in a rural area, surrounded by undeveloped land. Albin, who was called "Pen" by his family members, was known for his sense of humor and his love of shopping for items in thrift shops and flea markets. He was a favorite of his Aunt Daisy.[102]

In 2002, not long before the end of Pen's life, the couple entered into an arrangement to sell the development rights for a nearly eighty-acre parcel of their land to Bucks County for $35,000, when the property was valued at nearly $600,000. According to a county official, this was "the most significant charitable gift of development rights by a private property owner in Bucks County."[103]

---

100   1920 U.S. Federal Census, District 160, Ward 7, Philadelphia, Roll T625_1618, Page 3A, showing household of Joseph Sailer with Albin P., son, age 6 as of January 1920. 1930 U.S. Federal Census, District 280, Philadelphia, Page 8B, FHL microfilm no. 2341829, showing household of Mary L. Sailer with Albin P., son, age 16. Selective Service Registration Cards, World War II: Multiple Registrations 1940, online database at ancestry.com, original record viewed at fold3.com shows Albin Pennington [sic] Sailer, date of birth 8 December 1913, registered on 16 October 1940. Death notice, *The Intelligencer* (Doylestown, Pennsylvania), 13 February 2003, p. 71, reporting death of Albin P. Sailer at his residence in Tinicum Township, Pennsylvania, at age 89, stating he was the husband of Christine L. (Taub) Sailer.

101   U.S. Public Records Index, 1950–1993, Volume 1, online database at ancestry.com, showing Christine L. Sailer, birth date 4 March 1919, address in Pipersville, Pennsylvania, as of 1993. Obituary, *The Record* (Hackensack, New Jersey), 4 January 2013, reporting death of Christine L. Sailer, age 94, of Pipersville, Pennsylvania, on 1 January 2013; graveside service set for 4 January 2013 at noon at Beth El Cemetery, Paramus, New Jersey.

102   Email from Emily Starr to Alexander S. White, 23 April 2019.

103   "Upper Bucks to Preserve 177 Acres for Open Space; Development Rights for 78.7 Acres Were Sold for Fraction of Their Value," *The Morning Call* (Allentown, Pennsylvania), 6 February 2002, p. B6.

33. ix. ANNE WEST SAILER was born in Camden, Knox County, Maine, on 11 September 1916 and died in Philadelphia on 11 March 1922.[104]

34. x. VIRGINIA SAILER was born in Philadelphia on 1 December 1920 and died in Philadelphia on 1 December 1920.[105]

---

104   Maine Birth Records, 1715–1922, online database at ancestry.com, citing Maine State Archives, Augusta, 1908–1922 Vital Records, Roll no. 49, Record of a Birth, dated 11 September 1916, shows birth of Anne West Sailer in Camden, daughter of Joseph Sailer and Mary Strawbridge. 1920 U.S. Federal Census, District 160, Ward 7, Philadelphia, Roll T625_1618, Page 3A, showing household of Joseph Sailer with Anne West, age 3 3/12 as of January 1920. Pennsylvania Death Certificates, 1906–1966, online database at ancestry. com, citing Pennsylvania Historic and Museum Commission, Death Certificates, 1906–1965, certificate number range 26001–29000, certificate no. 26005 shows death of Anne West Sailer in Philadelphia on 11 March 1922, date of birth 11 September 1916. Birth place listed as Maine. To be buried in Woodlands Cemetery on 13 March 1922.
105   Pennsylvania Death Certificates, 1906–1966, online database at ancestry.com, citing Pennsylvania Historic and Museum Commission, Death Certificates, 1906–1965, certificate number range 121001–124000, certificate no. 121754 shows death of Virginia Sailer in Philadelphia on 1 December 1920, date of birth 1 December 1920, parents Joseph Sailer and Mary Lowber Strawbridge. To be buried in Woodlands Cemetery, 2 December 1920.

The Fifth Generation

26. ALICE WELSH[5] SAILER (*Joseph*[4], *John*[3], *Joseph*[2], *Wilhelm*[1]) was born in Philadelphia on 20 April 1904 and died in Philadelphia on 16 April 2002.[106] She married, first, in Philadelphia on 30 October 1930,[107] LAWRENCE LITCHFIELD, JR., who was born in Pittsburgh, Pennsylvania, on 19 June 1900, and died in Lower Merion Township, Montgomery County, Pennsylvania, on 28 October 1967, son of Dr. Lawrence Litchfield and Ethlwyn Herr Jones.[108] She married, second, in 1979, WILLIAM EZRA LINGELBACH, JR., who was born in Philadelphia on 22 May 1903 and died on 8 January 2001, son of William Ezra Lingelbach and Anna Lane.[109]

Although her sisters were all successful in various ways, Alice was the only one of the Sailer daughters to attend and graduate from a four-year college, Smith College in Massachusetts, where she was a member of the Class of 1925.

Figure 21. Alice Welsh Sailer Litchfield

She spent many summers in Camden, Maine, at her grandparents' or parents' summer home. During one summer visit she sent a brief note home to her father in Philadelphia with the latest news:

---

106   1910 U.S. Federal Census, Ward 7, Philadelphia, Roll T624_1389, Page 4B, showing household of Joseph Sailer, physician, with Alice W., age 6, and others. U.S., Social Security Applications and Claims Index, 1936–2007, online database at ancestry.com, showing claim of Alice Welsh (Litchfield) (Lingelbach) Sailer, birth date 20 April 1904, at Philadelphia, death date 16 April 2002. Obituary, *The Philadelphia Inquirer*, 21 April 2002, p. B6, reporting death of Alice Lingelbach on 16 April 2002.
107   "Litchfield–Sailer," *The Philadelphia Inquirer*, 31 October 1930, p. 17, reporting on wedding on 30 October at Old St. Peter's Church, Philadelphia.
108   Pennsylvania and New Jersey, Church and Town Records, 1669–2013, online database at ancestry.com, citing Historical Society of Pennsylvania, Philadelphia, Historic Pennsylvania Church and Town Records, Reel 196; register of St. Thomas' Episcopal Church, Whitemarsh, Pennsylvania, showing burial of Laurence [sic] Litchfield, Jr., on 31 October 1967, listing his date of birth as 19 June 1900 and date of death as 27 October 1967. "Lawrence Litchfield Jr., Alcoa Executive, Dies," *The Sunday Star*, Washington, D.C., October 29, 1967, p. C-7, reporting death on 28 October 1967 in Philadelphia.
109   U.S. WWII Draft Cards Young Men, 1940–1947, online database at ancestry.com, citing NARA in St. Louis, Missouri, Records of the Selective Service System, 147, Box 1482, original image of card viewed at fold3.com, showing William E. Lingelbach, Jr., birth date 22 May 1903 in Philadelphia. U.S. Social Security Death Index, 1935–2014, online database at ancestry.com, showing William E. Lingelbach born 22 May 1903, died 8 January 2001. "William E. Lingelbach, 97, Lawyer and Athlete," *The Philadelphia Inquirer*, 11 January 2001, p. B11, reporting his death on 8 January 2001 and saying he married Alice Litchfield in 1979, and that his first wife, Barbara, died in 1974 after 41 years of marriage.

Sunday, July 31 [1921]

Dear Daddy,

It is very foggy here today and we are having a thunder storm, only it isn't raining. Jack & George are up here now & I took them to church as Granny has a little pain over her eye.

They got the fire in Rockland out successfully, that is, they got it out before it caught any houses that would make it spread, but all the lumber was lost of course.

We expect the Churchills to-morrow and I guess the baseball team will soon be started. Mr. Theodore Justice said to tell you he missed you very much. Miss Palmer is not getting along with her candy and is starting to sell it at Pascals and some other places. Mother & I went to the Carrols for supper last night & played cards. We had a fine time. I hope you are well & the city is not fearfully hot. You missed a very hot spell here.

With love,

Alice[110]

In 1930, she married Lawrence Litchfield, Jr., a geologist with the Alcoa aluminum company. Lawrence was a man of many accomplishments and interests, having graduated from the U.S. Naval Academy, served for a while at sea, been educated in the United States, Switzerland, and Germany, and having a degree in mining engineering from Harvard University. He rose steadily through the ranks of Alcoa, eventually becoming president in 1960 and chairman of the board in 1963. He also held many civic positions and was involved with various charitable and arts-related organizations.[111]

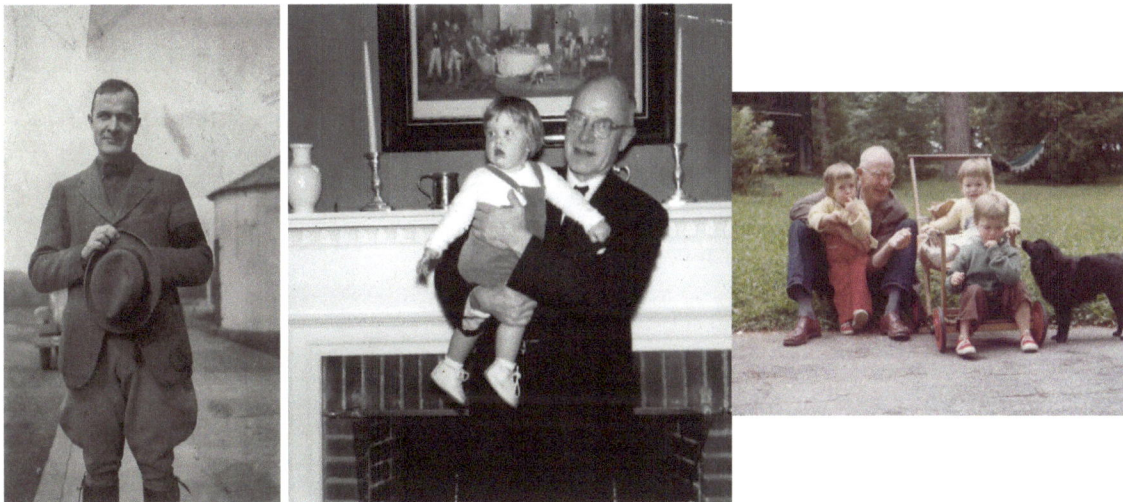

Figure 22. Lawrence Litchfield Jr.

In 1979, Alice married William E. Lingelbach, Jr., another highly accomplished man. He was a star athlete, having been a member of two U.S. Olympic soccer teams and a champion amateur tennis player. He earned a degree in international law as a Rhodes Scholar at Oxford University in England, and joined the Pennsylvania Bar in 1930.

---

110   Letter from Alice Sailer to Joseph Sailer, dated Sunday, July 31; year believed to be 1921 based on calendar and context; original in possession of the author.

111   "Litchfield Rites Slated," *Pittsburgh Post-Gazette*, 30 October 1967, p. 8.

He had a distinguished career for many years as a lawyer in Philadelphia, and continued to enjoy sports until late in life.[112]

Figure 23. Alice and William Lingelbach

Children of Lawrence Litchfield, Jr., and Alice Welsh[5] (Sailer) Litchfield:

35. i.   PRISCILLA SAILER[6] LITCHFIELD.

36. ii.   MARY LOWBER LITCHFIELD.

37. iii. LAWRENCE LITCHFIELD.

38. iv.   NICHOLAS CARVER LITCHFIELD.

27. MARY LOWBER[5] SAILER (*Joseph*[4]*, John*[3]*, Joseph*[2]*, Wilhelm*[1]) was born in Philadelphia on 19 January 1906 and died in Philadelphia on 15 November 1992.[113] She married, first, in Philadelphia on 27 December 1932,[114] WILLIAM WILSON WHITE, who was born in Philadelphia on 23 February 1906 and died in Lower Merion Township, Montgomery County, Pennsylvania, on 11 November 1964,[115] son of Thomas Raeburn White and Elizabeth Wilson White. She married, second, in Philadelphia, on 1 December 1967,[116] ROBERT BARCLAY

---

112   "Mr. William E. Lingelbach, 97," *The Philadelphia Inquirer*, 11 January 2001, accessed online on 16 April 2019 at https://www.genealogybank.com/doc/obituaries/obit/0F8EB35B56914498–0F8EB35B56914498.

113   1910 U.S. Federal Census, Ward 7, Philadelphia, Roll T624_1389, Page 4B, showing household of Joseph Sailer with daughter Mary L. Sailer, age 4, and others. U.S. Passport Applications, 1795–1925, online database at ancestry.com, citing Passport Applications, January 2, 1906–March 31, 1925, 1923, Roll 2377, Certificates 34850–346349, 12 Oct 1923–15 Oct 1923, application no. 346347, dated 9 October 1923, signed by Mary Lowber Sailer Jr., says she was born on 19 January 1906 and is daughter of Joseph Sailer. Death Notices, *The Philadelphia Inquirer*, 17 November 1992, p. 37, reporting death of Mary L. Knight, née Sailer, on 15 November 1992. U.S. Social Security Death Index, 1935–2014, online database at ancestry.com, showing Mary L. Knight, born 19 January 1906, died 15 November 1992.

114   "White-Sailer," *The Philadelphia Inquirer*, 28 December 1932, p. 6, reporting wedding of Mary Lowber Sailer to William Wilson White on 27 December at St. Peter's Church, 3d and Pine Streets, Philadelphia.

115   Pennsylvania Birth Certificates, 1906–1911, online database at ancestry.com, citing Pennsylvania Historical and Museum Commission, Harrisburg, Pennsylvania, Birth Certificates, 1906–1910, Box number 16, certificate number range 44701–47850, certificate no. 46614 shows birth of William Wilson White in Philadelphia on 23 February 1906, son of Thomas R. and Elizabeth Wilson White. Pennsylvania Death Certificates, 1906–1966, online database at ancestry.com, citing Pennsylvania Historic and Museum Commission, Death Certificates, 1906–1965, Box number 2411, certificate number range 108401–111250, certificate no. 108642 shows death of W. Wilson White in Lower Merion Township, Montgomery County, Pennsylvania, on 11 November 1964, date of birth 23 February 1906.

116   "Knight-White," *The Philadelphia Inquirer*, 2 December 1967, p.23, marriage announcement.

KNIGHT, who was born in Trenton, New Jersey, on 8 July 1899, and died in Portland, Maine, on 11 August 1984, son of Edward J. Knight and Katharine Scarborough.117

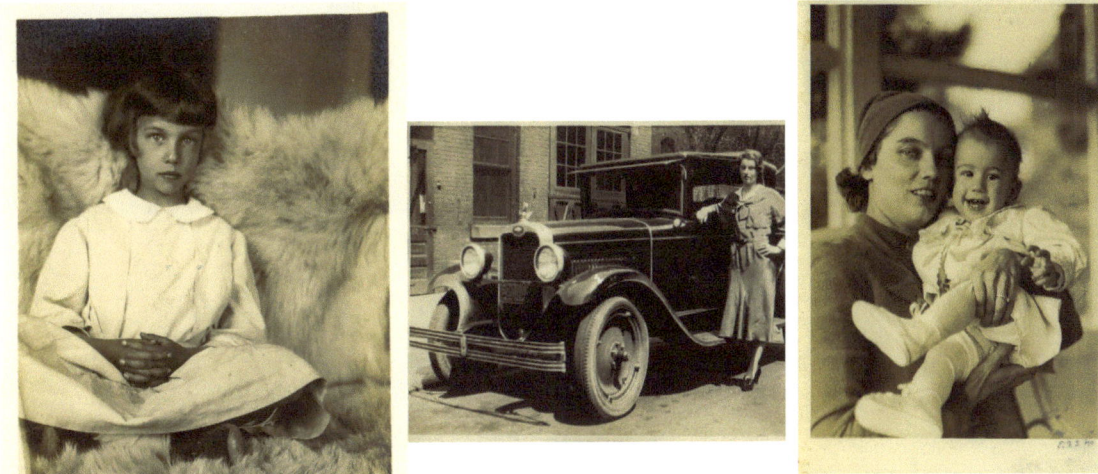

Figure 24. Left: Mary Sailer as a Child; Center: Mary Sailer in the 1920s; Right: Mary White with Her Son, Welsh, in 1940

Mary had a happy childhood in a house in central Philadelphia that eventually filled up with children. It was a privileged existence, with several servants and a rich variety of experiences. In the summer, the family traveled north by train to escape the heat and humidity of the city. For at least one year, they went to Jamestown, Rhode Island, where Mary's younger brother Joe Jr. was born in 1907. In later years, they traveled to Camden, Maine, where Mary's mother's parents, the Strawbridges, had a property called "Rockledge" on the ocean.

In later years, Mary's parents had an impressive summer "cottage" at the top of Chestnut Street in Camden, called "The Forecastle," which overlooked the ocean from its expansive rear porch. On most mornings, the family members who were staying at the house went down a steep hill to an undeveloped property with frontage on the beach, where the Atlantic Ocean met the shore. The beach was partly sandy and partly covered with rocks.

Figure 25. The "Forecastle," The Sailers' "Cottage" in Camden, Maine. Left, Possibly in the 1930s; Right, Possibly in the 1980s

117   1900 U.S. Federal Census, Trenton Ward 10, Mercer, New Jersey, District 87, Page 4, FHL film no. 1240983, showing Robert B., born in 1899, in household of Edward and Catharine Knight. U.S. Passport Applications, 1795–1925, online database at ancestry.com, citing NARA, Washington, D.C., Roll 1665, certificates 55876–56249, 20 Jun 1921–20 Jun 1921, application by Robert Barclay Knight dated 17 June 1921 says he was born in Trenton, New Jersey, on 8 July 1899. Maine, Death Index, 1960–1997, online database at ancestry.com, shows death of R. B. Knight in Portland on 14 August 1984, age 85.

On many afternoons, Mrs. Joseph Sailer drove a group of family members, including children, in the family's 1923 Moon automobile to Megunticook Lake, a few miles away from town, where the family had a small but comfortable cottage, with a wooden float and one or more boats, so the children could swim and play.[118]

In at least one of the summers in Camden, Mary and her sister Alice were tutored by Edna St. Vincent Millay, who was then a young student, not yet having achieved prominence as one of the most famous of American poets.

After Mary attended the Farnum School and then the Agnes Irwin School, from which she graduated in June 1923, her father wanted her to attend college, but she had no interest in doing that; she wanted to become a writer instead. She wrote to her father from the family's summer home in Camden to explain:

> Dear Daddy,
>
> I am sorry that you are so eager for me to go to college, as I so perfectly detest even the mere thought of it. I do not think that I possess those qualities which make you think college so necessary, but if I am wrong and I do, then I would rather never write at all than write at the price of going to college. If I cannot write without going to college, then I would consider my writing worthless if it were only the kind that college could inspire. I am afraid that you will think that this is lack of ambition, but I think that the desire to write rather than the ambition to become a writer is the only way to become a successful author. This may not be true, but if it is not true then all hope of my becoming a writer is lost. I hope that this explanation will satisfy you, for if it does not I can produce no other.
>
> If I had had any wavering thought of going to college, your letter would have clinched the matter and I would have gone. But I have never had any doubt. If in later years I regret my decision I can have no one to blame but myself, as you have given me every chance possible, and the best of reasons for your advice.
>
> I hope you will soon be up here as everything is fine in Camden now, and everyone is having a lovely time. We certainly are sorry you didn't hire the aeroplane and come from York Harbour.
>
> With love, Mary[119]

In late 1923 and early 1924, Mary traveled to France to study French and get an introduction to European culture. After returning home, she attended art classes at the Pennsylvania Academy of the Fine Arts, where she developed skills in oil painting and watercolors that she enjoyed throughout her life.

As a student, she came into contact with Miss Alice Kent Stoddard, a nationally recognized portrait painter. In 1926, Miss Stoddard produced a large oil portrait of Mary, which won a prestigious award. That portrait, shown below, is still in the family.

---

118   Personal knowledge of the author.
119   Letter from Mary L. Sailer to Joseph Sailer, M.D., 23 August 1923, in Sailer-Strawbridge family papers.

Figure 26. Portrait of Mary Lowber Sailer by Alice Kent Stoddard

In 1932, she married William Wilson White, a son of a prominent Philadelphia attorney, Thomas Raeburn White. He generally went by his middle name of Wilson. He started work in his father's law firm, and they started their family with William Wilson Jr. in April 1934.

Figure 27. Wedding of Mary Lowber Sailer and William Wilson White

Figure 28. William Wilson White

In September 1935, when Wilson was out at his father's estate in Penllyn, Pennsylvania, for a short time, he wrote Mary with the latest news, including his excitement about a new radio he had found:

> I am at this time listening to an excellent program over a very luxurious radio. It is about 2 years newer than the one I told you about, which was I think a 1933 model. This is a set never sold—was a floor sample (RCA Victor). It has as good a tone as any set I have ever heard; has short-wave; and the latest type of phonograph attachment, playing the new "long-playing" records—10 to 15 minutes—as well as regular records. Price $75—allowance for old set—$20—$55!! Came in all however, to $59.75, as I had a new part put on the speaker for $4.75. Not bad?
>
> I have many new records, 5 of which are specialties for you.[120]

Mary and Wilson continued their family with a son, Welsh Strawbridge, born in 1940; then Wilson went on active duty as a naval reserve officer in World War II, serving first on a submarine chaser and later as the executive officer on a troop transport, the U.S.S. General W.F. Hase (AP-146), rising to the rank of Commander.

Toward the end of the war, Mary moved with their two sons to 275 Denslowe Drive in San Francisco, the home port for Wilson's ship. She wrote many letters to her mother back in Philadelphia in 1945, discussing the boys' progress in their new schools, her relationships with neighbors and friends, and other matters of daily life. She sang the praises of Sarah, a maid who worked for Priscilla Deaver back in the Philadelphia area, who traveled to San Francisco to help Mary with the two boys and taking care of the house.

Mary and her mother also corresponded in some detail about the disposition of Mary and Wilson's possessions that were left behind in Philadelphia, and, after the death of her Aunt Nancy Penington on May 5, 1945, they discussed the disposition of Aunt Nancy's furniture and other possessions. They also discussed John Nutter, who had worked as the gardener for Mary's Aunt Anne West Strawbridge until her death in 1941. John had been very close to the family, and a great friend to young Welsh White, who missed him deeply. John became sick himself and died during this period. Mary also occasionally mentioned her brother John and Viking, a beloved pet dog they had had to leave behind in Philadelphia.

---

120   Letter from William Wilson White to Mary Lowber White, 6 September 1935, original in possession of the author.

Wilson wrote many letters to Mary from his troop transport ship and from the various ports the ship visited, but, because of wartime censorship rules, his letters were vague and uninformative about the ship's locations and any action that took place at sea.

One of Mary's first letters to her mother, written on stationery of The Chief, a Santa Fe Railroad train, gave an account of the train trip west:

Jan. 19 [1945]

Dear Mother,

I have written Aunt Nancy all about our excitement in catching the Chief. So for once all our precautions are justified and I am certainly glad Welfie & Sarah are coming a day early. Tell John the light baggage saved Bill & me because if we had had to wait for a porter or struggle with a heavy bag ourselves we would never have gone fast enough to make it. With Welfie I might have had a chance since they were holding the train, but I was glad I had Bill since he could go as fast as I could.

The Chief is a wonderful train & Bill & I have a magnificent lower. It is plenty big enough for two and we had a splendid night's sleep. Above is a girl named Valerie. She looks like a show girl and is very nice. Yesterday she played hearts with us for about one hour, but most of the time she spends in the club car being offered black market nylon stockings (this is a train racket) and being made up to by a couple of fur salesmen. She has a lot of light hair piled high on her head.

The Admiral, our train to Chicago, was an hour late leaving Phila. Then it did not have the right cars on it. There was no duplex, our space reserved by Mr. Dickenson. We were given a roomette and told to get a refund. However there was something wrong with the heating so that the blasts of heat filling the little roomette could not be cut off and it must have been over 90. I asked the conductor if he could change us and he got us a section in the last car. This was very nice but so cold Bill and I slept in the lower with all the blankets of both berths over us. Being in the last car made it even tenser catching the Chief, but our porter had our bags the first off and Bill & I were the first off and had gone the 14 car length before most of the other people were out of their cars. The porter said all the trains to Chicago have been running 3 or more hours late most of the time due more to the labour shortage in getting the trains made up than the weather. The Chief is now running an hour late & will lose more time.

With love,

Mary

In February, Wilson took Mary and their two small sons to tour his Navy ship, the General W.F. Hase, while it was in port in San Francisco.

[Postmarked 13 February 1945]

Dear Mother,

I just got a long letter from Alice saying you had talked to Mr. Smith about the house. However she did not seem overly anxious to sell so I guess the best idea is to wait for the spring boom. I thought when I told her we hadn't sold that she sounded very disappointed but if she doesn't mind holding I certainly don't as most of the renting worry will be your and hers instead of mine.

It was too bad about the little schnauzer. Priscilla L does not seem fated to have one. Certainly the Bauers can not have sent him in very good shape as he developed the skin disease & distemper but I guess Lawrence's theories of no germs didn't help any either.

Wilson has been gone a while. Before he left he took me & Bill & Welfie down to look over the ship. We stayed for lunch & the Captain then invited us for ice-cream & cake. It was a great success. We had lunch in the ward room. No one can sit down till Wilson comes in. There was lots of very fine food & a great many quick & efficient waiters to wait on every one. The room is full of round tables seating about 5 each. We saw the galleys, bake shop, & ice making room all working. We saw them peeling potatoes. They said it took 1200 lbs per meal.

There was great loading activity as they were soon leaving. Before we left we saw troops marching on board. Welfie took a great interest especially in the great quantities of potatoes being loaded on, and seeing the big guns & steering wheel. Bill saw a lot more than he did as Wilson took him on a separate trip down to the engine room etc. Every one was very nice showing us around. They seem to rather like visitors.

No furniture or cars yet, but they say the train the furniture is on is due Tuesday so maybe I will get some by the end of the week. The studio couch from Wanamaker's is here but no knowing when it will be sent up.

Saturday & Sunday, Bill, Sarah & I spent painting the living room. We used Kem-tone & it required two coats. Even then one side is quite streaky, but it turned out a beautiful color, aqua mixed with white. Sarah is far the best & does it very carefully and evenly.

To-day June Parsons & I did the dining-room. It turned out very well too, white with a touch of yellow. She is very gloomy & droopy to be with. She has nothing to do as she lives in a room that serves as bed-room, living-room & dining-room. Her sister died a short while ago & I do not think she herself is in very good health. She told me she could not force herself to work unless she was doing good to some one else. I am evidently the person she has picked out. She wants to come out here every day to paint, and when we have finished that she is coming every day to work in the garden. She & Rose Feuling do not speak so it is a rather difficult situation. I am trying to fill myself up with engagements so to escape her here & there. You will have to send me some of the "just say" advice.

Welfie is fine but rather bad. He, Sarah & Bill went to the zoo & beach to-day. Welfie got his feet wet, ran into the street & sat in the middle of the crowded trolley. I think he was tired as he had no nap.

Write me all about the dog show. I hope there is a ribbon or two. Did John Nutter mention the one for Viking?

Love,

Mary

A couple of months later, Mary wrote a letter that included her visit with Floy Larsen, a woman who had been a serious love interest of her brother, Joe, who was killed in the war in 1942. Floy was living in San Francisco, and they arranged to get together. The letter first discussed mundane details about clothes and furniture before turning to discussions of family and Floy Larsen:

May 1st [1945]

*　*　*

Wilson got ten days' leave and arrived last Monday night. Unfortunately Welfie was in bed with a bad cold, so we could not leave the house much. But as Wilson seemed tired this was just as well. Until to-day we have had gorgeous weather, sunny and warm. Welfie's cold is better and we have had him on one or two drives. I think he got run down by the measles and I will have to keep him out of school for a while.

I am glad John Nutter died peacefully. He seemed to be hopeful to the end which was a good thing. I received a letter from him two days before your telegram so I had no idea he was so much worse. I hope the doctor made things easier for him. The neighbors seemed very attentive, as they were all so fond of him. I can imagine the kick he got out of giving you the lettuce.

I had a very interesting letter from John. He seems delighted to be stationed in Phila. I hope he doesn't move again.

Floy Larsen came to supper last Wednesday. She was leaving S.F. the next day as she was not happy here, and indeed I could not make out why she had come, except that her job seemed about to fold in Washington, and her mother lives in Portland Oregon. She is not a bit pretty but very nice, I would say the sweet type, she is just my size with hair a touch darker. She and Joe seemed to have had a whirlwind affair, and she was very much in love with him. But I doubt if it would have lasted. She had written to him at least every other day, generally every day, and he wrote her once a week until he left the country. He had wanted her to drive out west with his car, but I think she is somewhat the helpless type without too much get up and go. She said she couldn't drive, and couldn't leave her job, though Joe was the main and greatest thing in her life and seems still to be. She has now gone back to Washington D.C. where she has an apt. she shares with her girl friend. Here her chief complaint was the living quarters, also she found her job very boring. She was going to phone John, but of course he will have gone. She said you had written her the most wonderful letters, and she treasures Joe's picture for which she has bought a beautiful leather frame. She brought it to show us. Wilson thought she was very nice.

*　*　*

In September 1945, Wilson wrote to Mary from his ship, telling her he expected to be able to leave the Navy sooner than expected:

8 September [1945]

Darling,

As I write this everything is in an excited state of uncertainty. I don't want to predict too much, so will say nothing except that I will be home at least as soon as I predicted when we sailed. Don't count on anything more yet. I will also tell you that I have been feverishly cleaning up all my work.

Had a long talk with Marshall about driving cross-country—he took the southern route and recommends it highly. You might get the AAA started on it, also I hope you are really busy on selling the house. It does look as if I might be getting a break at last, and

I have my fingers tightly crossed tonight. As you can readily conjecture, I am hoping to make myself the envy of John, Marshall, et al. That would be quite a scoop—to be the first to arrive in San Francisco!

All goes well on the ship, and as no one seems to be ready to stick a knife in me in spite of rumors of my going, I guess I didn't make too many enemies after all.

I hope you're wishing hard to see me—if you are, things may break right very soon.

All my love,

Wilson

Mary's last surviving letter from this time period was written on the road, with details about her trip from San Francisco back to Philadelphia. The letter was written on stationery from the El Rancho Hotel and Courts, Gallup, New Mexico. The first page of the original letter is shown below, followed by the full text:

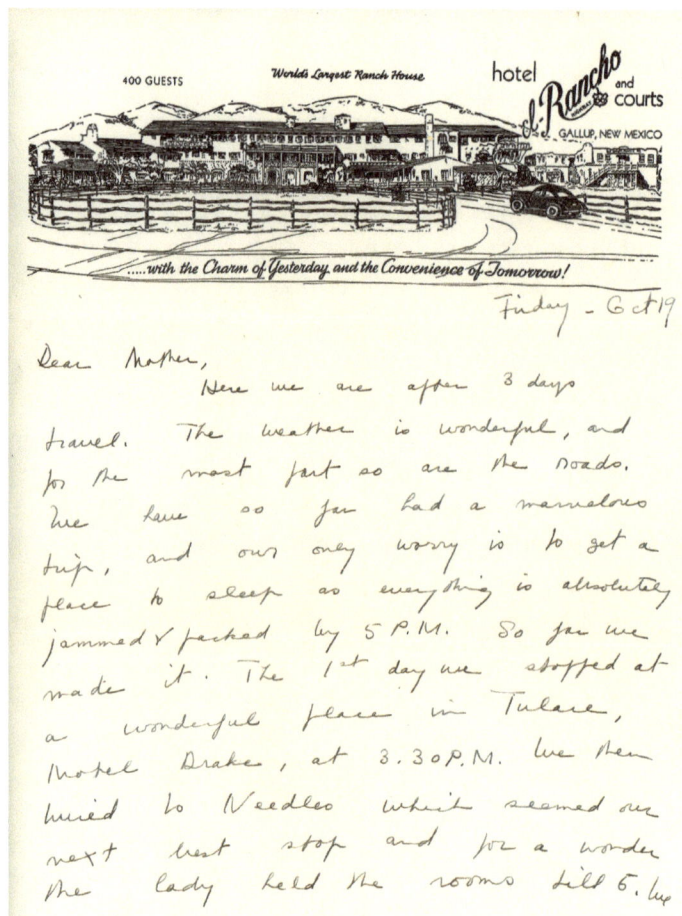

Figure 29. First Page of Letter from Mary White to her Mother, 19 October 1945

Friday, Oct 19 [1945]

Dear Mother,

Here we are after 3 days travel. The weather is wonderful, and for the most part so are the roads. We have so far had a marvelous trip, and our only worry is to get a place to sleep as everything is absolutely jammed & packed by 5 P.M. So far we made it. The 1st day we stopped at a wonderful place in Tulare, Motel Drake, at 3:30 P.M. We then hurried to Needles which seemed our next best stop, and for a wonder the lady held the rooms till 5. We just got there, though she was already turning people away when Wilson got there. To-day we couldn't decide where we wanted to go but as we saw signs for almost 400 miles to El Rancho we couldn't resist coming on and arrived here at 4:45—Wilson doing the last 101 miles in 103 minutes—though usually we don't do that well. It was just as well we did as they say they are full by 5:30 or 5 every day.

There are lots of cars on the road, but our car is much better than most and it seems as though lots off ex-war workers are going home, with all their family and possessions packed into an old car with a small trunk attachment on back. Often they just have the stuff piled in the back and tied on the top. There are also hundreds of trailers. I would say over 25% of the traffic. Welfie and Bill seem to enjoy it and are very good. We see wonderful scenery.

I have the Duncan Hines books that Reini gave me to come out. Yours didn't arrive in time, but these are 1944 and seem very good. We follow them, and AAA maps and suggestions. We had 2 tires recapped the day before we left and never go over 62 or 63 and generally less. The garage man told Wilson recaps won't stand more than 65 any length of time.

I was able to keep the washing machine and beds.

I will let you know when to expect us—but we will probably be 10 to 14 days on the way as we do not average over 300 [miles] a day.

Lots of love,

Mary[121]

After they moved back to Philadelphia, they completed the family with a third son (the author of this book) in 1948. Wilson was well-connected politically, and hoped to be appointed as a federal judge. He never achieved a judgeship, but he was appointed U.S. Attorney for the Eastern District of Pennsylvania in 1953, and later was appointed to two successive positions with the U.S. Department of Justice in Washington: Assistant Attorney General for the Office of Legal Counsel, and, after new civil rights legislation was enacted in 1957, he was named the first Assistant Attorney General for the Civil Rights Division. In that capacity, he was responsible for writing the legal opinion that authorized President Eisenhower to send federal troops to Little Rock, Arkansas, in September 1957 in support of the requirement for racial integration of the schools.

In December 1961, Mary traveled overseas with her middle son, Welsh, to bring back her oldest son, William Jr. (Bill), who had been taken sick while traveling in India and had been the object of a search by the U.S. State Department and others. Once Bill had been found, Mary and Welsh set out on this grueling trip. When they had located Bill in Baroda and determined he was safe, Mary sent a telegram to Wilson, who had had to remain back in Philadelphia.

---

121   Letter, Mary L. White to Mary L. Sailer, 19 October 1945, original in possession of the author.

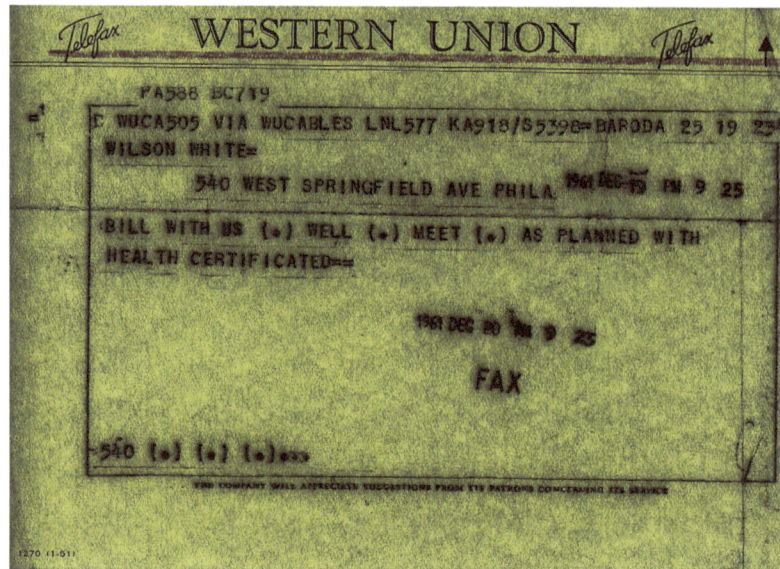

Figure 30. Telegram Sent by Mary L. White to W. Wilson White Saying Their Son Was Safe

After leaving government service, Wilson returned to the family law firm in Philadelphia, where he continued his career in private practice until his death of a heart attack in 1964.

Whenever possible, and particularly later in life, Mary had a space at home set aside for art, and she produced a great variety of canvases and watercolors over many years, mostly featuring flowers, dolls, and other everyday items, but occasionally animals, people, and other scenes that caught her fancy.

Figure 31. Paintings by Mary Lowber Sailer (White) (Knight)

In December 1967, Mary married Robert Barclay Knight, a retired stockbroker and advertising executive who had been a star athlete in his youth. They spent summers together in Camden, Maine, and for a while had a winter place on St. Croix in the U.S. Virgin Islands. They had an active social life until Barclay died in 1984.

Figure 32. Mary and R. Barclay Knight

Children of William Wilson White and Mary Lowber[5] (Sailer) White:

+ 39. i. WILLIAM WILSON[6] WHITE, JR., was born in Philadelphia on 18 April 1934 and died in Pittsburgh, Pennsylvania, on 1 February 2018.[122]

+ 40. ii. WELSH STRAWBRIDGE WHITE was born in Philadelphia on 17 April 1940 and died in Pittsburgh, Pennsylvania, on 31 December 2005.[123]

    41. iii. ALEXANDER STRAWBRIDGE WHITE.

29. JOHN[5] SAILER (*Joseph*[4], *John*[3], *Joseph*[2], *Wilhelm*[1]) was born in Philadelphia on 3 June 1909 and died in Philadelphia on 7 November 1981.[124] He married, in Palm Beach, Florida, on 31 March 1941,[125] MARION ALDRICH CROZER, who was born in Philadelphia on 27 May 1916 and died in Hilton Head Island, Beaufort, South Carolina, on 3 December 1999, daughter of Samuel Aldrich Crozer III and Helena Beale.[126] They divorced in 1947.[127]

John attended private schools in Philadelphia, graduating from Chestnut Hill Academy in 1927. After about a year of work as a clerk, he attended the University of Pennsylvania, where he graduated in 1932 with an AB degree. He

---

122   Personal knowledge of the author.

123   Personal knowledge of the author.

124   Pennsylvania, Birth Certificates, 1906–1911, online database at ancestry.com, citing Pennsylvania Historical and Museum Commission, Harrisburg, birth certificates, 1906–1910, Box number 248, certificate number range 965333–99228, certificate no. 97649 shows birth of John Sailer in Philadelphia on 3 June 1909, son of Joseph Sailer and Mary Strawbridge. U.S. Department of Veterans Affairs BIRLS Death File, 1850–2010, online database at ancestry.com, shows John Sailer, born 3 June 1909, died 7 November 1981. Death Notice, *The Philadelphia Inquirer*, 9 November 1981, p. 15-C, reporting death of John Sailer on 7 November.

125   Florida, County Marriage Records, 1823–1982, online database at ancestry.com, certificate no. 8667 shows marriage of John Sailer and Marion Aldrich Crozer on 31 March 1941 at Church of Bethesda-by-the-Sea , Palm Beach, Florida. "Miss Marion Crozer Marries John Sailer in Resort Church," *The Palm Beach Post* (West Palm Beach, Florida), 1 April 1941, p. 9.

126   1930 U.S. Federal Census, District 616, Philadelphia, FHL microfilm no. 2341838, Page 17B, shows household of Samuel A. Crozer and Helena B. Crozer with daughter Marion A., age 13, and others. U.S. Social Security Applications and Claims Index, 1936–2007, online database at ancestry.com, shows Marion Aldrich Crozer, also known as Marion Crozer McKinley, born in Philadelphia, on 27 May 1916, died on 3 December 1999. "Marion Crozer McKinley," obituary, *The News Journal* (Wilmington, Delaware), 8 December 1999, p. 20, reporting her death in Hilton Head Island, South Carolina, on 3 December 1999.

127   Florida Divorce Index, 1927–2001, online database at ancestry.com, record shows divorce of John and Marion Sailer, certificate no. 16009.

then attended the University of Pennsylvania Law School, where he earned his law degree in 1935. He eventually became a partner in the Philadelphia law firm of Pepper, Hamilton & Scheetz. He served in the U.S. Navy from 1942 to 1945.

Figure 33. John Sailer as a Child; in Uniform; at his Wedding

In 1918, when his father was serving in the U.S. Army in Georgia, John, who had recently turned nine years old, wrote him a letter postmarked July 18 from Camden, Maine, to update him on events at the summer place:

> Dear Daddy,
>
>   Our garden is growing very well. Aunt Nancy is very well. She seems to like Camden Maine. She comes to the lake with us. She has gone in bathing once. We have had very cool weather. I can not go in bathing, because my cold is not all better, Dr. Hart said that I can not go in bathing for a week. Our beach was not washed very much. It was very sandy. But then we had a bad storm, and [it] washed the sand all away, and then our beach was nothing but big stones. Our stone wall was not very much washed. It will do for another year.
>
>   With love from
>
>   John Sailer[128]

Children of John[5] Sailer and Marion (Crozer) Sailer:

42.   i. JOHN[6] SAILER.

43.   ii. CHRISTOPHER ALDRICH SAILER.

---

128   Letter from John Sailer to Joseph Sailer, postmarked 18 July 1918; original in possession of the author.

30. Priscilla Sparks[5] Sailer (*Joseph*[4], *John*[3], *Joseph*[2], *Wilhelm*[1]) was born in Philadelphia on 13 November 1910 and died in Camden, Maine, on 20 August 1994.[129] She married, first, in Philadelphia on 16 December, 1932,[130] Joshua Montgomery Deaver, who was born in Philadelphia on 10 October 1901 and died in Philadelphia on 12 November 1978, son of John Blair Deaver and Caroline Randall.[131]

She married, second, in Whitemarsh, Pennsylvania, on 10 February 1981,[132] Stillman Francis Kelley II, who was born in Massachusetts on 3 June 1906 and died in Rockport, Maine, on 3 March 1992, son of Stillman Randolph Kelley and Edith May Jouett.[133]

Priscilla was close in age to her slightly younger sister, Elizabeth ("Betty"), and the two of them made their "debut" into Philadelphia society at a series of parties, including one organized by Mr. and Mrs. Welsh Strawbridge and Anne West Strawbridge on September 21, 1929, at "Graeme Park," the historic house located on the Welsh Strawbridges' farm. Margaret Strawbridge recalled the event in an interview sixty years later. She said it was an afternoon event with a large number of guests invited, perhaps as many as one thousand, with a "very large reception," followed by a little dinner party and dancing:

> That was a lovely day. The weather was perfect. And, the two girls—Betty had an old dress which belonged to the period, about my—mine was 1810, and Betty. But Priscilla wanted a modern dress, so she wore a modern dress. And my father, and my aunt, and a number of my family were there.[134]

As shown in the photograph in Figure 34, Betty and Priscilla were both quite striking in their appearance, and it was difficult to tell them apart in some photographs. Although their Aunt Margaret recalled years later that they wore different styles of dresses, other relatives believe they both wore old dresses.[135]

---

129   Pennsylvania Birth Certificates, 1906–1911, online database at ancestry.com, citing Pennsylvania Historical and Museum Commission, Harrisburg, birth certificates, 1906–1910, Box number 356, certificate number range 178951–181950, certificate no. 180762, shows birth of Priscilla S. Sailer in Philadelphia on 13 November 1910. 1920 U.S. Federal Census, District 160, Ward 7, Philadelphia, Roll T625_1618, Page 3A, showing household of Joseph and Mary Sailer with Priscilla, daughter, age 9 6/12 as of enumeration date on 6–7 January 1920. Maine Death Index, 1960–1997, online database at ancestry.com, shows death of Priscilla S. Kelley in Camden on 20 August 1994, age 83, certificate no. 9406339. "Deaths Elsewhere," *The Philadelphia Inquirer*, 30 August 1994, p. 26, reporting death of Priscilla S. Kelley on 20 August in Camden, Maine.
130   "Deaver-Sailer," *The Philadelphia Inquirer*, 17 December 1932, p. 16, reporting wedding of Priscilla Deaver and Dr. J. Montgomery Deaver in Old St. Peter's Church, 3d and Pine Streets, on 16 December.
131   U.S. Passport Applications, 1795–1925, online database at ancestry.com, citing NARA, Washington, D.C., Roll no. 2461, certificates 387850–388349, 04 Apr 1924–05 Apr 1924, application by Joshua Montgomery Deaver dated 2 April 1924 states he was born in Wyncote, Pennsylvania, on 10 October 1901. Pennsylvania, WWI Veterans Service and Compensation Files, 1917–1918, 1934–1948, online database at ancestry.com; record shows Joshua Montgomery Deaver served in United States Marine Corps in 1918–1919, was born in Wyncote, Pennsylvania, on 10 October 1901. Online image at findagrave.com/memorial/89336534, photo of gravestone shows Joshua Montgomery Deaver, M.D., 10 October 1910–12 November 1978, and Priscilla Sailer, his wife, 13 November 1910–20 August 1994. Pennsylvania and New Jersey, Church and Town Records, 1669–2013, online database at ancestry.com, page of burial register of St. Thomas' Episcopal Church, Whitemarsh, Pennsylvania, shows Joshua Montgomery Deaver, M.D., died 12 November 1978, age 77, buried in West Laurel Hill Cemetery on 15 November 1978.
132   Pennsylvania and New Jersey, Church and Town Records, 1669–2013, online database at ancestry.com, citing Historical Society of Pennsylvania, Philadelphia, Historic Pennsylvania Church and Town Records, shows page from marriage register of St. Thomas Episcopal Church, Whitemarsh, Pennsylvania, with marriage of Stillman Francis Kelley II and Priscilla Sparks Sailer Deaver on 10 February 1981.
133   1920 U.S. Federal Census, District 170, Lexington, Middlesex, Massachusetts, Roll T625_710, Page 5B, shows Edith M. Kelley, head, with Stillman F. Kelley 2nd, son, age 13, born in Massachusetts, and others. U.S. Social Security Death Index, 1935–2015, shows birth date of 3 June 1906 and death date of March 1992. Maine Death Index, online database at ancestry.com, shows death on 3 March 1992 in Rockport, certificate no. 9202649.
134   "Now It Is All In Memory and I Shall Treasure It Always": Recollections of Margaret Marshall Strawbridge, transcript of interviews with Margaret Strawbridge (The Friends of Graeme Park, 1989) 76–77; copy in possession of the author.

135   Email message from Emily Starr to Alexander S. White, 4 July 2019.

Figure 34. Priscilla, Left, and Betty Sailer at Coming-Out Party at Graeme Park, 21 September 1929

In 1932, Priscilla married Joshua Montgomery Deaver, who went by his middle name of Montgomery. He was a prominent surgeon, eventually becoming chief of surgery at Lankenau Hospital in Lower Merion Township, just outside Philadelphia. Priscilla maintained a very active life in civic affairs, charity work, and the world of dog shows. She raised miniature schnauzers and was a nationally recognized expert on the breed, judging at dog shows including those of the Westminster Kennel Club in New York.

Figure 35. Left: Priscilla Deaver with Daughter Sally and Nephew Bill White; Center: Priscilla and Montgomery Deaver; Right; Montgomery Deaver with Mrs. Joseph Sailer

Priscilla and Montgomery were tremendously proud of their only child, Sally, born in 1933, who was a world-class athlete in more than one sport. She was at one point invited to become a member of the U.S. Olympic ski team, and in 1959 she was ranked among the top three American women skiers. She also was an excellent tennis player, and she excelled at equestrian events. Unfortunately, that skill led to her early death in Virginia in 1963, when she was killed in a fall as the horse she was riding failed to clear a jump. She was married in 1959 to Benjamin Murray, but they had no children.[136]

In 1945, while Montgomery was away for wartime duty, Priscilla wrote a letter from the family's summer place in Camden, Maine, to her sister, Mary White, who was living in San Francisco while her husband, Wilson, was at sea in the Navy. The letter was full of family news, including news of Priscilla's daughter, Sally; her niece, Priscilla Litchfield; her Aunt Daisy Sailer; and the family of her sister, Betty Churchman:

Sunday, July 9 [1945]

Dear Mary,

Have been meaning to answer your wonderful letter for weeks, but as usual haven't gotten around to it. I think it's heart breaking that Wilson is coming in in the east this time. It seems hard to know just where to live if you want to see him, but I guess the west really works out better anyway. Montgomery wrote that he may come home in a month or more although no orders have come through yet. He says C.O. Capt. Cook has gotten orders and I think left. He wanted to know your address which I sent him; so if he comes in you will see him before I do. If Wilse does come in where you think, tell him to call Willis & Eleanore DeLaCorr V.B 1374J. I know they would love to see him.

It is wonderful to be up here out of the heat. It was awful in Phila. We had a nice trip up, taking about a week. We stopped at New Canaan for five days; during that time I went back to Phila. & N.Y. for 2 days for a last little fling with Caroline & friends before the quiet of Camden; then we started off, stopping at Bennington Vt. the first night, where dinner was $4.00 a person. We had so many waiters hovering around, Sally could hardly eat. I took she & Pris, & for a wonder, the Plymouth held out; then we stopped at North Conway the next night, where I saw the Schneiders & Reids, my winter group. The children rode & swam & had a very gay time. It was awfully hot. From there we went to Prouts Neck & stayed with Dais. We had a lovely time there, but were beginning to get to the worn out stage by then.

She had a party for us. A girl of Mrs. Cates, age 14 or 15, for Pris & Sally who seemed definitely in the boy craze stage. Pris & Sally were completely out of it. She had Mrs. Cates & someone else for me for bridge. My bridge at best was not too hot but it was at worst that night; however, Dais was in a wonderful humor & never expects me to be very good.

She took us to the beach the next day, where she certainly is the queen. All of Prouts congregated under her umbrella. Dais was on a little mound of sand higher than the rest & held court. She introduced me to everyone. They all seem to have a very gay time there, but there was so much local talk I couldn't enter into. Dais had a pin, bracelet & watch all stolen from her bath house that day. My pocket book was in the next one to hers but was not touched, thank goodness.

We stayed there a day & night & arrived in Camden the next day to find everything in beautiful order. Mother, Churchmans & maids installed; so far all is peaceful except John Horace who is past being controlled by Mother. Thank God, Betty seems to take more interest in him than any of the children. She says he's such a strong character that even though he's the middle child he gets all the attention. Little Joe seems completely

---

"Sally Deaver Murray Killed as Horse Falls; Noted Skier, Socialite," *The Philadelphia Inquirer*, 15 August 1963, p. 29.

Hattie's. Of course, Hattie has nothing else to do up here. Betty is trying hard to get on & is lovely to the children. Mother has been wonderful. I am the complaining, difficult one. It's very easy to criticize the way some one else brings their children up. Of course, I had a lot of practice with the Uhle's.

The weather here has been heaven. The sailboat is in & we have done a lot of sailing. Pris & I went out alone this morning. We didn't put up a jib, much to disgust of family, but got along beautifully. Stokes hasn't arrived. I have gotten a G.I. Joe from Valley Forge Hospital for 30 days with one mutilated ear but other than that whole. He is to help with sailing & anything we want. Barrett Brown got him for me. He says he's totally reliable & not a wolf. Stokes was supposed to come yesterday but couldn't get reservations til next week, so is keeping my man to haul his luggage. He's had a coronary thrombosis but is supposedly well now. He called me & said he wanted a big strong girl to do the heavy work & he would supply the skill so the man is to do the heavy work.

The lake house is open & the float & boat in, so if the hubbub gets too great here it is a place to retire to. Mother & I have played a little golf & the children play tennis with me. With 3 maids, 2 cars, & the lake open, plus 2 sailboats, we are living like millionaires & getting fat & healthy. I wish you were here too.

Much much love,

Priscilla[137]

Many years later, Priscilla wrote another letter full of family news, this time a letter to her great-nephew David, a grandson of Priscilla's sister, Betty Churchman, to give him an idea of what her family life was like back in her childhood days, probably in response to some questions he sent her for a school project. The undated letter was written in about 1993:

Dear David,

In my day, [I] have started with getting around by horse and buggy & have lived to see us going to the moon & other marvels in space. Television did not start until after World War 2 & so we grew up with no television. We read more books. We had projects. I used to make scrap books of dogs & scrap books of great artists. I had sisters & brothers. We used to play store & we made paper money & divided it up & then had our possessions like shells & pretty glass washed up on the beach to sell & my brother John always ended up with the most money. We played with a wind-up Victrola & had records to play & my cousin Jack used to play the drum. We played double solitaire & parchesi & your grandmother & I played with our large baby dolls & pretended they were our own babies.

We lived in the city. Our father was a doctor & had his office in our house in the early years. Later, he moved to his own office. We had a cook & a butler. The kitchen was on the ground floor & the dining room on the 2nd floor. Julius (our butler) brought our food up on the dumb waiter. It had shelves & you pulled it up by a rope. The pantry was upstairs & Julius served the meals & then washed all the dishes.

We played in Rittenhouse Square. We had roller skates & tricycles. We played hopscotch & prisoners base. We skipped rope. We only got presents at Christmas & on our

---

137   Letter from Priscilla Deaver to Mary L. White, July 9, 1945, original in possession of the author.

birthdays. Occasionally we spent a weekend with our grandmother & our aunt. They had a wonderful farm in Mount Airy. They had horses, ponies, & all kinds of carriages, dogs, cats & kittens & vegetable gardens. Also rose gardens. We loved to go there.

Yes, we loved to go to school. We walked to school & started with kindergarten, then first grade & so on. Your grandmother & I had a nurse to take care of us & we loved her. Pen's nurse once told me if I was naughty the rag man would get me. I was terrified when he came down the street yelling any old rags today. The organ grinder & his monkey came down our street often. We would rush out & listen & give the monkey pennies in his hat. We went to the Mummers Parade every New Year's Day. It was wonderful, but freezing. During World War One we hated the Germans & sang patriotic songs like Johnnie Get Your Gun; Over There; It's a Long Way to Tipperary; and so on. We hated the Kaiser & we all bought Liberty Bonds. My father went to war & so did Uncle Jack Strawbridge.

There were four girls & three boys in our family. Three more were born but didn't live past five years. I was no. five & was teased a lot by the older ones, also squelched. You had to be tough & that was the hard part. My mother was very strict. I don't know whether this was good or bad. I do know it made your grandmother & me very shy.

We went to Camden, Maine, every summer. We went from Phila. on the Bar Harbor Express train. We took up one whole sleeping car with maids, children, cousins, etc. We took our own food in hampers. There were upper & lower berths & at Portland the trains separated & ours went to Rockland & the other set went to Bar Harbor. At Bath our train was put on the ferry to cross the river. We stayed in Maine for three months. It was my favorite time—except for two summers when your grandmother & I went to camp. We both hated it. We were not good athletes & they said we were detriments to our team. The other years we loved. We played at the beach & in the afternoon went to the lake if there was enough room in the Moon car for us. We climbed mountains & went fishing. Our grandmother had a place there too, on the water. We went to fairs & baseball games. It was such fun. We rented horses one year & a wagon & a saddle. We took them swimming in the lake one day & were very sad when we had to leave.

I forgot to tell when there were fires the fire engines were horse-drawn & would go galloping up the street clanging their bells, in the city. Also there were trolleys on our street that came by every 20 minutes. They were very noisy but we got used to it.

> All love,
>
> Aunt Priscilla[138]

In the late 1960s, a local newspaper named Montgomery Deaver "Citizen of the Week," and published a detailed profile of his life. It provides a good overview of his accomplishments and character:

> A 67-year-old gentleman farmer here in Ambler crosses the Schuylkill River every morning to breakfast in Overbrook at seven o'clock before a long day practicing surgery.

---

138   Letter from Priscilla Kelley to David Churchman, approximately 1993; copy in possession of the author.

Whether at "Brookside Farm" or in Lankenau Hospital, Dr. J. Montgomery Deaver knows the stimulation of congenial hard work. To diligence and skill he adds the gift of personality.

Clearly the grand old man of the hospital, who carried on a legend when he filled the post of Chief of General Surgery held by his father before him, "Monty" Deaver comes on debonair and modern.

The fact that he is also illustrious may be gleaned by an outsider from certain written materials, if not in verbal exchange.

 Most recent evidence of this is the establishment of the J. Montgomery Deaver Lecture in Surgery by the Department of General Surgery at Lankenau. It honors the man who was Chief of Surgical Service "A" for 24 years and of General Surgery for four years, until he was promoted last year to Senior Consultant in Surgery.

The last giant step relieved Dr. Deaver from administrative duties and meetings. It enables him to breakfast at seven, instead of 6:30 a.m. Otherwise, the change is miniscule.

"I try not to schedule more than one or two major operations a day," he says reasonably, explaining that "major" means of two or three hours' duration.

When the first Deaver Lecture was given on Oct. 11, by Dr. James T. Priestly of the Mayo Clinic, on "Surgical Lesions of the Pancreas," residents, interns and medical students from area institutions attended. That was particularly satisfying to Dr. Deaver, who began to develop a teaching service in Lankenau's Surgical Department when he became head of "A" in 1942.

Dr. Deaver explains that "the real beginning of Lankenau as a teaching hospital" came when Dr. John H. Gibbon, Jr., the father of the heart-lung machine, became Professor of Surgery at Jefferson Medical College, and sent surgical students out to Lankenau.

Dr. Deaver's connection with Jefferson deepened when he served as Associated Professor of Surgery at that Medical College from 1949 to 1964. Also in the teaching vein was Dr. Deaver's post as Professor of Clinical Surgery at the Graduate School of Medicine of the University of Pennsylvania.

A graduate of Penn's Medical School, following Hill School and Yale University, Dr. Deaver finished his internship at Lankenau in 1930, at the old Hospital, Girard Ave. and Corinthian St. He began his preceptorship there under his father, Dr. John B. Deaver, who was Chief Surgeon of Lankenau from 1886 until his death in 1931, and world renowned as a surgeon, teacher, and writer.

The John B. Deaver Centennial Lecture, given in 1960 by Dr. I.S. Ravdin, executive vice-president in charge of medical affairs for the University of Pennsylvania, contained this statement about the elder Dr. Deaver:

"His Saturday afternoon clinics at the Lankenau Hospital were attended by students from all our medical schools and by surgeons from all parts of the world. No surgeon came to Philadelphia but that he attended the Professor's clinics."

Those days are perpetuated in Sterner's floor-to-ceiling oil painting of Dr. John B. Deaver in this clinic situation, operating on the artist's wife, while ringed about with student observers. It hangs now on the lower level of the main hospital building at the Lancaster Ave., Overbrook location where the institution was relocated in 1953. A three-dimensional replica of the famous painting will be made for the entrance of the Archives Room in the now-in-progress Cyclorama of Life area, adjacent to the main hospital lobby.

This project is of vital interest to Joshua Montgomery Deaver, M.D., named for his grandfather, who was a country doctor in Lancaster County. The Cyclorama is a $369,500 investment intended to bring the latest in expanded health education programs to the public—particularly the teen-age public.

Dr. Deaver has already raised $102,292.93 for the Archives Room, which is an indication of his interest in preserving the valuable old within the framework of the exciting new.

Keeping up with the new is the purpose of the Cyclorama of Life. It will provide the hospital's Department of Health Education with a flexible tool to meet the expansion in medicine. Emphasis is on teen-age health problems, according to Dr. Deaver. Each major unit—tobacco, alcohol, drugs and sex—will have its own slide or film presentation, utilizing the most modern audio-visual techniques.

Since 22 different school districts now participate in Lankenau's health education programs, reaching 6,000 youngsters a month, the preventive health education benefits are incalculable.

The teaching impulse remains undiminished in Dr. Deaver. In a recent interview in his Lankenau Hospital office he commented on evolution in the field of surgery:

"Technical advances and bio-chemical advances in surgery have made it just like going into the Nuclear Age. There have been great advances, not only on mechanical lines, but in application of the basic sciences—chemistry, biology and physics. Today it is a far more complex thing than it was for my grandfather or father. It is more highly specialized. The field is so intricate that a man can no longer be a Jack-of-all-trades. It's been a gradual thing, but in my father's time, a man could still be a Jack-of-all-trades."

Dr. Deaver adds that he finds it satisfying "to have played a part in establishing the cardio-pulmonary and open heart surgery laboratory at Lankenau about seven years ago." He developed the department in conjunction with Surgical Service.

"I raised the money to get the lab off the ground," he recalls. "I don't like to raise money, but I felt I must go out and appeal—to tell them that one multi-channel recorder costs $44,780."

The surgeon expressed his gratitude for the financial support of Miss Ethel Pew in this lab development. Touring the lab area, he pointed out a multi-channel recorder used in cardiac catheterization. It is bigger than a breadbox; it looks as if it was worth every nickel.

A purposeful man at every phase in his life, Dr. Deaver earned a varsity letter, as an end on the football team at Yale University's Sheffield Scientific School in 1921, '22 and '23, while earning a B.S. degree.

He served with the U.S. Marine Corps in World War I and the U.S. Navy in World War II. For action in the latter war, he was awarded a Bronze Star.

Among professional groups where his active interest has been given, Dr. Deaver lists the American Surgical Assn., the Philadelphia Academy of Surgery, of which he is a past president, the American College of Surgeons, in which he is a Fellow, and the International Society of Surgeons.

Dr. Deaver is married to the former Priscilla Sparks Sailer, Philadelphia, daughter of the distinguished Dr. Joseph Sailer, whose name is associated with the University of Pennsylvania and Presbyterian Hospital.

The Deavers moved to Ambler in 1947. Dr. Deaver describes their "Brookside Farm" at 110 Skippack Pike, as "a working farm where hay, alfalfa, wheat and corn are the crops." His specialty is Black Angus cattle, while his wife raises miniature Schnauzers and is well known in the area as a judge for the breed.

They lost their only child, daughter Sally, in 1963 when she was killed while training a horse. Dr. Deaver's personal archives show Sally, radiant after winning a silver medal in the 1958 World Alpine Ski Championships, in Bad Gastein, Austria.

They show, by default, his conviction that the life of joyful participation extends itself, generation to generation.[139]

Montgomery died in 1978 and, in 1981, Priscilla married Stillman F. Kelley II, whom she had known during summers in Camden, Maine. Stillman was an excellent athlete, who won or placed high in the rankings in golf tournaments over the years in Maine. They moved to his house on Chestnut Street in Camden, where they lived until his death in 1992.

Figure 36. Priscilla and Stillman Kelley

Child of Joshua Montgomery Deaver and Priscilla Sparks[5] (Sailer) Deaver:

---

139   "Top Lankenau Surgeon Adds New Distinction to Old Name," *The Ambler Gazette*, approximately November 1968, page number unknown; clipping in possession of the author.

+   44.   i. SALLY LOWBER[6] DEAVER was born in Philadelphia on 14 November 1933 and died in Hot Springs, Bath, Virginia, on 14 August 1963.

31.   ELIZABETH TWELLS[5] SAILER (*Joseph*[4], *John*[3], *Joseph*[2], *Wilhelm*[1]) was born in Philadelphia on 27 January 1912 and died in Lafayette Hill, Montgomery County, Pennsylvania, on 19 March 1988.[140] She married, in Philadelphia on 23 December 1936,[141] JOHN HORACE CHURCHMAN, who was born on 9 December 1909 and died in Weymouth, Nova Scotia, Canada, on 4 August 1988, the son of Clark Wharton Churchman and Helen Norah Fassitt.[142]

Figure 37. Wedding of Elizabeth Twells Sailer and John Horace Churchman. Adults from Left: Priscilla Deaver, Elizabeth Sailer, J. Horace Churchman, Clark Wharton Churchman. Children from Left: William W. White Jr., Sally Deaver, Priscilla Litchfield

As noted earlier, Elizabeth (Betty) was close in age to Priscilla, and they made their social debut together in 1929. After finishing her studies at the Agnes Irwin School, Betty worked for a photographer for a while, and then

140   1920 U.S. Federal Census, District 160, Ward 7, Philadelphia, Roll T625_1618, Page 3A, shows household of Joseph Sailer with Elizabeth, age 7 11/12 as of January 1920. U.S. Social Security Death Index, 1935–2014, online database at ancestry.com, showing Elizabeth Churchman, born 27 January 1912, died 19 March 1988. "Death Notices," *The Philadelphia Inquirer*, 21 March 1988, p. 6-B, reporting death of Elizabeth T. Churchman, née Sailer, age 76, at her home in Lafayette Hill.
141   "Elizabeth Sailer Weds John Horace Churchman," *The Philadelphia Inquirer*, 27 December 1936, p. 46, reporting wedding on 23 December at St. Peter's Church, 3d and Pine Streets.
142   Pennsylvania Birth Certificates, 1906–1911, online database at ancestry.com, citing Pennsylvania Historical and Museum Commission, Harrisburg, birth certificates, 1906–1910, Box number 289, certificate number range 196745–199561, certificate no. 198407, shows birth of John Horace Cheachman [sic] in Philadelphia on 9 December 1909, son of C. Wharton Churchman and Norah Fassitt. U.S. WWII Draft Cards Young Men, 1940–1947, online database at ancestry.com, citing NARA St. Louis, Missouri, Records of the Selective Service System, record group 147, box number 412, original record viewed at fold3.com, dated 16 October 1940, shows John Horace Churchman, born 9 December 1909. U.S. Social Security Death Index, 1935–2014, shows J. H. Churchman, born 9 December 1909, died 4 August 1988. "Death Notices," *The Philadelphia Inquirer*, 6 August 1988, p. 5-B, reports death of John Horace Churchman in Weymouth, Nova Scotia, on 4 August 1988.

married John Horace Churchman, who went on to become a partner handling estate matters in the Philadelphia law firm of Drinker, Biddle & Reath. He loved golf, archery, badminton, and other sports, and enjoyed gardening.[143]

For his archery, he carved out two fields on the family's property, each one 80 yards long, and used a long bow with a heavy pull.[144]

His sports activities were hampered when, around 1944, he was hit in the eye by a badminton racket, causing serious injury to his eye.[145] He was heavily involved in affairs of Christ Church and Christ Church Hospital, serving as a vestryman of the church.[146]

Figure 38. Left: Elizabeth "Betty" Churchman, at Right, with her Three Sisters, 1981; Right: John Horace Churchman

Children of John Horace Churchman and Elizabeth[5] (Sailer) Churchman:

    45. i. EMILY WOODWARD[6] CHURCHMAN.

    46. ii. ELIZABETH TWELLS CHURCHMAN was born in Philadelphia on 24 April 1939 and died on 25 April 1939.[147]

    47. iii. JOHN HORACE CHURCHMAN JR.

    48. iv. JOSEPH SAILER CHURCHMAN.

  + 49. v. CHARLES WEST CHURCHMAN was born in Philadelphia on 23 January 1947 and died on 29 July 2018.

    50. vi. ALICE WELSH CHURCHMAN.

---

143   Email from Emily Starr to Alexander S. White, 29 April 2019.
144   Email from Joseph Churchman to Alexander S. White, 12 May 2019.
145   Email from Emily Starr to Alexander S. White, 29 April 2019.
146   Email from Joseph Churchman to Alexander S. White 14 May 2019.
147   Pennsylvania Death Certificates, 1906–1966, online database at ancestry.com, citing Pennsylvania Historic and Museum Commission, Death Certificates, 1906–1965, certificate number range 32001–35000, certificate no. 32913 shows death of Baby Churchman in Philadelphia on 25 April 1939, date of birth 24 April 1939, parents J. Horace Churchman and Elizabeth Sailer. To be buried in Woodlands Cemetery, 26 April 1939.

The Sixth Generation

NOTE: This chapter discusses only the few individuals from this generation who were deceased at the time of writing. Information about living persons has been withheld to the extent possible, in order to preserve their privacy.

39. WILLIAM WILSON[6] WHITE JR. (*Mary White*[5], *Joseph*[4], *John*[3], *Joseph*[2], *Wilhelm*[1]) was born in Philadelphia on 18 April 1934 and died in Pittsburgh, Pennsylvania, on 1 February 2018.[148] He married, first, in Philadelphia on 14 April 1962, INGRID MARIEANNE HUNGERSHAUSEN, who was born in Germany about 1939.[149] The marriage ended in divorce on 28 June 1968.[150] He married, second, in Santa Fe, New Mexico on 17 September 1976,[151] THELMA JEAN PIERCE, who was born in Quincy, Massachusetts, on 18 August 1957 and died in Batavia, Genesee, New York, on 5 November 2005.[152] The marriage ended in divorce on 27 September 1983.[153]

Wilson and Mary White's oldest son was always called Bill. He was a cheerful, intelligent, and athletic boy. He attended the William Penn Charter School in Philadelphia for several years, then traveled to San Francisco with his mother and brother, Welsh, for a time while his father served in the Navy. When they returned after World War II, Bill resumed studies at Penn Charter. By 1949, he was representing the school in a multi-school track meet, scoring points in the low hurdles and broad jump.[154]

Figure 39. William Wilson White Jr., Shown at Right on Wedding Day in 1962 with his Wife, Ingrid

In his early years, Bill led an active life, traveling in the summers to Maine, where he played with his cousins, particularly Priscilla Litchfield and Sally Deaver, who were close to him in age.

---

148   Personal knowledge of the author.
149   "Marriage License Applications," *The Philadelphia Inquirer*, 6 April 1962, showing application of Ingrid Marieanne Hungershausen, 23, and William White, Jr., 27. ""White-Hungershausen," *The Philadelphia Inquirer*, 15 April 1962, p. 79, reporting marriage on 14 April 1962.
150   Divorce papers from German court in family records.
151   Email from Delia White to Alexander S. White, 10 May 2019.
152   U.S., Social Security Applications and Claims Index, 1936–2007, online database at ancestry.com, citing death certificate number 721 TURNER FH 14020; email from Delia White to Alexander S. White, 18 May 2019.
153   Place of death and date of divorce provided by Delia White in an email to Alexander S. White, 18 May 2019
154   "Victory in Triangular Track Gives Bartram Perfect Season," *The Evening Bulletin* (Philadelphia), 26 May 1949, page no. unknown.

Figure 40. Left and Center: Bill White with his Cousin Priscilla Litchfield in Maine, 1930s. Right: Bill with his Cousin Sally Deaver

In 1950, he wrote a letter to his young brother, Welsh, at home in Philadelphia, from Camden, Maine, where Bill was already an accomplished sailor, taking his great-aunt and great-uncle for a trip:

July 21 [1950]

Dear Welfie,

You certainly have become a wonderful letter writer and I think your printing is a lot better too.

Today Uncle Welsh, Aunt Margaret, and I started out at 9:30 for Castine. We were planning to get there in time for lunch. Everything, however, seemed to be against us. The sail we were using had been used only twice before, and therefore had still to be stretched considerably before it was any good for tacking; the wind was dead against us so that we had to tack all the way; the charts we had on board did not go as far north as Castine.

After three and [a] half hours of sailing we reached the end of the chart and Castine was still a long way off. Therefore we decided to turn back. We thought that with the wind behind us we would be back in Camden in time for a late lunch.

For a while everything was fine; we breezed along nicely with spinnaker pulling and thought we would be back in time. Our dreams were short-lived, however. The wind died out, and after a few minutes came up from the South, directly opposite from what it had been. After four hours of beating back and forth with the wind dying out every now and then, we reached Camden—at 5:30, and still without any lunch.

We rushed off to a restaurant, but couldn't eat too much as it was only an hour before supper.

We all had a lot of fun however, and it certainly made supper taste good.

In the last two races we came in 7th out of 11 and 4th out of 12.

I hope your snake lives and you continue to be the center of attraction.

Love, Bill[155]

---

155   Letter from William Wilson White Jr. to Welsh White, 21 July 1950, original in possession of the author.

Bill graduated from Penn Charter with honors in 1951 and went off to Princeton, where he did well academically, studying the poet Gerard Manley Hopkins in particular, and graduated with honors in 1955. Later that year he traveled in Europe, and enjoyed the benefits of having an uncle, Lawrence Litchfield Jr., who had close ties to Europe through his family. Bill told the story of his encounter with a great movie star in Paris in a letter home:

Dec. 31 [1955]

Dear Mom,

I missed being home for Christmas though I did have a very interesting time. I spent three days with the Van Boetzelaers, who were extremely nice to me, but live in a world apart—and a rather dull one at that. By far the most interesting episode was Christmas dinner with Audrey Hepburn. Mel Ferrer, Mrs. Tripp (the late Mrs. Ferrer), and her two children came to lunch. The whole thing was somewhat of an ordeal for everyone concerned as the Ferrers have almost no avenue of rapport with the Van Boetzelaers (Audrey is a niece—I believe—of Mrs., which accounts for the connection in the first place). Mel and Audrey arrived half an hour late (Mrs. had almost phoned) and, perhaps a bit ironically, went into ecstasies over the flowers (which adorned every nook and cranny of the downstairs rooms), Christmas tree, creche, etc. Audrey was taking obvious pleasure in playing her role rather after the pattern of Roman Holiday.

At dinner the conversation revolved around truffles, pine cones, swans at Les Bois de Boulogne, and occasionally spiraled to the heights of perfume. I was sitting between Margaret and Audrey and must admit I was at a bit of loss to know how to talk to her (Audrey), but we talked a bit about my plans (going to Switzerland) and about Audrey's plans for the near future. She is making one film in the spring and may make another before it, but refuses to say any more until she can be more definite. I was very taken with Audrey and she was very charming to me the little we conversed. Both she and Mel can give the impression of being very ingenuous and sincere people but whether they are just superb actors I do not know. The one time they became completely real—in the sense of not acting—was when they were discussing the floods in view of a film that Mel Ferrer wants to make. He and Audrey then moved into a sofa together and became engrossed in a book of flood pictures, and he was telling her how he would direct the film.

The relationship of Mrs. Tripp is a fascinating question. She seems like an extremely nice woman but was rather left out during most of the incredibly trivial conversation. Her two children—named, ironically, Mel & Melee—are quite shy and very nice looking; and she apparently brought them to Paris—from Switzerland—in order to see Mel for Christmas. I cannot begin to comprehend the relationships but to the rumors that Mel & Audrey are somewhat tense with one another and that Audrey was more than friendly with Billy Wilder, you may add the fact that Susie, whom I like very much (in spite of her complete lack of poise and retraction into a world shut in by horses and dogs she has a certain sincerity), went with Audrey and the children the next day to see "The Lady and the Tramp"; Mrs. Tripp did not go, however, as Mel was going to the studio in half an hour and she had "so much to talk over with him."

 * * * [The letter went on to say he was leaving Paris the next day and going to Duvos.]

Love, Bill[156]

Bill continued his travels in Europe for quite a while, attending graduate courses there, and also spent some time in graduate studies at Yale University back in the United States. By this time, though, he was increasingly suffering from effects of a congenital disease, retinitis pigmentosa, which seriously affected his vision and made it impossible to drive a car or carry on other activities he had been accustomed to doing.

By the early 1960s, he had met Ingrid Hungershausen in Germany. At some point, he traveled to India in his continuing quest for information about the world and his own existence. He evidently became disoriented and was cut off from communication with his family in the United States. His father, who had returned to private law practice from federal service, turned to his contacts with the government, who enlisted the assistance of the U.S. Department of State. Bill was eventually located in India, and his mother, Mary, traveled to India with her middle son, Welsh, to bring him back.[157]

Bill spent some time recuperating in a hospital in Philadelphia. Then, in March 1962, his fiancée, Ingrid, traveled from Germany to Philadelphia to join him.[158] They were married in Philadelphia on 14 April 1962.[159] They lived at various times in Philadelphia, New Mexico, and Germany. In June 1968, they were divorced in Munich, Germany. Ingrid stayed in Germany and Bill returned to the United States.

In the mid-1970s, Bill met Thelma Jean Pierce, who was born 15 August 1957. They married in New Mexico in 1976 and had one child. The marriage eventually ended in divorce, and Thelma died on 5 November 2005. Bill lived with his mother in Philadelphia for a number of years, then, after her death in 1992, moved to Pittsburgh, Pennsylvania, to be near his brother, Welsh, and Welsh's family, who helped raise Bill's daughter.

Over the years, Bill created many oil paintings and other works of art and literature. He created striking paintings despite his visual impairment. The painting shown below is an oil portrait he did of his brother, Welsh.

---

157   "Missing Son of White Found in India Hospital," *Philadelphia Daily News*, 12 December 1961, p. 3.
158   New York State, Passenger and Crew Lists, 1917–1967, online database at ancestry.com, citing NARA, Washington D.C., NAI number 2990227, Records of the Immigration and Naturalization Service, 1787–2004, Record Group 85, Series A4115, Roll number 705; original record shows arrival of Ingrid Hungershausen in New York, New York, on 22 March 1962, on the German M/S Berlin.
159   "White-Hungershausen," *The Philadelphia Inquirer*, 15 April 1962, p. 79, reporting marriage on 14 April 1962.

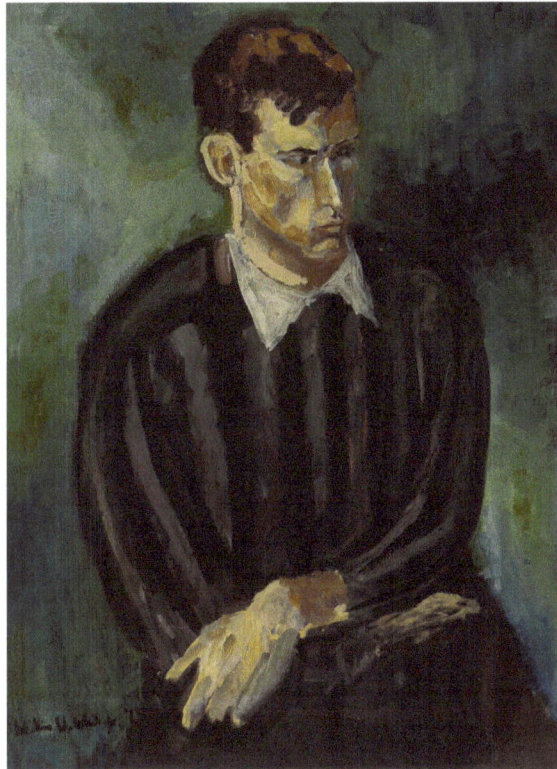

Figure 41. Portrait of Welsh S. White Painted by his Brother, William Wilson White Jr.

Bill died in Pittsburgh on 1 February 2018.

40. WELSH STRAWBRIDGE[6] WHITE (*Mary White*[5], *Joseph*[4], *John*[3], *Joseph*[2], *Wilhelm*[1]) was born in Philadelphia on 17 April 1940 and died in Pittsburgh, Pennsylvania, on 31 December 2005.[160] He married, first, in Philadelphia on 15 May 1965, JOYCE McELHENY, who was called "Kate" by Welsh and his family. The marriage ended in divorce in October 1974. He married, second, on 1 June 1979, LINDA MAY TIMMONS.[161]

Welsh grew up in Philadelphia as a boy who loved sports. He excelled in soccer, tennis, and squash, and loved to follow professional boxing, baseball, and basketball. He also was an excellent student, starting at Chestnut Hill Academy and later transferring to the William Penn Charter School. For a short time in 1945, he attended school in San Francisco, where his family moved while his father was serving on a Navy ship. Welsh discovered Shakespeare at an early age, and loved to perform long passages he had memorized, for family members. He won prizes for English and French on graduation.

---

160   Personal knowledge of the author.
161   Personal knowledge of the author.

Figure 42. Welsh Strawbridge White: Center, with Brother Bill; Right, with Brothers Alexander and Bill, and Their Father

Welsh enjoyed going to his grandmother's summer place in Camden, Maine, during the summers when he was younger, before he started going to overnight summer camps. Later in life, he wrote his recollections of those days, for inclusion in a family newsletter:

> During the forties, I spent most of my summers with my grandmother (Mary Lowber Sailer) and some of her other grandchildren in her big house on Chestnut St. in Camden, Maine. My memories of the summers of 1947–48 are fairly good; so I will recount some of them. One of my favorite parts of the summer was the train trip from Philadelphia to Camden. The train would leave 30th St. at Philadelphia in the early evening and would arrive in Rockland the next morning. We would have dinner on the train, sometimes in the restaurant car, and would sleep in a bunk bed. In 1947, I went up on the train with cousin John Stokes; in 1948, I traveled with Hattie, one of Granny's two maids. When I traveled with Hattie, I remember that we could not eat in the restaurant car because they would not serve black people there. We had the dinner brought to our seats. I remember that my meal, which included steak, cost $4, which seemed an outrageously high price at that time. The house on Chestnut Street was a huge green wooden house. It had a somewhat spooky appearance and was wonderful for exploring. Even though I spent many summers there, I don't think I ever saw all the rooms. Granny would sometimes have 7 or 8 grandchildren staying for most of the summers, 3 or 4 guests visiting for shorter periods, and always 2 maids sleeping in the maids' rooms. Yet there always seemed to be plenty of space. During the summers of 1947–48, I slept in a room that was at the very end of the house and had a nice view of the bay. You could see boats bobbing in the blue ocean. Other cousins also generally kept the same rooms. I remember that Priscilla, the oldest grandchild and Granny's favorite, had the room next to Granny. The grandchildren, especially the younger ones, followed a regular routine. We always went to the beach in the morning and the lake in the afternoon. During those years, I especially liked the walk to the beach. It seemed as if we were on a path in the middle of the woods when all of a sudden a magnificent view of the beach appeared. Granny always drove us to the lake in her old green car, a 1926 [sic; actually 1923] Moon in excellent condition. The color of the Moon matched the color of the house.
>
> The part of the day I least liked was right after lunch. All the younger grandchildren would have to take a nap. The nap probably lasted only an hour, but it seemed longer. Aside from going to the beach and lake, some of my favorite activities involved playing in the den. The den was totally child oriented. It had a wonderful supply of blocks and I used to spend hours building elaborate houses. We would also sometimes play croquet or other games outside the house.

Granny was strict. If you disobeyed, you were punished. But in those summers, I can't really remember any punishments. Everyone knew that you had to do what Granny said. Certain basic principles were drilled into our heads: "No one says 'no' to Granny; no one says 'won't' to Granny." If you recognized that Granny was in charge, it was easy to get along. Granny was born in 1875. At 73 and 74 (her ages in 1947–48), she looked old because her hair was gray and her face was very wrinkled. Nevertheless, she was ramrod straight and vigorous both in mind and body. She would generally walk three miles a day for her "constitution" and she played competitive duplicate bridge until she was well into her eighties.

Granny was fair; but she did make mistakes. I remember in one of those summers my cousin Larry and I were at the Camden library. For some reason, I was waving my hand in front of Larry's face; irritated, he gave me a little bite on one of my fingers. It was no big deal; but at lunch somebody asked me about the mark on my finger. Without thinking, I responded, "Oh that's where Larry bit me." Larry's mother, Aunt Alice, said, "Oh Larry, how could you?" But Larry immediately said he hadn't done it. Then, Granny looked closely at my finger and decided that the mark didn't look like a bite. She thought rather it had been caused by a stone. During the regular nap hour after lunch, Granny interrogated me about the mark on my finger. For quite awhile I adhered to my story, since it was the truth. But Granny had a variety of effective interrogation techniques. I remember one central theme was that people who tell the truth are respected. If you tell a lie, you're not respected. She told me some of the people who were respected because they told the truth. My father was one, cousin John Stokes was another. Then she came up with what was probably the clincher. She said, "You were somebody who was respected because you tell the truth. Until this incident, everybody thought you were an honest honorable person." I was concerned about this and asked if people's opinions about me were irrevocably changed. Granny said, "No. Its never too late to tell the truth. If you admit that you lied about Larry and say what really happened to your finger, then people will respect you just as they did before." That was enough for me. I then admitted that I had lied about Larry and had really hurt my finger on a stone. After my admission, I had to apologize to Larry for falsely accusing him. Larry graciously accepted my apology.

Although Granny was certainly an honest and honorable person, in the interest of a greater good, she would occasionally tell a falsehood herself. During one of those summers, I asked her what happened to the maiden who fell off Maiden's cliff. Granny told me that the girl was very badly hurt and was in the hospital for a long time. But she said that the young have remarkable recuperative powers and, in fact, the girl completely recovered and was now an old woman living in Camden. I completely believed this story. In fact, about 20 years later, I was telling some of my relatives and others about how the girl who fell off Maiden's cliff went on to make a complete recovery and to lead a long productive life. I never finished the story, however, because it was interrupted by laughter. As I later learned, Ms. French, the girl who fell off Maiden's Cliff died after the fall, which occurred during the 1860s. I guess Granny didn't want an eight year old boy to confront this grim reality.[162]

---

162   Recollections by Welsh S. White, undated document in possession of the author.

Welsh went on to study at Harvard College, again with academic success. He continued with sports, though not at the intercollegiate level, playing squash and soccer. He started out majoring in mathematics, switched to economics, and ended up with English, because of his continued love of Shakespeare. He kept up a lively correspondence with his mother, often filling her in on the mundane details of college life, but occasionally bursting into youthful playfulness:

[postmarked 23 January 1960]

Dear Mom,

Thank you for your letter. It ran my streak to twelve. I have been studying very hard for the exams and everything seems very tense, though Dean maintains his customary good spirits. Yesterday I took the Physics exam and I think I did well; but I felt at times like a pitcher who had once had a great fast ball, but had lost it and had to rely on his cunning and wiles to get by. Well, well, I see I talk but idly and you laugh at me.

I still think I got a B on the exam and if I could [get] a B on it, I should be able to get B's in my other subjects. Bob and I saw the fight last night; it was very poor and though neither man fought at all, I think the decision going to Pender was a mistake.

I have still not yet completely decided my major though I have officially changed in to economics, I can easily change again into anything I want to, that includes a dragon, a bear, or a lion, but not of course a hippopotamus.

Love,

Macbeth[163]

After college, Welsh attended the University of Pennsylvania Law School, where he applied himself enthusiastically to his studies and did very well. After law school, he worked for a time in the law firm that had been his grandfather's, and where his father and uncle were partners, White & Williams. He fairly soon found that corporate practice was not where his interests lay, and he went to work as an Assistant District Attorney in the office of District Attorney (later U.S. Senator) Arlen Specter.

After a few years in the District Attorney's office, Welsh moved into the field of teaching, which turned out to be his true calling, and where his achievements earned him great respect and honors. He was a long-time professor at the University of Pittsburgh law school, where he was "a devoted teacher, who was beloved by his students, and a committed colleague, who always found time to serve as a thoughtful and caring mentor."[164]He published numerous articles and several books on the death penalty, and he worked steadily to save clients from death sentences and to work toward the eventual abolition of the penalty.

Welsh was a devoted family man, with children from two marriages. He continued a very active life until he was stricken with lung cancer in 2005 and died on the last day of the year.

41. SALLY LOWBER[6] DEAVER (*Priscilla Deaver*[5], *Joseph*[4], *John*[3], *Joseph*[2], *Wilhelm*[1]) was born in Philadelphia on 14 November 1933 and died in Hot Springs, Bath, Virginia, on 14 August 1963.[165] She married, in Philadelphia

---

163   Letter from Welsh S. White to Mary L. White, postmarked 23 January 1960, original in possession of the author.
164   "Welsh S. White: Pitt Law Professor, Leading Authority on Death Penalty," obituary, *Pittsburgh Post-Gazette*, 1 January 2006, p. 21, quoting University of Pittsburgh Chancellor Mark A. Nordenberg.
165   Online image at findagrave.com/memorial/89336533, photo of gravestone shows Sally Deaver Murray, 14 November 1933–14 August 1963. Virginia, Death Records, 1912–2014, online database at ancestry.com, citing Virginia Department of Health, Richmond,

on 21 December 1959, BENJAMIN HUGER READ ("LADDIE") MURRAY, who was born in Baltimore, Maryland, on 6 June 1928, and died in Owings Mills, Baltimore, Maryland, on 11 September 1964, son of Samuel Murray and Anne Cleland Read.[166]

Sally enjoyed summers in Camden, Maine, with her cousins, perhaps especially Priscilla Litchfield and Bill White, who were close to her in age.

Figure 43. Sally Deaver as a Child in Maine; on the Ski Slopes; at her Wedding

Figure 44. Sally Deaver, Left, in Maine with her Cousins Priscilla Litchfield and Bill White; with Hattie, One of the Maids Who Lived in their Grandmother's House to Cook, Do Housekeeping, and Watch the Children

---

Virginia Deaths, 1912–2014; Certificate of Death no. 23331, shows death of Sally Deaver Murray at Community House Hospital, Hot Springs, Bath, Virginia, on 14 August 1963; birth date shown as 14 November 1933.

166   WWII Draft Registration Cards, online database at fold3.com, citing NARA, St. Louis, Missouri, Records of the Selective Service System, Record Group 147, Box 374, Roll 44015_03_00029, card serial number W681, order number 13247, dated 7 June 1946, shows registration of Benjamin Huger Murray, born in Baltimore, Maryland, on 6 June 1928, son of Samuel Murray. Online image at findagrave.com/memorial/85770609, shows gravestone for Benjamin Huger Read Murray, 6 June 1928–11 September 1964, son of Anne Cleland and Samuel Shoemaker Murray; "Murray–Deaver," *The Philadelphia Inquirer*, 22 December 1959, reports wedding of Sally Lowber Deaver to Benjamin Huger Read Murray at St. Peter's Church, 3d and Pine Streets, Philadelphia, on 21 December 1959.

When she was ten years old, she attended the North Country School at Lake Placid, New York, where she learned to ski. She also had skiing lessons during holidays at North Conway, New Hampshire. She took up skiing again in 1951, when she attended Vassar College. During the summer of her sophomore year, she skied at a resort in South America, in the Andes mountains, and became more serious about skiing.[167]

In 1956, she won the National Women's Giant Slalom Championship and the National Women's Slalom Championship, both at Squaw Valley, California.[168] In 1957, she won the National Women's Giant Slalom Championship at Aspen, Colorado.[169] In the 1958 World Alpine Championships in Austria, Sally came in second in the giant slalom competition, which was the best showing for a U.S. skier in several years.

In reporting on her second-place finish, an Associated Press news story stated:

> Miss Deaver's achievement was an outright embarrassment to the experts and to the Swiss, Italian and Austrian girls who usually dominate. She wasn't rated with the world's best and when she drew the No. 1 starting post even her friends didn't give her a chance. The No. 1 skier must help blaze a trail with a resultant loss in time.
>
> Actually, the 23-year-old Miss Deaver might have won. She took one of the 55 gates on the course the wrong way and lost valuable time correcting the error.
>
> As it was, her time of one minute, 55.1 seconds for the course that drops 1302 feet in its 5280-foot length was only a half second slower than Miss Wheeler's.[170]

Sally was invited to join the 1960 U.S. Olympic Team's training squad, but she was planning to be married, and so declined the invitation. She was elected to the U.S. National Ski Hall of Fame in 1978.[171] For many years, the Camden Snow Bowl in Camden, Maine, has hosted The Sally Deaver Memorial Citizen Super G Race, which was established after her mother, Priscilla Kelley, moved to Camden.[172]

Sally also enjoyed tennis, golf, skating, and riding. At the age of 15, she won the Penllyn Club Open Horsemanship Trophy for riders under age 19.[173] The following year, at age 16, she came in at or near the top placement in several areas of competition at the Philadelphia Horse Show for Juniors.[174] She continued competitive riding into her twenties, winning more honors in 1959 at the annual horse show in Buxmont, Pennsylvania.[175]

In August of 1963, though, when she had been married to Benjamin "Laddie" Murray for not quite four years, she was putting an unfamiliar horse through its paces in jumping over obstacles, when the horse failed to clear a jump and fell on top of Sally, causing a severe brain injury that took her life.[176]

---

167   "Sally Deaver Murray: Hall of Fame Class of 1978," online article at site of U.S. Ski and Snowboard Hall of Fame, https://skihall.com/hall-of famers/sally-deaver-murray, viewed on 8 May 2019.

168   "National Slalom to Sally Deaver," *The Philadelphia Inquirer*, 8 April 1956, p. 93.

169   "Yankee Skiers Sweep Aspen Slalom Tests," *The Montana Standard* (Butte, Montana), 3 March 1957, p. 34.

170   "North American Girls Stun Alpine Ski Stars," *The Boston Sunday Globe*, 9 February 1958, p. 60.

171   "Sally Deaver Murray: Hall of Fame Class of 1978," online article.

172   "Sally Deaver Race at Camden Snow Bowl Makes History with Redesigned Super G Slalom," *Penobscot Bay Pilot*, online article at https://www.penbaypilot.com/article/sally-deaver-race-camden-snow-bowl-makes-history-redesigned-super-g-slalom/114805, viewed on 8 May 2019.

173   "Girl, 4, Thrown by Pony at Penllyn Hunter Show," *The Philadelphia Inquirer*, 18 September 1949, p. 10.

174   "Texas Girl Wins 2 Riding Titles," *The Philadelphia Inquirer*, 11 June 1950, p. 25.

175   "Perfect Weather, Many Entries Mark Horse Show," 23 July 1959, *News Herald* (Perkasie, Pennsylvania), pp. 1, 7.

176   "Fall from Horse Kills Socialite," *Philadelphia Daily News*, 15 August 1963, p. 4.

49. CHARLES WEST[6] CHURCHMAN (*Elizabeth Churchman*[5], *Joseph*[4], *John*[3], *Joseph*[2], *Wilhelm*[1]) was born in Philadelphia on 23 January 1947 and died on 29 July 2018.[177]

Charlie was a very accomplished individual. Throughout his life, he was something of a rebel, not fitting into the mold of the society around him and occasionally creating friction with relatives and others. He did not go to college, but he made great use of his talents at figuring out the inner workings of mechanical and electronic devices. He repaired and rebuilt jukeboxes, video equipment, and antique automobiles, among other things. He was an expert in transferring old movies to digital form for organizations such as the Prelinger Archives, colleges, and others with challenging restoration and digitization tasks.[178]

After his untimely death in 2018, Charlie received a tribute from a man who had done business with him. This gentleman placed the following posting on his own website, with the heading, "My Friend Charlie Churchman":

> When my cell phone rang in the car on the afternoon of July 29, and Rick Lombardi showed up on the caller ID, my stomach dropped. I knew it would be something too important to wait for Monday. He called to tell me Charlie had died earlier in the day of an apparent heart attack.
>
> Charlie Churchman was notoriously prickly, ornery, or cantankerous, depending on where you grew up. When I first called Skip Elsheimer about acquiring a film scanner, he suggested I talk to Charlie. But first he needed to tell me that dealing with Charlie could be difficult. Over the next few years my staff and I would get to know a side of Charlie few people got to see.
>
> Visitors to his home and shop in Lafayette Hill would quickly be overwhelmed by the abounding clutter. He probably had 20 film scanners, some working, some "hanger queens," hundreds of vector scopes and waveform monitors, videotape machines, especially quads, and—if you looked carefully—a vast collection of cathedral radios, jukeboxes and player pianos. His forklift (an electronic model with 63 hours on it) dazzled guests. And the cars. Charlie loved cars as much as he loved film. There was a red Bentley, a 1960s Land Rover he managed to put air conditioning in, a 1950s Olds 98.
>
> Charlie enjoyed a good laugh. When he knew you well enough and knew he could trust you, there was nothing he liked laughing about more than himself. I once texted him, "Hey Good Looking!" He didn't miss a beat. He said, "You must have the wrong number." Or after a rough visit where he scared the staff half to death, I messaged him saying, "They think you're the devil." He replied, "Call me Beelzebub, please."
>
> Coming up to his 70th birthday, Charlie had to lay down the law to his assistant and associates: there would be no celebration. But he had not told me. He would only allow me to take him to lunch. When he showed up in the parking lot, I dragged him in "to show him something special." The entire staff assembled to sing "Happy Birthday" and share ice cream. On the way out he grumbled, "I knew something was up." We went to his favorite lunch place, the Fairlane Grill. It was my first visit. He was a regular and all the staff greeted him by name when he came in. I turned to one of the waitresses and

---

177   Death notice, *The Philadelphia Inquirer,* online site viewed through genealogybank.com. Web site with tribute, https://www.georgeblood.com/news/2018/8/2/my-friend-charlie-churchman.

178   Personal knowledge of the author; online article, "Meet a Lafayette Hill man who's a 'savant' at restoring old sports videos," at https://www.philly.com/philly/sports/eagles/charlie-churchman-nfl-films-sports-videos-highlights-20170626.html, viewed on 26 May 2019.

whispered, "Today is Charlie's birthday." She winked and said she would make sure the staff did something about that. Sure enough, all the regular staff came out and sang "Happy Birthday" to him. He blushed and looked at me wide-eyed, "How did they find out?"

He loved to tell stories about growing up in the area. His parents had bought the property in the '60s. He knew which store was where in old Chestnut Hill. He could point out the hi-fi shop where he worked, tinkered, and learned his trade. For a time he was a factory service center for JVC professional video equipment. He was in the shop on Christmas Day when the phone rang. "Don't you know I was dumb enough to answer it!" Somebody had gotten a consumer camcorder as a present and couldn't get it to work. They'd found him in the phone book under JVC video repairs. Charlie said, "I had to think real quick. I put on a fake accent and said I was the cleaning company. The shop was closed for the holiday."

Monday was a quiet day at my shop as the staff reflected on the sad news. James Voges, one of our video digitization engineers, said in an email, "Charlie was an absolute pleasure, I enjoyed every minute with him. Very sad to hear about this. We would often stand in his yard and talk about the cats that adopted him, great guy, big heart." Eddie Austin, who does film prep and would go to Charlie's, wrote, "I really enjoyed chatting with Charlie about his work as a projectionist, Ernie Kovacs, and diners in Philly while working in his barn or on the schlep down the hill. He was gracious enough to make repairs to a projector of mine while cleaning films. Very sad to hear of his passing, I felt a camaraderie with him."

I know that feeling. When I was having a really rough time, Charlie said something that had me rolling on the floor with laughter. I saw him the next day and thanked him. I was having such a rough day, and he made me laugh. "You're such a great friend to me, Charlie." He said, "Yeah, well it cuts both ways."

You were my friend, Charlie. We were your friends. We will miss you always.[179]

---

179   George Blood, "My Friend Charlie Churchman," online posting at https://www.georgeblood.com/news/2018/8/2/my-friend-charlie-churchman, viewed on 1 May 2019, used by permission of George Blood. Photograph of Charlie in workshop courtesy of George Blood; used by permission.

Figure 45. Charlie Churchman as a Child and in his Workshop

PART B: THE STRAWBRIDGES

The First Generation

1. JOHN¹ STRAWBRIDGE was born in Ireland, probably about 1715, and emigrated in about 1752 to America, where he settled with his family near Back Creek on the Eastern Shore of Maryland.¹⁸⁰ He died in Cecil County, Maryland, on 31 July 1768. He married, probably in Ireland, a widow named JANE MILLER, who was born about 1715 and died on 7 April 1799.¹⁸¹

Children of John¹ Strawbridge and Jane (Miller) Strawbridge:

+ 2. i. JOHN² STRAWBRIDGE was born in Ireland in about 1746 and died in Philadelphia on 16 September 1793.

3. ii. ANN STRAWBRIDGE was born about 1746 and died on 29 April 1823. She married, on 17 June 1768, SAMUEL MAFFITT, who was born on 24 May 1742 and died on 31 May 1815, a son of William Maffitt and Mary Scott.¹⁸²

4. iii. MARY STRAWBRIDGE was born on 2 January 1747 and died on 30 June 1806, and was buried at Sharp's Graveyard near Fair Hill, Maryland. She married, on 31 December 1770, THOMAS MAFFITT, who was born on 8 June 1739 and died on 25 January 1815, and was buried in the Rock Presbyterian Church graveyard in Lewisville, Chester County, Pennsylvania, another son of William Maffitt and Mary Scott.¹⁸³

5. iv. JAMES STRAWBRIDGE was born about 1749 and died on 14 November 1805 in Philadelphia.¹⁸⁴

---

180   "Autobiography of John Strawbridge," an account written by the grandson of this John Strawbridge (1780–1858), set out in the text below, in connection with that person; also available at https://strawbridgefamily.net/documents/john-strawbridge-autobiography-complete-version/.

181   Johns, John Henry, *A History of the Rock Presbyterian Church in Cecil County, Maryland* (unknown publisher 1872); at page 38, list headed "Persons Buried in Sharp's Graveyard, Fair Hill, Cecil Co., MD," includes John Strawbridge, died 31 July 1768, and Jane Strawbridge, died 7 April 1799. Available online at https://archive.org/details/historyofrockpre00john/page/38.

182   Lyons, Nathalie Fontaine, *The Ancestry of Nathalie Fontaine Lyons* (privately published, Salisbury, North Carolina 1981) 206, citing Family Bible of Henry C. Mackall and Records of Frank E. Moffitt.

183   Lyons, *Ancestry of Nathalie Fontaine Lyons* 203, citing Prerogative Court Accounts, Liber 68, folios 174–176 and Cecil County Accounts, Box 11, folder 57. As can be seen from the information in the text, the two Strawbridge sisters married two Maffitt brothers.

184   U.S. Presbyterian Church Records, 1701–1970, online database at ancestry.com, citing Presbyterian Historical Society, Philadelphia, *Interments 1851–1867*; Accession Number: V MI46 P533b v.5; original page from Record of Interments in the Second Presbyterian Church Yards of the City of Philadelphia, 1851, states that the remains of "James Strawbridge buried 1805 aged 56," along with others, were removed from the Arch Street burial ground on 12 November 1851. Philadelphia County, Pennsylvania, Will Index, 1682–1819, online database at ancestry.com, citing *Philadelphia County Wills, 1682–1819*, Historical

James did not marry or have children, but he lived an interesting life. In addition, he has the distinction of being the oldest Strawbridge ancestor for whom a portrait appears to be available. The likeness shown below is taken from a miniature that, as of 1906, was in the possession of his great-grand-niece, Miss L. Murry Ledyard, of Cazenovia, New York.[185]

Figure 46. James Strawbridge, About 1749–1805

In 1904, Mr. Charles Tubbs was asked to write a history of the "Pioneer of Tioga County, Pennsylvania," a label given to James Strawbridge. As he explained in his prefatory remarks to this work, Mr. Tubbs initially had difficulty in uncovering any facts about James. He persisted, though, and his explanation in 1906 of how he eventually had some success is instructive enough to be included here:

> It was matter of common knowledge that John and James Strawbridge were patentees of land, but their names had disappeared from our annals in the first years of the last century. Did they have descendants; and, if so, where were they? And did they possess any old papers? A branch of the family at one time resided at Cazenovia, New York. I ventured an inquiry directed to the postmaster of that place.
>
> After many days my inquiry was answered by Helen Ledyard, wife of the Honorable Charles S. Fairchild, of New York city. She is a descendant of John Strawbridge.

Society of Pennsylvania, 1900; index shows James Strawbridge, merchant in City of Philadelphia, will proved 29 November 1805, left his estate to John, George, James, Joseph, and Jane Strawbridge, and to sisters Ann Moffitt, Mary Moffitt, and Margaret Lawson. Septimus E. Nivin, *Genealogy of Evans, Nivin and Allied Families* (2d ed. International Printing Co., Philadelphia 1930) 235, Appendix C, reprinting a letter by Jane Strawbridge Ledyard to her daughter, 6 April 1852, with details about family history, viewed at ancestry.com online database on 21 April 2019. That letter is also available at https://strawbridgefamily.net/documents/jane-ledyards-letter-to-her-daughter-1852/.
185   Charles Tubbs, "James Strawbridge: Pioneer of Tioga County, Pennsylvania," reprinted from volume containing monographs contributed to Tioga County Centennial Celebration of 1904 (Agitator Print: Wellsboro, Pennsylvania, 1906, unnumbered page in front matter). Author has copy obtained from Lorenzo Historical Site archives, Cazenovia, New York.

In her second letter to me, replying to many questions, she wrote: "In 1900 Miss Sarah Strawbridge, of New Orleans, presented to Princeton University, through me, a copy of her father's, Judge Strawbridge's, little autobiography. He was a graduate of Princeton. If you could see it, you could find some information."

It was thus I discovered the "document," on which this monograph is founded.

It is desirable to base historical statements on original documents. The disquieting word therefore in my correspondent's letter was the word "copy." Mrs. Fairchild thus authenticates the Princeton copy: "The original of Judge Strawbridge's Memoirs I returned to his daughter. When the copy was made from the original my cousin and I compared it most carefully."

An application to Miss Sarah Strawbridge for the original revealed the fact that she had died in 1903, aged 84 years, and that a painstaking search through her effects, made by her nephew, Edward H. Strawbridge, Esq., of Saint Landry Parish, Louisiana, had failed to find it.[186]

Mr. Tubbs went on to describe the early actions of James Strawbridge in 1785 in exploring the land that became Tioga County, quoting from the autobiography written by James's nephew, George:

"Now, it so happened that my father's only brother, (James Strawbridge) who had been an officer in Smallwood's Maryland Brigade had to retire from the army (of the Revolutionary War) on account of a terrible abscess of the lungs, which nearly cost him his life; he chose on partial recovery the life of the woods. The land office of Pennsylvania was recently opened: with good guides he penetrated the woods and located a considerable body of the choicest lands of Pennsylvania. They lay principally in Tioga County on the waters of the Tioga and Cowanesque rivers."[187]

At the end of his monograph, after recounting the story of how James met with violence and fraud that deprived him of the enjoyment of his lands, Mr. Tubbs provided a brief biography of the "pioneer":

It only remains to give the few personal items that are known about James Strawbridge, our premier pioneer. He was the second son of John Strawbridge, who came to this country from the North of Ireland about 1752. The family settled at Back Creek and afterward, lived at Fair Hill near Elkton, Cecil County, Maryland. In Maryland he grew to manhood and as already noted in due time became an officer in General William Smallwood's Brigade in the Revolutionary War. Existing records of the part taken by Maryland in that war are meager, and from them, it is impossible to state his rank, or the details of his service, except that Smallwood and his men were engaged in battle at Brooklyn Heights, White Plains, Fort Washington and Brandywine. From this service he was discharged for physical disability, and at the close of the war removed to Philadelphia. Upon the sale of the lands by the State of Pennsylvania in the "New Purchase," he and his brother, John, who was a tobacco merchant on Walnut street wharf, purchased 30,000 acres. As has been seen it was the intention of James Strawbridge to become a permanent resident of what is now Tioga County, and the manner in which his design in that direction was frustrated has been related. He

---

186   Tubbs, "Pioneer of Tioga County," unnumbered page in front matter headed "Prefatory."
187   Tubbs, "Pioneer of Tioga County" 6.

returned to Philadelphia and took up his residence in a fashionable boarding house at Fifth and Market streets, where he retained rooms as long as he lived.

He exerted his utmost ability to secure legislation to dispossess those who were occupying his lands. The legislature in those years held its sessions at Philadelphia, and he had easy access to it. The legislation was obtained, but so long as he lived it did not prove effectual. The laws could not be enforced. Juries would not convict. He was a prominent member of the Land Owners' Association. He attended all its meetings, and gave it information derived from actual experience.

He died on Thursday, the 14th day of November, 1805, aged fifty years, and was buried in the cemetery of the Second Presbyterian church. He was never married. In face and figure he was an exceedingly handsome man. He possessed a magnetic nature and his family and friends were devotedly loyal to him. As a man of affairs, as a soldier and a citizen he enjoyed a deserved popularity.[188]

6. v. MARGARET STRAWBRIDGE was born in Philadelphia and died probably in Lycoming County, Pennsylvania. She married JOHN LAWSON and moved with him to Lycoming County in about 1787.[189]

---

188   Tubbs, "Pioneer of Tioga County" 13.
189   "Autobiography of John Strawbridge."

The Second Generation

2. JOHN² STRAWBRIDGE (*John¹*) was born in Ireland in about 1746 and died in Philadelphia on 16 September 1793.[190] He married, in Wilmington, Delaware on 23 July 1778,[191] HANNAH EVANS, who was born on 23 September 1758 in Chester County, Pennsylvania, and died in Wilmington, Delaware, on 1 November 1811, daughter of George Evans and Rachel Gilpin.[192]

Following is a letter written by Hannah Evans Strawbridge (1758–1811) to her daughter Jane (1793–1855) on May 25, 1809. Some of the words are unclear; I have made my best guesses. The "king's evil" was a term for a disease called scrofula, or tuberculosis of the lymph glands, especially the neck. The John who had this disease was John Ralston Strawbridge, Hannah's grandson and the son of John Strawbridge, born in 1780. John Ralston was to die, presumably of this illness, in June 1809 at the age of two. John Strawbridge, born in 1780, whose first wife, Elizabeth Stockton, died in 1807, married Frances Taylor in 1810. The letter also mentions Stockton, another child of John and Elizabeth, born in 1805.

> Miss Jane Strawbridge
> at Mr Ward's
> Elkton
> Maryland
>
> My Dear child
> I was very much gratified at receiving a few lines from you and your friend and in next week I shall expect a double pleasure by seeing you untill that time comes I wish you to make yourself as contented as possible by doing all you can to promote happiness in your friend, and remember through life after haveing keep [?] as close to the line of your duty as possible to leave all to providence and take all enjoyment you can as troubles will come soon enough without going to meet them—the family all are well as you left them Stockton wishing for Papa and Aunt Jane he has done very well at night but the first word in the morning is aunty—John [Hannah's grandson, John Ralston Strawbridge] has been very poorly but is better. Dr Tilton came the day after you left us and has been to see him every day since. He agrees with Dr Smith that his complaint is the king's

190   U.S. Presbyterian Church Records, 1701–1970, online database at ancestry.com, citing Presbyterian Historical Society, Philadelphia, *Burial Records 1758–1808*; Accession Number: V MI46 P533b v.1, original record is page from births and deaths register of Second Presbyterian Church, Philadelphia, showing death of John Strawbridge, age 47, on 16 September 1793. See also "Autobiography of John Strawbridge." 1790 U.S. Federal Census, Water Street East Side, Philadelphia, Series M637, Roll 9, Page 34, Image 365, FHL film no. 568149, shows John Strawbridge, Mert (merchant), at 71 Walnut Street. Pennsylvania, Wills and Probate Records, 1683–1993, online database at ancestry.com, copy made and certified in 1901 of last will and testament of John Strawbridge, which was admitted to probate in September 1793.

191   Delaware, Marriage Records, 1750–1954, online database at ancestry.com, page in register of marriages conducted at Trinity Church, Borough of Wilmington, Delaware, shows marriage of John Strawbridge and Hannah Evans in July 1778, date probably 23 (hard to read).

192   Nivin, *Evans, Nivin and Allied Families* 43, viewed at ancestry.com online database on 20 April 2019.

evil but says little respecting a cure but from his constant attendance I flatter myself he has hopes—James was to see us on Sunday and I look for John and George [Hannah's sons] to be here next Sunday and one of them I expect will go for you—Tell Maria I will say nothing of what I expect of her till I see her as that will be soon. Offer love and compliments to Mr and Mrs Ward, and a double portion to my dear child believe me as ever your aff. Mother H Strawbridge

May 25 1809

[note, evidently on outside of letter:]

Your little box has got a tennant and a very busy one this minute [?] going in with its furniture.

Children of John² Strawbridge and Hannah (Evans) Strawbridge:

+   7.   i.   JOHN³ STRAWBRIDGE was born on 25 April 1780 and died in Philadelphia on 4 April 1858.

    8.   ii.   GEORGE STRAWBRIDGE was born in Philadelphia on 31 October 1784 and died in New Orleans, Louisiana, on 11 March 1859.[193] He married, probably in Philadelphia, on 18 November 1816, FRANCES HEPBURN, who was born in Philadelphia on 13 January 1792 and died in New Orleans on 12 June 1871, daughter of Stacy Hepburn and Sarah Duffield.[194]

Figure 47. Judge George Strawbridge, 1784–1859

193   U.S. Presbyterian Church Records, 1701–1970, online database at ancestry.com, citing Presbyterian Historical Society, Philadelphia, *Register of Baptisms and Marriages etc 1744–1833*; Accession Number: V MI46 P533r v.2, original record is page from baptisms register of Second Presbyterian Church, Philadelphia, showing birth of George Strawbridge, son of John and Hannah Strawbridge, on 31 October 1784. Louisiana Statewide Death Index, 1819–1964, online database at ancestry.com, citing State of Louisiana, Secretary of State, Division of Archives, Records Management, and History, Vital Records Indices; index shows George Strawbridge, born about 1784, died in New Orleans on 11 March 1859. Untitled note, *The Times-Picayune* (New Orleans, Louisiana), 12 March 1859, p. 1, states that Judge Strawbridge will be laid to rest on this date, an esteemed resident of New Orleans for forty years.
194   Louisiana, Wills and Probate Records, 1756–1984, online database at ancestry.com; original record is handwritten will of Frances Hepburn Strawbridge, stating her date and place of birth, date of marriage, and names of her parents. New Orleans, Louisiana, Death Records Index, 1804–1949, online database at ancestry.com, showing death of Mrs. Francis [sic] H. Strawbridge, age 80, on 12 June 1871.

Following is a brief excerpt from the very long letter written in April 1858 by this George Strawbridge, brother of Jane Ledyard, to his son, Henry H. Strawbridge. (The letter, or "autobiography," was discussed earlier in connection with James Strawbridge.) This George was a judge in New Orleans, and ultimately a justice of the Supreme Court of Louisiana. This text is taken from a typed transcription of the letter. This excerpt contains about the first 4 of 42 typed pages; the transcription notes that it omits at least 10 other pages, so the full letter would consist of at least 52 typed pages. This first portion recounts the family history.

My dear Son:

It was at your desire I write this sketch, which I now commit to your discretion. When I began, I found the task irksome and unpleasant. I was in ill health, scarcely looking to recovery; my spirits depressed: my property embarrassed and destroyed, with other misfortunes, which made life a burden and made it questionable whether it would be borne. In fact, without that feeling, which ever has been uppermost "love for my family", it is not likely this work would ever have been undertaken; now that the struggle is over I ask myself "What have I to live for?" I cannot answer the question, but to say "To suffer". That history full of errors as it is, has been varied enough to have been of some interest under a different tone of mind, but with the consequences of these errors and sins severely visited on me in these latter days, it is left a meagre statement of family history, chiefly useful as it may guard you against the like, so little are the better portions of my character known or appreciated in this community, where I have now resided nearly forty years, that they are scarcely worth being spoken of.

It will be of interest to my children, however, to know:

That John and Jane Strawbridge, my grandparents, came from the north of Ireland, about the year 1750, and settled in Cecil County, Maryland—where two families of the name of Moffat or Maffit (for singular to say it, they spelled their names differently, charging each other jocularly, with not knowing how to spell the name) yet reside; a third daughter married John Lawson and settled in Lycoming County, Pennsylvania, where I found quite a large family. Lawson, the father, being dead and several of his children grown up and providing for themselves.

My father was the eldest son and took the real estate, according to the common law then in force. His brother, James, lived a batchelor and died in Philadelphia, I think, in 1806. He was a very fine looking man, an officer in Smallwood's Maryland brigade. My father was sheriff of the County, and ex officio Col. in the Militia, in which capacity he was called on by Genl. Washington, when, in company with Lafayette, he was making a reconnaisance of the country around the head of the Chesapeake, there being an apprehension that the British army might transfer their operations from New York. The sheriff of the district, and of course, well acquainted with it, accompanied them and gave them such information as led them to believe that no such attempt would be made there. On parting, Genl. Washington proposed to him to join the army, offering his interest to obtain the same standing he held in the militia: this was declined. Three years afterwards, he was again thrown in Washington's presence, who recognized him and renewed the offer.

At the close of the revolution, he sold his property, went into Virginia, invested the proceeds in tobacco, established correspondence with the planters, and settled himself in Philadelphia, then the great tobacco mart, as a factor. I believe most of the business of that city passed through his hands. I can remember when his counting house on

Walnut Street was lumbered with tobacco samples. I should judge, if my memory serves, the business was much more extensive than since. At any rate, he found it a lucrative business. Since I was married, I passed some short time in Virginia, where I met some of his former correspondents, who spoke in very favourable terms of their connexion.

He died in the yellow fever of 1793 (16th Sept): a handsome tribute was paid to his memory in a pamphlet published afterwards, giving a history of that sad visitation, not forgotten to this day. I have heard my mother say I was his favorite child: it may be so, there was a distinction made. I can remember several pretty smart floggings, which my brothers did not share in, or receive separately the like.

My mother was the eldest of eleven children of George Evans and Rachel Gilpin of Delaware. He was unfortunate enough to survive them all, and died at the age of 84, since your birth, my son, though too young to have any recollection of him. He was an active Whig during the Revolution, was at the Crossing of the Delaware with Washington, and I think, at Trenton and Brandywine, on which latter stream he was for many years, a miller. The Gilpin family were from that neighborhood. It is said the original couple took up their first residence in a cave on the Brandywine, where they lived to rear a family of 16 sons and daughters, and see this numerous progeny around at once. They were distinguished by the old citizens, as "The descendants of the Cave."

I have heard of an amusing scene, which occurred on a public stage between Wilmington and Philadelphia.

There happened to be amongst the passengers, a gentleman full of himself, full of politics and full of religion, and very dogmatic with all. He was very annoying and disagreeable to the company. My mother, in a good humoured way, engaged with him, and soon showed herself an overmatch. There was amongst the passengers, also, a certain Johnny Webster, a well-known apothecary, a humorist and gossip, knowing and known to everybody, who encouraged the fun, roaring out at every advantage "hurra for the Cave" "I know thee for one of the descendants of the Cave." Till at last the man was silenced by laughter and the journey finished without further declamation.

After the death of my father, she retired to Wilmington, where she quietly passed the rest of her days, respected and esteemed by all who knew her, from the gay French emigrants of St. Domingo, who formed an important part of the population, to the plain Quaker, who formed even a more numerous sect.

She was a woman of clear, strong understanding and sound judgement, of a plain and even temper, which I have very rarely known to be ruffled, yet with quite as much firmness and decision as generally belongs to the sex. Clear and exact in her own principles, but most liberal and tolerant to others; even Quaker exclusiveness gave way to it, and it was considered by the aforesaid Johnny Webster, that friend Strawbridge might make a tolerable Quaker, nay, might sit in the gallery, if she would only take that cockade out of her bonnet.

John Dickinson, author of the celebrated Farmers Letters, and the only member of the Federal Convention who refused to sign the Declaration of Independance, which greatly helped to open the Revolution—the Farmers Letters—said to her one day, "Friend Strawbridge, I know of no one who is entitled to so much credit for the manner of bringing up their children as thee."

My eldest brother, John, is yet living in Philadelphia: his intellect has failed and he is bedridden, but surrounded by a large and kind family.

My brother, James, died in Philadelphia on the day the news of the capture of the Guerriere by the Constitution arrived; he was a seaman who, in consequence of a quarrel with his Captain, left his place as Mate in Smyrna, and to get home, took the same place on board an English vessel bound to London. In the English Channel, they were attacked and captured by two French privateers and carried into, I think, L'Orient. As Mate of the English vessel he was treated as an Englishman and imprisoned. It so happened that at this time the U. S. Ship Hornet entered the port, on board of which his cousin, Sam Moffit, happened to be Purser. How the communication between them was established, I do not know, but through him, he was able to establish his citizenship and discharge. Much censure fell on the Captain for discharging an American in a foreign port; I can't say how wrongfully. That Captain, afterwards, fell into the power of John Strawbridge, who let him off, pardoned. I am not sure I should have been so forgiving of his trespasses. However, James was put by the American Consul, on board the Hornet and had a very rough passage to the United States, and arrived with health much shattered; in fact, his lungs were affected, which shortly closed his career.

My brother, Joseph, was brought up, as we say, in a counting house, but before he had grown up, the same disease of the lungs, which was fearfully prevalent in Wilmington, laid hands on him. He went with two gentlemen I knew well, to Canton, but returned worse. His good temper, capacity for business and drollery, which after his death, I found by accident, had made him his mother's favourite and cherished one, in fact had made him so with all his acquaintances: we lost him a few months later at the age of 18. It is a fearful thing to look back on the ravages of that disease; I am sure I have aided to carry at least a dozen of my fellows to the grave, victims of that disease. Give me New Orleans, Havana, Batavia, Cholera and yellow fever, but keep me from the healthy North, where consumption bides it's time to take, at 18 or 20, the fairest flowers. I know not whether it yet dwells there. I have reached mature age through climates called unhealthy, but I'll take them again rather than the beautiful, healthy city of Wilmington.

My only sister, Jane, did not much resemble her mother, except in manner; you all remember her, as her death is quite recent (4 Feb. 1855, age 61). She married J.D. Ledyard, Esq. of Cazenovia, N.Y. and reared a large family, of which connexion, it is best to say briefly, she was the head, in which it is not possible to fill the vacancy, and where, had she lived, I might have passed last summer with great advantage to my health and happiness. She should have given us the family history, and had abundant material which she gave and which has, I understand, been published, at least so much as gives the history of Wilmington in those days.

9. iii. JAMES STRAWBRIDGE was born in Philadelphia on 14 April 1787, baptized on 31 May 1787, and died in Philadelphia on 3 September 1812.[195]

---

195   U.S. Presbyterian Church Records, 1701–1970, online database at ancestry.com, citing Presbyterian Historical Society, Philadelphia, *Register of Baptisms and Marriages etc 1744–1833*; Accession Number: V MI46 P533r v.2, original record is page from baptisms register of Second Presbyterian Church, Philadelphia, showing birth of James Strawbridge, son of John and Hannah Strawbridge, on 14 April 1787, and baptism on 31 May 1787. Register of burials from same source shows death of James Strawbridge on 3 September 1812 at age 25.

Some of the little information available about James's life is set forth directly above, in the long letter written by Judge George Strawbridge to his son. There is some more information in the long family history letter written by James's sister, Jane, who married Jonathan Denise Ledyard, set forth later in this section. As is recounted in those letters, James worked for a while in a mill, where his lungs became irritated. He then went to sea, but suffered setbacks in that career as well, resulting in a failure of his health that led to his early death.

10. iv. JOSEPH STRAWBRIDGE was born, probably in Philadelphia, about 1788, and died, probably in Wilmington, Delaware, about November 1808.[196]

In the family records are several letters written by Joseph Strawbridge. These letters are fascinating documents, but very fragile and fairly hard to read. (For example, he used the old-fashioned "s" that sometimes looks like an "f".) Following is the text of one of these letters. There are a few gaps because of tears in the old paper, and one or two places where the writing could not be deciphered. Following is the text of the letter:

Addressed to: Mrs. Strawbridge, Wilmington, Del.

Postmarked: New-York April 22 (year not legible)

Canton December 10, 1802

Dearest Mother

Having written two letters by the Ship Tyre who still remains, to sail in Company with the Ship George Barclay, I rather expect you will have a number of Letters, arriving about the same Period, & tho our extreme hurry & Impatience to expedite our Return is very little favorable to writing much or frequently to Friends, yet am resolved no American shall depart without having information of our progress and wellfare.

Our whole Time and Attention is so much engaged by the variety of our business, that I can yet give very little Information or Idea to you of the Singularity of the manners and Customs of the Chinese.

Every thing however particularly at first sight, reminds You, of your being an Antipodean to America, they are generally very attentive & polite to Strangers, tho there is no other Intercourse than that of business. The mode of living here is entirely European, & Foreigners are separate from the natives in their Houses, tho the Servants are generally Chinese & very active & Faithfull—We have a very delightful Factory or Residence, with every Accomodation a most excellent & well furnished Table & number of Servants, altogether quite an Establishment.

Notwithstanding the plenty & variety of things & the luxury of the Principal Persons, we are constantly shocked with the most disgusting Figures or moved with the most distressing spectacles, who here extort money from the Chinese, by sticking close to them till removed by a few cash. We see more (?), blind & miserable wretches in one hours walk thru the streets than in a twelvemonth at home.

The Country as far as we can see, especially in our passage from Whampoa (?) about 12 miles distant where the Shipping lay, is very pleasing, the richness of the Landscapes,

196   Nivin, *Evans, Nivin and Allied Families* 49. According to that source, he was buried in the Presbyterian Churchyard, Wilmington, but his remains were later removed to Riverview Cemetery, Wilmington. Similar information is given at findagrave.com/memorial/124186415.

the variety of Trees, shrubs, & birds, you see, is quite exhilarating to an Eye wearied with contemplating an unbounded waste of Nature.

In your approach to the City, the boats which since you made the Land are constantly in motion, become for miles to throng, that they are divided into squares or rows like houses, where thousands of the Poor reside, scarcely ever putting their foot on shore during their Lives, where business of all kinds is conducted & every thing is like a town, some are handsome & capacious, having one or two rooms, like (?)'s back parlor in size, but generally they are small, with a cover higher tho resembling in appearance the Tub of an old Fasticone Cradle, where in the space of ca. 4 feet by 3 a whole family constantly live, the mother, having her youngest child slung on her back, sculling the boat or house & the other children if very small having Cords tied to them, to support them in case of falling overboard. They live principally on Rice or Fish, both of which Providence has supplied them with in great abundance, tho an occasional Scarcity produces the most dreadfull Consequences.

We learn much of their Rogueary at home, which to be sure, is not always exaggerated tho said to be much more general than I believe. They are Capital Artists, every thing that is shown them, they can imitate exactly & their Shows display the most astonishing variety, suited to the Taste or Caprice of all Nations—Here we are a curious Assemblage all in harmony, pursuing our disparate interests, besides the Variety among the Chinese, Americans, English, Swedes, Danes, French, Spaniards, Portuguese, Dutch, Italians, Armenians, Moors, Malays, & an endless variety more who are bringing to the Chinese the Supply of their wants, are received with equal Indifference.

A Person having no business to attend to, might spend a month very agreably, notwithstanding the limited space, we are circumscribed in, as you meet, besides the paucity of every thing, with a number of very gentle or agreable People—There are still a few American Ships here, but suppose all of us will be ready to sail before about the 1st February, at which period, the Resident Agents Supercargoes & (?) go down to Macao, which is a very pleasant place, somewhat under the Portuguese Authority, to remain till the next season for business generally commencing in August. Altho like other Young Men, apt to regard Wealth, as an object of much desire, & independant of any affection or Friendship at home, I should very little covet residence for some years in this place, tho as a certain consequence, I should be wealthy as a Nabob. It is generally the case that their Constitutions are somewhat impaired, which is a poor reward for their Labors. The Weather since our Arrival has been truly delightfull, (?) our month of October & we have still the greatest Variety of Fruits & Vegetables, which are here in constant succession. I have made it a point to request some seeds for you, the Possession of which, will make us almost rival (?) exotics. I rather despair of much success, as the Experiment has failed, and I do not intend for some time, to raise my Elegant / never to be sufficiently admired hot House / which I defer as have often told your dear friend Susan Read, till I can retire. "Otium cum Dignitate." A period notwithstanding her unbelief, I hope not very far distant, I made an assurance of paying my homage to that Lady from this place, which I shall undoubtedly fullfill by this or the next opportunity & "not when more important business permits" for what can to me be a more delightfull Employment.

We are generally very healthy, excepting very slight Indispositions, no where can there be better Health, in so great a number. Our business is progressing & we hope to sail about the 1st of February. Every thing is very scarce & high, I fear our Owners will not make much, tho we will exert ourselves, for their Interest to the utmost & hope at all events to give satisfaction.

The Anticipation of seeing all Friends well, makes me allmost indifferent about my own. As regards what it is or what it sells for, tell George, if he should choose to go behind the Counter, I will give him employment, to sell ------ provided he gives good security that neither, Friends, you or ------ self, will plunder any, as I think I shall be too much of the Fine Gentleman to do any thing but overlook. I would be pleased to put something in any young man practicing his way. My Duty to Gran & Aunt B, embrace the Children, say all of my constant & lively affection & how happy I shall be by any little in my power, to reward their Diligence & good Conduct—

If time permits, I will write to Uncle or George by this Vessel. Remember me in much sincerity to Mr. Stockton & all the Family & their friends, & may Dear Mother, every blessing be your remaining portion. I am your affectionate Son, J.S.

The next passage, below, is a transcription of an old document found among the Sailer-Strawbridge papers, which appears to be an original account from about 1808 of a sea voyage to China from America in 1807. The document consists of eight pages of clear handwriting, written to the edges of the pages. Because of the lack of margins, a few words are missing where the bottom of a page is worn away. The pages were attached on the left side by two small bits of black thread.

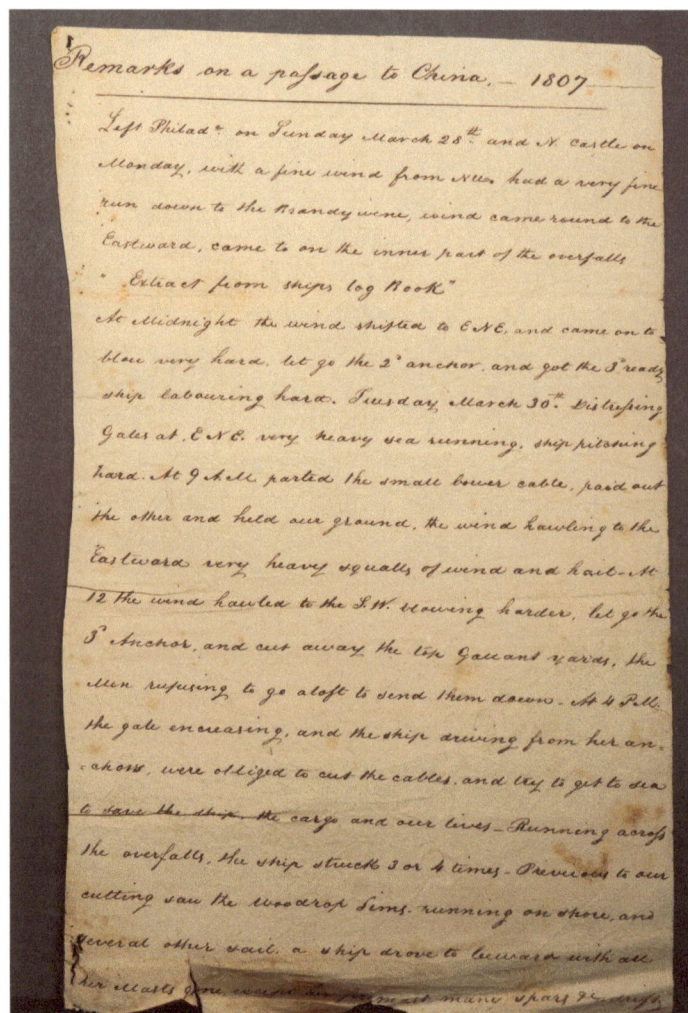

Figure 48. First Page of Document with Remarks on a Passage to China

Because this document was included with other old Strawbridge family papers, including several letters of Joseph Strawbridge, and because George Strawbridge, in his letter to his son, says that Joseph went to China in about 1807, it appears that this account was written by Joseph.

The text below omits several charts showing the ship's progress, listing destinations and mileages. Apart from those omissions, there are only a few minor edits, and some obvious misspellings and inconsistent spellings have been left in the text.

Remarks on a passage to China—1807

Left Philada on Sunday March 28th and N. Castle on Monday, with a fine wind from NW. Had a very fine run down to the Brandywine, wind came round to the Eastward, came to on the inner part of the overfalls.
"Extract from ships log Book"
At midnight the wind shifted to ENE, and came on to blow very hard. Let go the 2d anchor, and got the 3d ready, ship labouring hard. Tuesday, March 30th. Distressing Gales at ENE. Very heavy sea running, ship pitching hard. At 9 A.M. parted the small bower cable, paid out the other and held our ground, the wind hawling to the Eastward very heavy squalls of wind and hail. At 12 the wind hawled to the S.W. blowing harder. Let go the 3 Anchors, and cut away the top Gallant yards, the men refusing to go aloft to send them down. At 4 P.M. the gale encreasing, and the ship driving from her anchors, were obliged to cut the cables, and try to get to sea to save the ship, the cargo and our lives. Running across the overfalls, the ship struck 3 or 4 times. Previous to our cutting saw the Woodrop Sims running on shore, and several other sail. A ship drove to leeward with all her masts gone, except her foremast mane spars adrift.

After we were clear, stood for New York, lost most of our stock, three of the men gave out. April 1st hard gales and squalls of wind running along shore in from 15 to 18 fathom water, wind at west, under short sail. At 4 P.M. set the fore sail and Main top sail. At midnight tacked in 8 fathom water. April 2d begins with moderate breezes, and clear weather, out all reefs. At 3 P.M. tacked to the north. At 5 saw the land on Long Island. At 8 calm. At 9 got a breeze from ENE. At 12 mer. saw the high lands of Nover Link. Thick weather and rain, wind beginning to blow hard, etc. 3 P.M. ran in by the Light House, with the Jack hoisted and firing guns, no pilot to be got, a brig in Co. The gale encreasing and hawling to the S.E. Could not get to sea, and having no anchors to bring her up, and no pilot boat in sight, found it absolutely necessary to run the ship on shore, the brig in company running on shore at the same time. Furled the sails and cleared the decks, and took every possible measure to save the ship and cargo. 3d begins with heavy gales at N.W., wind hawling round to W. At 6 A.M. got down the fore top G. mast, & struck yards & top masts & f. water along side, signal of distress hoisted, no boats passing_____ three apprentices _____ of P____ from Jamaica _____.

Dist. Yr. Log. 15930 miles average pr day 124 ½, days: 128

From leaving America, we had pleasant weather, until we made Tristian da Cunha, and had but one gale 5 days out, in which time we saw two sail, one a schooner which we spoke, from Martinique, and a ship, which we were in sight of two days, standing on our course. From or near Tristian da Cunha, the weather was cold and rough until we began to run down our lattitude from St. Pauls. In this time we were continually surrounded with numbers of birds, of different kinds, caught severall Large Albatross, and many cape pigeons. In rounding the Cape we had several very heavy gales from the west, lasting for several days.

In the Straits of Sunda we experienced a very heavy squall, which came up very suddenly, when we were near 4th point, being obliged to scud the ship were in much danger of running on some of those islands, it being so dark you could [not?] see the length of the ship. Fortunately, the Lightning was bright; and we could at times see the Land. Next day came to at Anjire Point. Found there ship Mercury of P. which had left America 6 days [?] since we had. Went on shore and were very politely received by the Dutch Com., who permitted us to walk thro' the village which is considerably larger than it appears from the ship. We here procured stock for the remainder of our voyage, which is very cheap indeed. Fowls were 18 for a dollar, ducks 12, and very fine Turtle a dollar each weighing from 45 to 80 lbs. By getting the stock of the Dutch boat, which always boards you, it is cheaper than from the Malays. Letters left at Anjire will be forwarded to America via Batavia.

In sight of Java fell in with an English ship Bound to Borneo, and agreed to keep company thro' Gasper. We entered Straits about 2 P.M. with a fine breeze, and at 9 we were past Gasper Island, had a current with us. From Pulo Domar till we had passed the Macclesfield Shoal we had much light weather [?]. On making the Lema islands we got a pilot who takes you to Macao. Found him of considerable use from his knowledge of the currents. They are very exorbitant in their demands at first.

Captain Beare, of the ship Martha, lately arrived from Calcutta, has favored the editors of the N. York Gazette with the following memorandum, which, no doubt, will prove a useful caution to navigators from the E. Indies. On the 17th June 1808 [?] saw the island of St. Paul's. By a good-time keeper and a lunar observation in the morning he found its true situation in lat. 37"55 N., long. 29"30 W. from London, which is 1.45 further west than laid down in the latest publication. Its extent is not more than 1 ½ miles. Capt. B found a strong current setting to the westward for three days before and after, making it, at the rate of 24 to 30 miles per day. As this island is immediately in the track of our homeward bound India men, he thinks it extremely dangerous to pass its latitude in the night, without being well assured of their longitude.

In passing this island in the La Carolina we found [it] to lie about 100 miles to the Eastward of our reckoning, tho we had several very good observations for several days before. Capt. A thought at the time it was laid down wrong.

Capt. A and Captain Gilchrist of the Caravan of Boston having agreed to keep co., sailed the 21, Nov. from Wampoa. On leaving the coast of China we had a very fresh breeze, and being bound down the inner passage made it quite a free wind. The evening before we made Sapata, we had a very heavy squall from the S. of W. and another severe one the next day. After passing Sapata, the wind which had hitherto been fresh, left us and we had light winds to the Straits of Banca.

We had just got a good entrance in the Straits, when we experienced a very heavy squall which scarcely permitted us to lay along. It lasted about 1 hour, and blew very fresh. Having a fine Moon light night we continued under sail till we arrived at 1st point when we anchored, and the next morning by 11 we were fairly clear. Had a very fresh breeze but scant to North Island. We lay at North Isl. 36 hours, and procured some wood and water from Sumatra. From N. 1st till we were clear of the straits the wind was ahead, blowing fresh up the straits, and sometimes squally. We came up with at No. Isl. the ships Fair Leader, Cooper, Trident, Blakeman, Frances Henrietta Skinner. We were joined at No. Isl. by the Mercury Arnold and passed the Straits in Company of those vessels. We had fine weather, and a good breeze for some days after, and saw the Mercury when three days out.

Off the Island of Madagascar we had very disagreeable weather, the wind shifting very suddenly. The Wind from this to the Cape of Good Hope was mostly to the Westward, had one gale from West off Augullas. Spoke the Mercury in Long. 76, Lat. 34, and saw a brig supposed the Caravan. Had fine weather from the Cape to Line.

We crossed the Equator the 19 February, and had little or no calm weather, and not much light w. Between Latt. 3 & 4 we took the N.E. trade winds which lasted without intermition for 8 or 10 days blowing a fresh Top Gal't breeze generally. The ship for 7 days averaged rather more than 8 miles pr. Hour. In Lat. 22 Long. 62. Fell in with a french privateer 3 days from Gaudaloupe, from whom we received the unpleasant news, that there had been an embargo laid throughout the United States, in consequence of Bonaparte's having demanded of America to declare for or against England. We also learned from him that peace had been made between Russia and France, that the court of Portugal had removed to Brazil, and other news, the purpose of which was that the U. States could not be long at Peace, at the same time advising us to keep well to the West to avoid British ships. We fell in with a brig 2 days after standing NW. March the 4 saw a ship standing WNW, supposed for Charleston. Since speaking the French vessel the weather has gradually grown colder.

11. v. JANE STRAWBRIDGE was born in Philadelphia in 1793 and died in Cazenovia, New York, on 4 February 1855.[197] She married, in Philadelphia on 26 October 1819,[198] JONATHAN DENISE LEDYARD, who was born in Middletown Point, New Jersey, on 10 June 1793 and died in Cazenovia, New York, on 7 January 1874, son of Benjamin Ledyard and Catherine Forman.[199]

In 1819, a few months before Jane's marriage to Jonathan Ledyard, Jonathan's sister, Helen Lincklaen, wrote a warm letter welcoming Jane to the family at Cazenovia, New York. Helen was born November 15, 1777, in Middletown Point, New Jersey, and died April 10, 1847, in Cazenovia.[200] The "V d Kemp" couple mentioned in the letter probably are John Vantarkamp (or Vandekemp) and his wife, Juliana, born Taylor. Juliana was the sister of Frances Taylor, the wife of Jane Strawbridge's brother John.

Cazenovia 8th of May 1819

My Dear Miss Strawbridge,

Altho' I have a great aversion generally to the use of the pen, I cannot refrain from addressing a few lines to you, merely to say, how very happy you have made us all by

197   Cass Ledyard Shaw, *The Ledyard Family in America* (Phoenix Publishing, West Kennebunk, Maine 1993) 80. Death notice, *The New York Post*, unknown date, reporting death of Jane Ledyard in Cazenovia on 4 February 1855.

198   U.S. Presbyterian Church Records, 1701–1970, online database at ancestry.com, citing Presbyterian Historical Society, Philadelphia, *Register of Baptisms and Marriages etc 1744–1833*; Accession Number: V MI46 P533r v.2; original record is page from marriages register of Second Presbyterian Church, Philadelphia, showing marriage of Jon. D. Ledyard and Jane Strawbridge on 26 October 1819.

199   Shaw, *The Ledyard Family in America* 80.

200   Shaw, *The Ledyard Family in America* 73.

consenting to become an inhabitant of our Dear little village. May you never have cause to repent of this goodness—that a much loved brother's happiness will be secured by being united to one who I know is possessed of every enviable quality. I have not the least doubt and be assured my dear Jane, we will all strive to make you as happy as you have us, and trust we shall in some measure succeed. It is true, we cannot offer you the conveniences and amusements of a city, which you have always been accustomed to, but we freely give you warm affectionate hearts, and will endeavor to be unto you, as the sisters and brothers you will leave. I will not trust myself with stating the many excellencies that we think our brother J possesses, but will leave them for you to find out. I long for the time to arrive, when I may welcome you here, and hope you will give us that pleasure before the roads become bad in the fall. Sister Catharine is much engaged in the necessary business of spring house cleaning, which she requests me to say prevents her from doing herself the pleasure of writing you this Mail. We are both much gratified with the pretty little cases of Needles you have had the goodness to send us. Nothing could have been more acceptable, as we were both much in need of this useful article, and they are Doubly valuable on account of the Dear Donor. The weather here is very fine at present. I wish you could join me in a walk, that I intend taking this afternoon, on the banks of the Lake to look at a certain tree, with the initials of a young Lady's name cut on it. Be pleased to remember us affectionately to your brother and sister, Mr. & Mrs. V d Kemp, and accept for yourself the love and best wishes of Mr. L in addition to that of
yours sincerely and
affectionately

Helen Lincklaen

The following letter, which comes from the archives at the Lorenzo historical site in Cazenovia, New York, is from Samuel F. B. Morse, the painter and inventor of the telegraph, to Jonathan Denise Ledyard, the husband of Jane Strawbridge Ledyard. Morse did portraits of both Jonathan and Jane. It's not clear who is the Miss Strawbridge that Morse mentions in the letter; Jane did not have any sisters, but she did have a number of nieces, and one of them may have been visiting Cazenovia in the summer when Morse evidently was there doing the portraits.

New York Oct. 11, 1827

Gen. J. D. Ledyard

Dear Sir,

I owe you an apology for not informing you before this of the cause of the delay in forwarding the frames for your pictures. I was anxious that they should be more than ordinarily good, and, therefore, preferred choosing myself the patterns and style of moulding, rather than trust to the taste of the gilder. The moment I arrived I gave orders for the frames, and I am happy in informing you that I have just seen them safely put on board the Constellation steam boat for Albany to the care of J.N.M. Hurd as you requested; they are contained in one box. I hope they will arrive safe, and be satisfactory.

I shall long remember with pleasure the agreeable time I passed at Cazenovia under the hospitable roofs of Mrs. Lincklaen and Gen. Ledyard.

Please give my best wishes to Mrs. Ledyard, Mrs. Lincklaen, Miss Helen Ledyard, Mr. Walters, Mr. Child's family, and all Cazenovia friends; I know not if Miss Strawbridge is with you, if she is, she will think it "a shame," and "too bad" if I omit to name her among those who will be always pleasantly associated with my thoughts of Cazenovia. Pray, therefore, remember me to her.

To Mr. Brown your good clergyman I would also ask to be respectfully remembered.

With respect & esteem

Dear Sir

Y. Ob. Serv.

Samuel F.B. Morse

Figure 49. Detail from 1827 Portrait of Jane Ledyard by Samuel F. B. Morse

In 1852, Jane wrote a wonderful letter to her daughter, Helen, giving an account of their family history:

Cazenovia, New York
April 6th, 1852

My dear daughter:

It is a stormy afternoon, & I am not likely to be interrupted, so I will undertake what you have so urgently urged me to do (and what I have felt so disinclined to engage in). A little narrative of family matters, & particular notices of those with whom I was most intimately associated & to whom I was most fondly attatched.

Your Uncle John's account of the Strawbridge family is much more accurate & interesting than I could have given, for I was in infancy when my father died, and of course have no recollection of him whatever. Having had 4 sons, he was delighted by the birth of a daughter, & I have been told was continually calling on my name during his last hours. From all that I can learn he was a father whose memory ought ever to be revered by his children, having been one of the noblest & best of men in all the relations of life.

His sisters the two Mrs. Maffitts Anne & Mary I remember perfectly well & also their husbands, & children. My uncle Thomas Maffitt owned a farm & mill on the North East river Cecil County Maryland.

The situation was pleasant by the waterside, where there was a fine fishery; I recollect having seen them draw a seine there and catching a great quantity & great variety of fish—the North East herring are quite celebrated & often sent to Philadelphia. I was often very successful fishing there myself just by the Mill door, with only a thread line &

bent pin for a hook and the sight & sound of the mill, are always in my mind associated with agreeable recollections.

My mother was several times obliged to fly from Wilmington on account of the prevalence of Yellow fever, of which she felt naturally a great dread, having lost her husband by this dreadful malady, & suffered from an attack of it herself subsequently.

Her place of refuge, was with our Maryland friends, who always made her and myself, & sometimes my younger brothers welcome; & our visits were very delightful.

Our first stage always brought us to Elkton, where an Aunt of my Mother's, a Mrs. Gilpin, a fine hospitable old lady, resided. She had then several married children around her, all long since dead & all their children, unless it may be those of their eldest son John Gilpin who married a Miss Hollingsworth; she was a widow when I was last there & managing her young family & farm most admirably. On the occasion of this last visit I accompanied a young school friend to whom I had officiated as brides maid (the Hon. Lewis McLane was the other attendant), Maria Reading, who married W. H. Ward & who took possession of the same house (modernized & improved) that had been formerly occupied by Aunt Gilpin.

My Uncle Samuel Maffitt lived 6 or 8 miles from North East. He was a magistrate & a great Politician, & had a fine family of, I think, 10 children. Some of the older ones, as your Uncle J. observes had been partly educated in my father's family in Philadelphia, & seemed to be greatly attatched to us.

My venerable Irish grandmother lived here aged 90 years. My only recollection of her is of her calling me to her to inquire if the stumps in the field & woods around the house were not men & of my being directed to say "Yes" as she in her dotage believed them to be & the family found it necessary to indulge her in such fancies. Some of the mischievous grandsons set fire to some of the stumps, to satisfy, or convince her they were not human beings but this savageness (as she thought) nearly threw her in hysterics. I was named after her and born (as I forgot to say) in Walnut St. below 3d in Phila., in a 3 storied brick house which stood there when I left the city.

Of the Maryland connexions I had not heard for many years, until last summer when Mrs. Aertsen of Phila. visited us & as you may recollect told me she had occasional intercourse with them, & that several of the name yet remained at N.E.

You have frequently heard me mention my father's only brother "Uncle James," to whom I was excessively attached; he was our guardian & as fond, & indulgent to us as a father. We have, you know, his miniature, given to me when a little girl. He never married—was a most amiable excellent character, & the very handsomest man in face & figure my eyes ever saw. He always lived in Phila. at the corner of 5th & Market Sts. then a fashionable boarding house, where he retained his place no matter who kept the house.

My beloved mother was Hannah Evans. She married young, was a handsome woman—taller than myself, & of rather full habit, as I recollect her, & of a very florid complexion, large dark blue eyes, regular features & beautiful soft brown hair, which never became gray, as was the case with nearly all of our relatives, many of them at quite an early period of life. She was a pious woman, a member of the Presbyterian church, but much attatched to the Society of "Friends." She passed through many trials but had strong faith to support her and entire submission to the will of God. Was a person of strong mind—very energetic, active, & managing in her family & a general favorite among her pleasant & large circle of friends & neighbors.

She was greatly blessed in her sons, who were all dutiful & affectionate, & very upright & correct in conduct; & did every thing in their power to promote her comfort & happiness. She used to remark that she "had observed that the sons of widows generally turned out well." As I said, I was her youngest child & only daughter, and "the most troublesome when young to manage," but afterwards "her greatest Earthly comfort." She said she "always felt the greatest confidence in me—I was always concientious." It is pleasant my dear daughter to dwell upon her memory!

My childhood was a most happy one—Now when I look back, I think I had too much liberty.—In consequence perhaps I went too much to the other extreme in bringing up my own family, though I may say, I was watchful & unwearied in endeavouring by every means in my power, to render them happy at home.

Our home being so delightful, retired & with extensive grounds, made my task easier; she resided in a large town & I could not look out of either door or window without being hailed by young companions and for some reason—I know not why—Jane Strawbridge was a great favorite with her school mates. Our house was on the public promenade to Brandywine & there was always some novelty & variety to be seen.

The schools at Wilmington were excellent and I had many opportunities for improvement until I was 12 or 14 years of age, when our property (a handsome one) was thro' mismanagement nearly lost to us (about a 3d part of it was restored to the family in 1819, the year I was married) & we were obliged to forego many advantages & enjoyments, that we had previously been favored with & to struggle through many trials and privations for a long period of time.

My eldest brothers John & George were graduated at Princeton & both read law with James A. Bayard, quite a distinguished public man. John tired of it & went into a counting house at Phila. where after a time he was employed as supercargo twice to India, & his profits were so handsome that he was enabled to establish himself in business & married Miss Elizabeth Stockton, the only daughter of Gen. John Stockton of Delaware.

After George completed his course of study, he went to New Castle 5 miles below Wilmington, to be near us & with the hope of there pursuing his profession. Business came slowly, he had no other means of support, so after my mother's death he quit practice, & went out supercargo for brother John—but previously passed many months in Western Pennsylvania to look after lands belonging to the family & which had been neglected until necessity obliged us to sell off tract after tract for support.

After this George went abroad several voyages & was quite fortunate until the last war, when the vessel he was in was captured by an English frigate & he was detained prisoner on board six weeks—was at length landed at Georgetown N.C.—where he formed many pleasant acquaintances & was treated with the greatest hospitality & when leaving, was supplied with a variety of nice things for the return voyage.

Soon afterwards he engaged in Manufacturing which proved so profitable that he felt encouraged to settle down at a pleasant place near Frankford, & married Miss Fanny Hepburn—immediately afterwards, Peace was declared & the manufactory (where they had contracts from government to make cloth for the Army) was no longer to be depended upon.

He made other experiments—but only to experience other reverses of fortune, until at length he was induced to go to New Orleans—about the year 1824—and resumed his profession and after reading the Napoleon Code engaged very successfully in practice & was enabled to educate his children, & afford them every advantage. He yet lives there highly respected & esteemed, & last summer, as you know, we had the pleasure of seeing him here, in good health, & spirits. He has ever been distinguished for his perseverence, & integrity—has of late years been 1st judge of the Supreme Court, & afterwards of the commercial court, but now about retiring to private life.

James, my 3d brother, had a plain English education, was not of studious habits: but very steady healthy and industrious. He chose to enter into one of the Brandywine mills as an apprentice, & remained until he had a thorough knowledge of the business, but the dust of the mills irritated his lungs (as was often the case), & he was obliged to quit, &, as there was no other opening for him, he went to sea "before the mast," in one of brother J's ships & was soon advanced to the rank of Mate—when some how—returning from England in a British vessel, passenger—the ship was captured by the French & he with others thrown into the fortress of Cherbourg, on the Coast, exposed to chill sea air passing thro' a grated window, & there remained 2 or 3 months until the family heard of his situation, & thro' the government or our consul there, and had him released. He returned with impaired health & died in Philadelphia after I went there to reside, about the year 1814.

Joseph, my youngest brother, had a classical school education—went early into a counting house at Philadelphia, was very closely confined, & growing rapidly became weak & disabled & was advised to try a sea voyage. He made a trip to Martinique enjoyed it & was benefitted so much, that he concluded to go again & having obtained a very desirable berth as assistant supercargo on board a fine ship. went to Canton, & gave great satisfaction to his employers by his steadiness & capacity. I have many of his letters written as you know in the most beautiful manner. On the return voyage near home his health gave way—& after lingering several months he died at home, in the 19th year of his age. This was my first great sorrow. Many other rapidly followed— among these the sudden death of brother John's lovely wife, leaving an infant, & Stockton a pale delicate boy two years old. My mother brought them to our house, where she devoted herself to the infant, & I to the frail looking boy, who immediately attached himself to me, & we were rarely separated for years afterwards. At 18 months old the infant died but S. remained in W. with us (his father had again married—to Miss Frances Taylor) until my mother's death in November 1812; immediately after I went to reside in my brother's family at Philadelphia until I married your father in 1819. My home there was a most pleasant one as my sister Fanny was an estimable woman, and did every thing in her power to place me at ease & render me happy in her house.

My beloved mother had always enjoyed fine health & had a strong constitution—but taking cold at a critical period of life fell into ill health thro' which I nursed her 18 months when she was made willing to leave us to the care of that God in whom she had so long put her trust.

It was a great trial to leave Wilmington. All my early attatchments & associations were formed there. It is a beautiful place—the society was of a superior sort—many old settled respectable families, a great number of them Quakers—Many Marylanders who came to educate their children—the schools being excellent—many people educated & agreeable who lived there because it was retired & suited to moderate incomes, and a great many French Emigrants, both from the Continent & West Indies who built handsome houses & made beautiful gardens. I paid 2 visits after our family were broken up there, but they were sad melancholy ones, tho' I was received in the most cordial manner by our old friends, & neighbours. My last one was probably 36 years ago. I have an irresistable desire to go there once more, but will not probably accomplish such an excursion & perhaps it is best that I should not. I hope one of these days you may get there my child, tho' perhaps you might be disappointed in the place.—Of course it is greatly changed, & then we have been so accustomed in this country to fine scenery that it might suffer by comparison.

Uncle John you are aware has always remained at Phila., has had various changes & trials, but always been highly esteemed & respected by his old friends and connexions. Has had fine health & retained his natural gaiety of Disposition. He is a talented well educated man—was in youth very handsome—had all the beauty of the family. I will not enumerate or mention the younger branches—your cousins—with whom you are individually acquainted—all are correct & respectable and none have brought trouble, or disgrace upon the name.

I am sorry I have not arranged these reminiscences in a more connected manner.—I must however endeavour to give you some account of my Mother's family from recollection, aided by my friend Miss Lovering's notes. You must carefully preserve these notices of hers. From these we learn the Ancestors of the Gilpins (my maternal grandmother's name) came from England in 1696—among those embarkations which were invited to emigrate & settle in Pennsylvania under the immediate patronage of William Penn. They were driven by stress of weather into James' river, Virginia—but afterwards arrived at their place of destination on the Brandywine 12 or 15 miles above Wilmington, where as there were no buildings—they were obliged (until they could provide better quarters) to live in a cave. This cave is yet preserved and is on a farm occupied by one of the descendants of the same name. I believe it is in the neighborhood of Chad's ford, where the memorable battle was fought. I regret that I have not visited it.

This Joseph Gilpin & Alice[201] his wife (he was born in 1664 died 1741) came over as I remarked in 1696—He had two children before leaving England, a daughter, & son— this son was our ancestor. He afterwards had 13 children—12 of them married & had families—of course the number of descendants is immense & scattered far & wide— Many of them were Quakers as their progenitors were & all prided themselves upon being "descendants of the cave." When a child I used occasionally to go to a Druggist's store in Wilmington, kept by an eccentric old man by the name of Webster—who always asked my name, & when told who I was, invariably replied "Ah! Thee's one of the cave, thy scissors will cut sharp." But to return to Samuel eldest son of Joseph Gilpin, born

---

201   The reference to "Alice" evidently was a mistake; other records show that Joseph married Hannah Glover.

as supposed at Dorchester in England—married in Phila. Jane, daughter of John Parker whose Mother's name was Doe (She who marked the sampler now in my possession & presented the old blue smelling bottle to her daughter-in-law Jane Parker, my great grandmother, so that I am named after grandmother on one side, & great grandmother on the other) the daughter of Richard Doe who came from France to avoid the persecution there.

Samuel Gilpin settled after marriage at Nottingham Maryland & had 6 children the youngest of whom <u>Rachel</u> was my mother's mother. Her initials are upon our old silver sugar bowl. She married George Evans. I am sorry I do not know more of his (my grandfather's) family. I think he had 2 or 3 brothers: 1 was a judge in Pennsylvania—one a farmer in Montgomery Co., &, there may have been another. I recollect the daughter of the judge dying possessed of some property & leaving my mother 50 £ & a silver cream jug, perhaps the one I now have; but am not certain as there was another—a larger one. The old silver ladle we use I believe was her father's. It is marked J.M.E., John & Mary Evans.

My grandfather George Evans was an active man during the Revolutionary War—held various offices, was a commissary & afterwards a Col. (I believe) & was called Col. Evans—was in many engagements. I used to sit in a little chair by his side and listen to his accounts of the "war" & particularly remember his speaking of the battle of Princeton where his coat tail was shot off by a cannon ball, & of his describing the sensation—the shock being so great, that he at first thought that he had lost a limb. He is mentioned in a printed notice in my possession as having by his activity and patriotism made himself very obnoxious to the British—who when in possession of Wilmington were anxious to secure himself and family as hostages, but they were secreted for a time by their friends & and afterwards one at a time removed to the country. He was an excellent upright man—but as I recollect him rather melancholy having buried his wife, & 7 children. He resided with my mother for many years, who made him as comfortable as possible, but he survived her a few years and then resided with his brother in Montgomery County making occasional visits to us at Philadelphia.

Through the kindness of your Uncle Forman you have the genealogy of the Forman & Ledyard families for many years—and some account of the Strawbridge family through your Uncle John—&, here all I know of my maternal ancestors, so that you know nearly as much as most in the Republic, of your "great forbears"—and I earnestly hope that my much loved family may bring no stain upon their creditable descent—and that God may bless & strengthen them to walk in his fear, & uprightly in their intercourse with their fellow beings—& to be useful members of society, is the prayer of your affectionate mother. Jane Ledyard[202]

---

202   Letter from Jane Strawbridge Ledyard to Helen Lincklaen Ledyard, 6 April 1852; available online at https://strawbridgefamily. net/documents/jane-ledyards-letter-to-her-daughter-1852/; also reprinted as Appendix C in Nivin, *Evans, Nivin and Allied Families* 235, viewed at ancestry.com online database on 29 April 2019.

The Third Generation

7. JOHN[3] STRAWBRIDGE (*John[2], John[1]*) was born in Elkton, Maryland, on 25 April 1780 and died in Philadelphia on 4 April 1858.[203] He married, first, on 18 September 1804,[204] ELIZABETH STOCKTON, who was born about 1782 and died in Philadelphia on 4 June 1807,[205] daughter of John Stockton and Ann Griffith.

Children of John[3] Strawbridge and Elizabeth Stockton:

12. i. STOCKTON[4] STRAWBRIDGE was born, probably in Philadelphia, in 1805 and died in San Francisco, California, on 29 January 1861.[206]

13. ii. JOHN RALSTON STRAWBRIDGE was born in Philadelphia in about 1807 and died in Philadelphia in about June 1809.[207]

JOHN[3] STRAWBRIDGE married, second, in Philadelphia on 14 April 1810,[208] FRANCES TAYLOR, who was born in Philadelphia on 8 February 1781 and died in Philadelphia on 18 April 1836, daughter of John Taylor and Ann Huston.[209]

In 1802, while on a trip overseas in the merchant trade, John wrote a letter home to his mother and other relatives and friends. This letter, one of the few original documents surviving in the family from that era,

---

203   Philadelphia, Pennsylvania, Death Certificates Index, 1803–1915, online database at ancestry.com, citing FHL film number 1976715; record shows John Strawbridge, born about 1780, died at Philadelphia on 4 April 1858, burial at Laurel Hill Cemetery.

204   "Old Philadelphia Families," by Frank Willing Leach, *The North American* (Philadelphia), 10 March 1912, p. 6, giving date of marriage. Article available online at https://strawbridgefamily.net/documents/old-philadelphia-families-article-from-the-philadelphia-north-american-newspaper-march-10-1912/.

205   U.S. Presbyterian Church Records, 1701–1970, online database at ancestry.com, citing Presbyterian Historical Society, Philadelphia, *Register of Baptisms and Marriages etc 1744–1833*; Accession Number: V MI46 P533r v.2; original record is page from births and deaths register of Second Presbyterian Church, Philadelphia, showing death of Mrs. Elizabeth Strawbridge on 4 June 1807. Online image at findagrave.com/memorial/143935113, photo of gravestone showing Mrs. Elizabeth Strawbridge died June 1807 (day not legible), aged 24 years.

206   Nivin, *Evans, Nivin and Allied Families* 60. California, County Birth, Marriage, and Death Records, 1849–1980, online database at ancestry.com, showing death of Stockton Strawbridge in San Francisco on 29 January 1861, aged 52 years, native of Philadelphia. The age must be inaccurate, because that would set his birth in 1808 or 1809, and his mother died in June 1807.

207   Pennsylvania and New Jersey, Church and Town Records, 1669–2013, online database at ancestry.com, citing Historical Society of Pennsylvania, Philadelphia, Historic Pennsylvania Church and Town Records, Reel 801. Image of List of Names on Monuments and Tombstones in Graveyard of First Presbyterian Church, of Wilmington, Delaware, item no. 87, shows death of John R. Strawbridge in June 1809, aged two years.

208   Nivin, *Evans, Nivin and Allied Families* 48.

209   U.S. Presbyterian Church Records, 1701–1970, online database at ancestry.com, citing Presbyterian Historical Society, Philadelphia, *Church Register 1760–1806*; Accession Number: V MI46 P477rr v.2; original record is page from baptisms register of First Presbyterian Church, Philadelphia, showing Francis [sic], child of John and Ann Taylor, was born on 8 February 1781 and baptized on 20 May 1781. Philadelphia, Death Certificates Index, 1803–1915, online database at ancestry.com, citing Death Records housed at Philadelphia City Archives; record shows Frances Strawbridge, born about 1781, died in Philadelphia on 19 April 1836, buried at Second Presbyterian Burial Ground; online image at findagrave.com/memorial/40745852, photo of gravestone shows Frances Strawbridge died 18 April 1836, age 55..

is difficult to read, and this transcription has some gaps. The enclosure mentioned in the letter is not present. It was written from the ship Mount Vernon while it was at anchor in Anjir Roads, or Anjeer Roads, which apparently is an obsolete name for an anchorage in what is now Indonesia, near the Sunda Strait, in the area of Java and Sumatra. Here is an image of the first page:

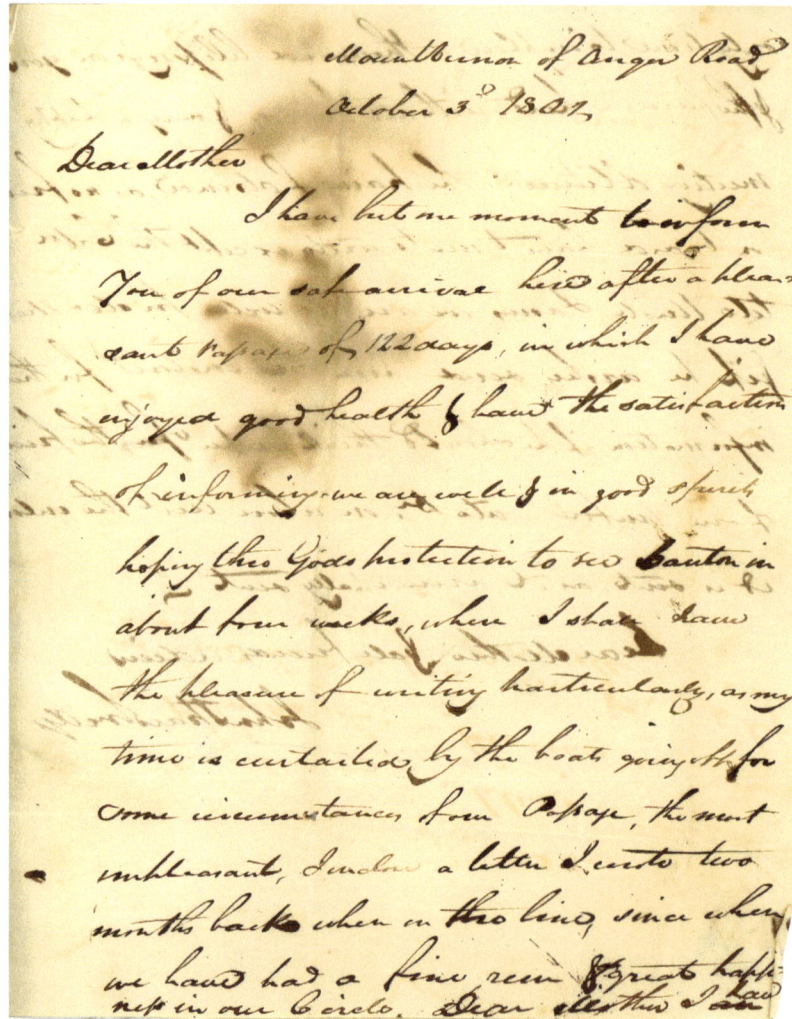

Figure 50. First Page of Letter from John Strawbridge to his Mother, 1802

Following is the text of the letter:

> Mount Vernon of Anjir Road
>
> October 3, 1802
>
> Dear Mother
>
> I have but one moment to inform you of our safe arrival here after a pleasant passage of 122 days, in which I have enjoyed good health & have the satisfaction of informing we are well & in good spirits hoping thro Gods protection to see Boston in about four weeks, when I shall have the pleasure of writing particularly, as my time is curtailed by the boats going off for some circumstances of our passage, the most unpleasant. I enclose a letter I wrote two months back when on the   , since when we have had a fine new & great happiness in our Circle. Dear Mother I have only time to implore a thousand blessings on your and the family's head, with all friends, & may a happy meeting obliterate the pain of absence, as no friends   have time to write

except the Calm   Uncle James we are all well for all   & if he wishes send him the enclosed for the information if he should think proper of the friends of our unfortunate Dr, on whose acct the enclosed   is sent, as it principally

Dear Mother & all Friends, Adieu

John Strawbridge[210]

In 1843, John Strawbridge wrote a brief "autobiography," which has been passed down through the generations. In it, he provides some good details about his family history:

John Strawbridge, my grandfather, emigrated from the north of Ireland about 1752, and settled near Back Creek, Eastern Shore of Maryland. He had previously married a Widow Miller, who survived him to the great age of 90 years and died in 1796, when I was about sixteen years old. Of my grandfather who died many years before I was born, I have heard only that he was a good tempered, indolent man of very moderate education. The support of her young family, three daughters and two sons devolved on the energy of my grandmother, who well discharged her duty assisted by my father who although a very young man and with but an imperfect education, as was common in those days, came to be considered the head of the family and received a large share in his mother's pride and affection. His attention to her and to his sisters and their children was constant and untiring. In after years his mother with sons of his nieces or nephews passed several months of every winter at his house, all receiving kindness and many presents, three or four of them were well educated by him.

His mother after forty years was nearly as Irish in her dialect and notions as ever. She was a strict Presbyterian and very religious, yet too indulgent to her grand children. She never could bear to hear any of us scolded. Her children were Anne and Mary, who married brothers, Samuel and Thomas Moffitt, respectable men, living near North East, Cecil Co., Maryland, Peggy who married John Lawson, and in 1787 emigrated to that part of Pennsylvania now Lycoming Co., then a wilderness. They had children of whom I have seen several. The Moffitt's are very numerous; but since my father's death our intercourse has in a great measure ceased.

John, my father, was the next child and the youngest was James. Considerably before the Revolution, the family left Back Creek, and owned a farm (a poor one when I saw it) three or miles from the Pennsylvania line, and afterwards a very pretty residence (Fair Hill eight or nine miles east of Elkton), both places in Cecil Co. I suppose they lived comfortably. I know they were highly respected by all the old neighbors. John must have been greatly esteemed as during the war, he was sheriff of the county and I have heard a major of the militia. It may be here noted that at this period, excepting Continental money, there was no currency but tobacco, and the rates of taxes, debts, etc., were estimated in pounds of that article as I have seen in the sheriff's books.

It was at this time (August 1777) when my father was circumstanced as I have described that the British fleet, which had sailed from New York several weeks previous and was supposed to be destined for Philadelphia, after various demonstrations off the Capes of the Delaware came to the Chesapeake, and landed a large force at Court House point,

210   Letter from John Strawbridge to James Strawbridge and others, 3 October 1802, original in possession of the author.

under Gen. Sir. William Howe. General Washington with the Marquis De Lafayette was in the neighborhood of Newport watching and expecting his arrival in the Delaware. My father was the first to communicate the news at camp. After being subjected to a searching examination, he was desired to accompany Washington and Lafayette, who, attended by the staff and escort, proceeded to Iron Hill to test the truth of his intelligence. My father rode between the two Generals. It was a very hot day, and he noticed that Lafayette wore long boots, but no stockings. When they attained the top of Iron Hill, a commanding emminence near Elkton, by the aid of glasses they could discern the British fleet and encampment. The Americans were brought up, several sharp skirmishes ensued, and on the 11th of Sept., the severe and unfortunate battle of Brandywine took place and the result was the loss of Philadelphia. Washington was highly pleased with my father and before they separated urged him to accept a captain's commission in the continental army. This compliment he was compelled under all circumstances respectfully to decline.

About the year 1778 my father was married to Hannah Evans, daughter of George Evans, then a very respectable miller on the Brandywine. Often have I heard her tell as passing through our army with her family, they and all they could gather in a wagon, on the day before that battle was fought, and of hearing the cannonading all day. Her description of their alarm and anxiety and of the looks and sufferings of the poor sick and wounded was truly graphic. "God bless your pretty face" said one of the soldiers. "Don't be afraid, you'll see how we will whip the d–d rascals." In her youth, my mother was very handsome, one of the best of wives, mothers, sisters and daughters. She remained a widow, irreproachable in all her relations and died at Wilmington, Delaware in November 1811. As long as she lived her house furnished an asylum for her aged father who survived her six or seven years and died in Philadelphia 1817 while on his way to his brothers in Montgomery Co., PA, his age was about 85 years. He was a good man of the Baptist persuasion and is buried in their ground of the Second st. Church. My son Stockton ought to remember these last two.

At the peace of 1783, my parents removed to Philadelphia and occupied a small house in Third st. below Market. My father's store was on Walnut Street wharf. They lived like most people in those days plainly but comfortably. Notwithstanding some heavy losses, he got on fast and at the end of ten years seemed desirous to arrange his affairs and go to the country, more especially there to bring up his children. He was fond of rural life and topics and used to entertain his family with conversations on such subjects. He was disposed to make investments in the Back Lands of Pennsylvania as they were called, which in that day were thought highly of, as a mode of investment. We had a quantity of them, but they never came to much in our hands. In 1792 he was about buying a large property in Washington Co. for himself, this fell through and in the summer of that year he rented Peale Hall (the site of Girard College) and set about winding up his business.

In August, 1793, the yellow fever made its appearance in Philadelphia. My father visited the city daily. On the 7th he had adjusted all, the 9th, he was attacked, and died prepared, and resigned on the 16th of September 1793 taking leave of my mother and uncle with entire composure, of his children he could not bear to take leave. I passed his door twelve hours before his death, and still remember his face and position, he was 44 years of age, of middle size, very square and stout, good face, hazel eyes, and possessed a wonderful constitution. He was always a temperate and religious man. As one of the victims of '93 his name appears in the record of that melancholy period as one of the most useful, benevolent citizens and intelligent, active merchants.

I may mention here as the evidence of the alarm and distress then prevailing in Phila. that in six hours, my good father was hurried to the grave. My uncle and two negroes alone attending him to our Arch St. ground. There is a monument with a long inscription by Dr. Green, which my mother never liked nor considered (however, just) as suited to his retiring modesty. For nearly five weeks after his decease, we were shut up, and nearly starved, such was the difficulty in procuring provisions. No one came near us, at last George Evans our grandfather took us to Newark, Delaware where we lived six months, then removed to Wilmington where my mother ended her days. My father had few close city friends but they were highly respectable. Dr. Ashbel Green then our young minister was one of them. I do not believe there was a more liberal and benevolent man in the city. He gave largely through others and was always retiring and unostentatious. Congress and Legislature both met here, he knew many of the members and their visits occupied most of the evenings. The events of the recent war, the Indians, then hostile within 100 or 150 miles of us of "old time" stories, of his family records of his youthful days, with indigents of country life were such interesting topics to me that many a time I had to be forced to go to bed and leave this delightful circle. I remember two of these gentlemen, Gen. William Montgomery and Judge Allison; on their knees I have sat and listened for many an hour, when about the age of Johnny C. Browne.

There was another class of tales which old Grandmother told me privately, which scared me so that I remember getting a whipping for telling my father flatly when sent to bed "I would not go." After which I heard my indulgent mother say he grieved much and tried to put an end to such doings with his mother's ancient tales and foolish fables.

James Strawbridge, my uncle, took charge of my father's large estate. He was a kind, honest, liberal man. About the year 1801 he embarked all he had and our property in some investment which proved unfortunate, and nearly the whole was consumed. This for years occasioned hard suffering on my mother's part. James S. was one of the handsomest men I ever saw. He never married and these untoward events ended his days (1806) in much trouble. I never think of him but with affection and regret. These misfortunes seem all for the best, they sobered my high notions considerably.

From 1794, I never lived at home, though a constant visitor there. Uncle James was indulgent, and I gay and extravagant, but not dissipated for I had then as my friends and patrons some of the best men in Phila., such as Robert Ralston, Samuel Archer, Alexander Henry etc. I was well educated, graduated at Princeton College 1797. George graduated at the same college 1802, the others James, Joseph and Jane had not much chance. After considerable trouble Mr. Ralston partially started me, in 1802 I made two prosperous voyages to India and settled in 1804.

To these reminiscences I now only add for the benefit of my children, my sincere conviction that I now for sixty three years have been most favorably dealt with by a kind Providence.

I have committed many errors and suffered for them, but I believe never forfeited the claim to honesty, and fair conduct in domestic relations, which after all is the only happy path.

Few have been more desirous of discharging the moral duties of husband and father. This I can say truly—but to God, the gracious Benefactor how far have I come short!

Philadelphia, April 1843[211]

Children of John[3] Strawbridge and Frances Taylor:

14.　iii. ANN TAYLOR STRAWBRIDGE was born in Philadelphia on 6 April 1811[212] and died in Philadelphia on 1 January 1881.[213] She married, first, in Philadelphia on 15 October 1836, PETER BROWNE, who was born on 8 February 1803 and died on 25 March 1840, son of John Coats Browne and Hannah Lloyd.[214] She married, second, between 1845 and 1850, WILLIAM CAMPFIELD KENT, who was born in Moorestown, Burlington County, New Jersey, on 12 September 1810 and died in Philadelphia on 24 April 1881, son of Rudolphus Kent and Mary Tuthill.[215]

Figure 51. Ann Taylor Strawbridge Browne Kent and William Campfield Kent

211　"Autobiography of John Strawbridge," an account written by John Strawbridge (1780–1858); also available at https://strawbridgefamily.net/documents/john-strawbridge-autobiography-complete-version/; also reprinted as Appendix B in Nivin, *Evans, Nivin and Allied Families* 230, viewed at ancestry.com online database on 29 April 2019.

212　U.S. Presbyterian Church Records, 1701–1970, online database at ancestry.com, citing Presbyterian Historical Society, Philadelphia, *Register of Baptisms and Marriages etc 1744–1833*; Accession Number: V MI46 P533r v.2; original record is page from baptisms register of Second Presbyterian Church, Philadelphia, showing Ann Taylor Strawbridge, daughter of John and Frances Strawbridge, was born on 6 April 1811 and baptized on 11 May 1816.

213　Online image at findagrave.com/memorial/129762402, photo of gravestone shows Anne T., wife of W. C. Kent, born 6 April 1811, died 1 January 1881. Other information at site says she married her first husband, Peter Brown [sic], on 15 October 1836. Death notice, *The Philadelphia Inquirer*, 3 January 1881, p. 5.

214　Keith, Charles Penrose, *The Provincial Councillors of Pennsylvania, who Held Office Between 1733–1776: And Those Earlier Councillors who Were Some Time Chief Magistrates of the Province, and Their Descendants* (Philadelphia 1883) 214 (available for download at books.google.com), setting forth birth date of Ann and marriage date for her and Peter Browne. U.S. Presbyterian Church Records, 1701–1970, online database at ancestry.com, citing Presbyterian Historical Society, Philadelphia, *Church Register 1827–1870*; Accession Number: V MI46 P533r v.3; original record is page from marriages register of Second Presbyterian Church, Philadelphia, showing marriage of Peter Brown [sic] and Ann T. Strawbridge on 15 October 1836.

215　Online image at findagrave.com/memorial/129762315, photo of gravestone showing William Campfield Kent, 12 September 1810–24 April 1881. Obituary, *The Philadelphia Inquirer*, 25 April 1881, p. 3, saying William Campfield Kent died on 23 April at his residence, 903 Clinton Street; he was born 13 September 1810 at Moorestown, New Jersey; his parents were Rudolphus Kent and Mary Tuthill. Death notice, *The Philadelphia Inquirer*, 3 January 1881, p. 5, announcing death of Anne Taylor Kent, wife of William C. Kent and daughter of the late John Strawbridge; her residence was No. 903 Clinton Street.

15. iv. JOHN TAYLOR STRAWBRIDGE was born in Philadelphia on 11 December 1812[216] and died on 16 July 1829 in Newtown, Bucks County, Pennsylvania.[217] He died of drowning while swimming with his brother, George, and a teacher from his school in that area.

+ 16. v. GEORGE STRAWBRIDGE was born on 18 November 1814 and died on 28 September 1862.

Following is a transcription of a letter to this George Strawbridge from his father, John, with an addendum by Mr. Strawbridge and a short note added by George's aunt, Elizabeth Taylor (probably the sister or sister-in-law of George's mother, who was born Frances Taylor).

The John Strawbridge who wrote this letter was born in Elkton, Maryland, in 1780 and died in Germantown (now part of Philadelphia) in 1858. He was the brother of Jane Strawbridge, who married Jonathan Denise Ledyard. John's second wife, Frances Taylor (George's mother) died in 1836, two years before this letter was written.

The letter was prompted by the family's relief that George was not one of the victims of a very recent steamboat catastrophe on the Mississippi River. On April 21, 1838, the steamboat Oronoko exploded on the Mississippi River, killing possibly 100 persons.[218] I am not sure if George was on the boat (which seems doubtful) or just was in the area and might have taken that boat. His father also mentions another great steamboat disaster at about the same time, which he calls the Cincinnati Affair (though he spells it a little differently). In that incident, the steamboat Moselle blew up on the Ohio River at Cincinnati, killing more than 100 people, according to one contemporary account.[219] This was a particularly bad time for steamboat accidents; safety valves had not yet been put widely into use, and inspections were not regularly required. After a third such accident in the spring of 1838 (involving a boat called the Pulaski), Congress in July 1838 passed legislation instituting some new safety measures. There were several other bad steamboat accidents in 1837 and before; this letter speaks of three accidents, but it is not clear which was the third one alluded to.[220]

After a rather brief discussion of the steamboat disasters, the letter moves into a fairly intense discussion of business affairs. John Strawbridge was a merchant who got his start through trading voyages to China and India, and he had a lot of advice to give his son about commercial matters.

Here is the text of the letter, as well as it could be made out, starting with the address, which appears on the outside of the folded letter. (Evidently envelopes were not used at this time.)

Mr. George Strawbridge
Care of
Messrs Forster & Foxx
Nashville Tennessee

My dear Son

216   U.S. Presbyterian Church Records, 1701–1970, online database at ancestry.com, citing Presbyterian Historical Society, Philadelphia, *Register of Baptisms and Marriages etc 1744–1833*; Accession Number: V MI46 P533r v.2; original record is page from baptisms register of Second Presbyterian Church, Philadelphia, showing John Taylor Strawbridge, son of John and Frances Strawbridge, was born on 11 December 1812 and baptized on 11 May 1816.

217   Rhode Island, Vital Extracts, 1636–1899, online database at ancestry.com; original record reports death of John Taylor Strawbridge, son of John in 17th year, drowned near Newton, Buck County [sic], Pennsylvania, on 16 July 1829. Death notice, *The National Gazette* (Philadelphia), 23 July 1829, p. 2, article reports death of John Taylor Strawbridge on 16 July near Newtown, Bucks County, by drowning in the Neshaminy Creek when swimming with his brother; says he was buried at Newtown.

218   "Steamboat Accident," *Richmond [Virginia] Enquirer*, 4 May 1838, p. 2.

219   "Most Awful Steamboat Accident—Loss of 125 Lives," *The [Baltimore] Sun*, 30 April 1838, p. 1.

220   For information about other steamboat disasters, see "Steamboat Disasters," online compilation at genealogytrails.com/ark/greene/SteamboatDisasters.htm, viewed on 28 May 2019.

Thanks to a merciful Providence you are safe from the fatal accident of the Oronoco, & our great anxiety relieved. Tho you mention slightly, it ought to produce permanent & sincere Gratitude in every one of our Minds—near 300 have been murdered in this & the Cincinatti Affair—

Most of these losses are owing to misconduct or ignorance & the Surviving Officers (& some of the missing [?] Passengers) ought to be hanged. It was so near your fixed time of return & Route, we were very wary [?], tho the lists of sufferers did not include your name. As neither Congress [?] nor the States will act any traveller must go in slow lines & wait for experienced old-fashioned Masters. Your Express from Randolph reached here in 14 days, about 3 longer than the Mail at Memphis. You will get mine of 5th & 14 April at Nashville. 24 March 18 April when Fanny [George's sister Frances, probably] wrote you 24 April Ann [his sister] 5 May.

All as usual, anxious for your speedy & safe Return, & none wishing any other than a temporary absence, this to be considered your home & place to start, let the turbulent S & West contain the adventurous, who have neither Friend nor means & some no Character but for such as you, here there only is your Effort to start, with Prudence & Industry, you have as much Capital as is good for a beginner & I never saw (& others say so too) a better time than the present. Times are in every respect mended. N York & the Eastern Banks pretend to pay species, ours under 1$ & to extend gradually.

All have given fair dividends & want good paper, except S to Tennessee, Alabama, & particularly Mississippi, considerable ----- excellent Receipts & more cash than usual— marketing is quite easy. Goods rising & earn at Auction, Exclusive—improved, & million specie in NY, tho Tennessee Bonds sold in NY,—cashed them here & with 500,000 Planters Port etc, you must find it easier to ------.

As yet neither Cotton nor Cash to me from Memphis, I have left all to your discretions, as for the 500 endorsement note I asked of you, I got it on deposit my Kensington [?]—

Denman [?] leaves Louisville for Nashville about now & will be there at same time as yourself. I have suggested your proper Course in any Event, if he wishes you to return here or give up the (poor trifling unfettered friends) do so on his written receipt, taking care to retain—in Notes if there is no Cash a very handsome allowance for your great Responsibility, toils & dangers—look at the note below. I and the 2 Ds appear to think you might as well stay & allmost work for nothing as you would find few openings here—at least such is the import of their Words. They magnify your cleverness but trebly glorify the value of this chance of distinguishing yourself & the ------ it will give you as an agent, not dreaming you can (& will) go on your own—.

If you are to return, write all interested per express mail and obey their orders strictly. Anyhow I cannot see the use of your remaining out longer than 1 July, all the crop is realized by 1 June.

One word as to carrying money or Notes about You, tis my greatest fear, do be careful & put all in Banks wherever you stay a few days. As to your—Union (no dividend yet) 92 Planters 93 Memphis the safest 85—watch well there & I will sell if you have any suspicion of their solvency. As they constitute your all, this is the more necessary; if it were as ¼ of my property, I would see it out as long as they are solid, they pay good dividends. But Memphis is in poor credit, the ------ sells at 74, the interior Shops nobody likes.

All the Cotton Country will come round but the price is so bare that it requires 2 Crops to pay their debts for lands & negroes, they must work close & learn to save, or they never will get square. As to what plans you may bring home, I cannot tell; you ought to know & be respected by most of the clever People & if you do start, come in as a good beginner for the best chances & much of that Cash which every one new must bring more or less, but they cannot as a Mass expect such indulgence as heretofore & no Man would be fool enough to risk the Large Capital requisite to ------ on the old plan, he could live like a prince on its income here.

The effort is to mix a little of this, with other cash & short Credit trade in 3 or 400 miles Vicinity. Never were better times in this line.

But on all those matters when we meet, that I ------- in my letters to such matters that you may found good houses as you go along.

Hughes is law clerk to Brown & Co. of Pittsburg his brother poor Jos. fell down the ------ hatch & broke his Thigh & Leg. What a distrest Family. C & D let poor H 10 penny less -------, even for his work done & terrible duty he performed since 15 February. All last year his work was most horrible to any sensitive minds & yet he is only secured by assign. If you return thro Pittsburg call & see him, he is attached to You.

By the bye, coming that route do look at our canal.

You are affectionately & favorably mentioned by many & your course commended. The more so, tho most think you had a bad Pattern in every way. An auditor showed a copy of WL's statement, miserable indeed. You have an agent for Banks & others 15 times as much to collect - don't be influenced by old rates or serving Mr. C cheap, he has no heart nor D either.

A second note or addendum followed, on the same paper, as follows:

May 8, 1838
Dear George

On reflection I leave this part open, as I may tonight hear from you at Memphis to 26 or 27th April. The SW Express Mail is discontinued as well it may if it took 14½ days from Randolph. The 3 Steamboat disasters, excite a strong feeling! Will it do any good, or procure any Law. You are in peril of life & from Robbers, abounding in S. Boats & Hotels, do be carefull & especially try & get home without losses of money Notes etc.

I understand Bill [?] & Penn [?] have written you. In meal or malt your faithfull prudent deportment must do you good. Be not afraid to ask & insist on a satisfactory compensation from Mr. D who is nominally somebody but really nobody as the Banks hold the leading strings, as Mr. C, you cannot expect any thing from head or heart either. He has dwindled to nothing, all the Anecdotes of his Career are unfavorable. You now are in truth looked to & depended on alone. I pray God help & keep you.

Affectionately, JS

Finally, one more note followed, from another relative:

Dear George

I have just heard of the wonderful escape and preservation you have had from the steam boat. I cannot express to you my gratitude and thankfulness, to Almighty God for this great preservation. May you be always sensible of it and may you be always greatful and thankful for all his goodness and mercy unto you. I hope you will [write?] to me soon. I remain your ever affectionate Aunt Elizabeth Taylor

17. vi. FRANCES REBECCA STRAWBRIDGE was born in Philadelphia on 14 December 1816[221] and died in Boiling Spring, Albemarle County, Virginia, on 30 January 1886.[222] She married, on 27 September 1866, CEPHAS GRIER CHILDS,[223] who was born in Plumstead, Bucks County, Pennsylvania, on 8 September 1793, and died in Philadelphia on 7 July 1871.[224]

18. vii. THOMAS STRAWBRIDGE was born in Philadelphia on 20 December 1818 and died in Philadelphia on 11 September 1840.[225]

19. viii. JULIA ELIZABETH STRAWBRIDGE was born in Philadelphia on 20 December 1818 and died in Philadelphia on 9 September 1887.[226] She married, in Philadelphia on 20 April 1843,[227] SAMUEL W. BORDEN, who was born in New Jersey in 1817 and died in Philadelphia on 17 April 1857, son of Josiah Borden and Mary Robbins.[228]

---

221   U.S. Presbyterian Church Records, 1701-1970, online database at ancestry.com, citing Presbyterian Historical Society, Philadelphia, *Register of Baptisms and Marriages etc 1744–1833*; Accession Number: V MI46 P533r v.2; original record is page from baptisms register of Second Presbyterian Church, Philadelphia, showing Frances Rebecca Strawbridge, child of John and Frances Strawbridge, was born on 14 December 1816 and baptized on 23 January 1819.

222   Philadelphia, Death Certificates Index, 1803–1915, online database at ancestry.com, citing Death Records housed at Philadelphia City Archives; record shows Mrs. Frances R. Childs died on 30 January 1886 in Boiling Springs [sic], Albemarle County, Virginia, buried in Laurel Hill Cemetery. Online image at findagrave.com/memorial/19421888, photo of gravestone shows Frances Strawbridge, Wife of Cephas G. Childs, 14 December 1816–30 January 1886.

223   War of 1812 Pension and Bounty Land Warrant Application Files, documenting the period 1812–ca. 1900, NARA Roll RG15–1812PB–Bx0690, available online at fold3.com; original record shows Cephas Grier Childs married Frances R. Strawbridge on 27 September 1866 in Philadelphia.

224   "Childs, C.G.", online article at https://digital.librarycompany.org/islandora/object/digitool%3A78982. Philadelphia, Death Certificates Index, 1803–1915, online database at ancestry.com, citing Death Records housed at Philadelphia City Archives; record shows Cephas Grier Childs, born about 1793 in Plumbstead [sic], Bucks County, died 7 July 1871 in Philadelphia, buried in Laurel Hill Cemetery.

225   U.S. Presbyterian Church Records, 1701-1970, online database at ancestry.com, citing Presbyterian Historical Society, Philadelphia, *Register of Baptisms and Marriages etc 1744–1833*; Accession Number: V MI46 P533r v.2; original record is page from baptisms register of Second Presbyterian Church, Philadelphia, showing Thomas Strawbridge was born on 20 December 1818 and baptized on 23 January 1819. Philadelphia, Death Certificates Index, 1803–1915, online database at ancestry.com, citing Death Records housed at Philadelphia City Archives, FHL film no. 1976401; record shows Thomas Strawbridge, born about 1819, died on 12 September 1840 at Philadelphia. Online image at findagrave.com/memorial/40745852, photo of gravestone shows Thomas Strawbridge, died 11 September 1840, aged 21 years 8 months.

226   U.S. Presbyterian Church Records, 1701-1970, online database at ancestry.com, citing Presbyterian Historical Society, Philadelphia, *Register of Baptisms and Marriages etc 1744–1833*; Accession Number: V MI46 P533r v.2; original record is page from baptisms register of Second Presbyterian Church, Philadelphia, showing Julia Elizabeth Strawbridge was born on 20 December 1818 and baptized on 23 January 1819 (along with her twin, Thomas). Philadelphia, Death Certificates Index, 1803–1915, online database at ancestry.com, citing Death Records housed at Philadelphia City Archives; record shows Julia E. Borden, born about 1819, died on 9 September 1887 at Philadelphia, burial 12 September in Laurel Hill Cemetery. Death notice, *The Philadelphia Inquirer*, 12 September 1887, p. 5, reporting her death on 9 September; her late residence is listed as 4309 Spruce Street; she was wife of the late Samuel Borden.

227   Keith, *Provincial Councillors* 214.

228   1850 U.S. Federal Census, Spring Garden Ward 2, Philadelphia, Roll M432_818, Page 368, shows Samuel Borden, dry goods merchant, age 34, born in New Jersey, with Julia E. Borden, age 32, and others. Philadelphia, Death Certificates Index, 1803–1915, online database at ancestry.com, citing Death Records housed at Philadelphia City Archives; record shows Samuel Bordon [sic], born about 1817, died in Philadelphia on 17 April 1857, age 40. Online image at findagrave.com/memorial/73327324, photo of gravestone at Laurel Hill Cemetery shows Samuel Borden, 1817–1857.

Figure 52. Julia Elizabeth Borden

20. ix. ELIZABETH JANE STRAWBRIDGE was born, probably in Philadelphia, on 29 January 1821, and died in Virginia on 4 February 1886.[229] She married, on 11 March 1845,[230] JOHN WYCKOFF GIBBS, who was born in Philadelphia on 28 March 1820 and died in Philadelphia on 18 May 1878,[231] son of Josiah Willard Gibbs and Hannah Vanarsdall.

21. x. JAMES VANDEKEMP STRAWBRIDGE was born, probably in Philadelphia, on 9 December 1823, and died, probably in Philadelphia, on 2 January 1836.[232]

229   1850 U.S. Federal Census, Spring Garden Ward 2, Philadelphia, Roll M432_818, Page 394A, showing John W. Gibbs, cloth merchant, age 30, with Elizabeth J. Gibbs, age 29, and others. Keith, *Provincial Councillors* 215. Death notice, *The Philadelphia Inquirer*, 9 February 1886, p. 5, reporting death of Elizabeth Gibbs on 4 February at her residence in Boiling Springs, near Warren, Albemarle County, Virginia.

230   Keith, *Provincial Councillors* 215.

231   Information online at findagrave.com/memorial/105654575, giving birth and death dates for John W. Gibbs, stating he is buried in St. Thomas Episcopal Church cemetery, Whitemarsh, Montgomery County, Pennsylvania. Philadelphia, Death Certificates Index, 1803–1915, online database at ancestry.com, citing Death Records housed at Philadelphia City Archives, FHL film number 2030525; record shows John W. Gibbs, born about 1820 in Philadelphia, died in Philadelphia on 20 May 1878. Death notice, *The Philadelphia Inquirer*, 20 May 1878, p. 5, reporting death of John W. Gibbs on 18 May at his residence in Chestnut Hill in 59th year of his age.

232   Online image at findagrave.com/memorial/40745852, photo of gravestone of John and Frances Strawbridge also shows James V., died 2 January 1836, aged 12. Pennsylvania and New Jersey, Church and Town Records, 1669–2013, online database at ancestry.com, citing Historical Society of Pennsylvania, Philadelphia, Historic Pennsylvania Church and Town Records, Reel 848; record shows page of funeral notes for Laurel Hill Cemetery, saying James V., aged 12 years, who died 2 January 1836, son of John Strawbridge, was moved, along with his mother, Frances, from burial ground of 2d Presbyterian Church at Arch Street, to a single grave at Laurel Hill, 15 March 1837. Nivin, *Evans, Nivin and Allied Families* 60 gives dates of 9 December 1823–2 January 1836.

The Fourth Generation

16. GEORGE⁴ STRAWBRIDGE (*John³, John², John¹*) was born in Philadelphia on 18 November 1814[233] and died in Philadelphia on 28 September 1862.[234] He married, in Philadelphia on 23 June 1842,[235] JANE VAN SISE WEST, who was born in Philadelphia on 12 September 1820 and died in Philadelphia on 13 July 1894, daughter of Joseph H. West and Ann Van Sise.[236]

Figure 53. Left: George Strawbridge; Right: Ann Van Sise West, his Mother-in-Law

Children of George⁴ Strawbridge and Jane Van Sise West Strawbridge:

---

233   U.S. Presbyterian Church Records, 1701–1970, online database at ancestry.com, citing Presbyterian Historical Society, Philadelphia, *Register of Baptisms and Marriages etc 1744–1833*; Accession Number: V Ml46 P533r v.2; original record is page from baptisms register of Second Presbyterian Church, Philadelphia, showing George Strawbridge, son of John and Frances Strawbridge, was born on 18 November 1814 and baptized on 11 May 1816. 1860 U.S. Federal Census, District 1, Ward 22, Philadelphia, Roll M653_1173, Page 248, shows George Strawbridge, age 45, merchant, with Jane V., age 35, and others.

234   Philadelphia, Death Certificates Index, 1803–1915, online database at ancestry.com, citing Death Records housed at Philadelphia City Archives, FHL film number 1003691; record shows George Strawbridge, born about 1814, died in Philadelphia on 26 September 1862. Pennsylvania and New Jersey, Church and Town Records, 1669–2013, online database at ancestry.com, citing Historical Society of Pennsylvania, Philadelphia, Historic Pennsylvania Church and Town Records, Reel 196; record shows page of burial register of St. Luke's Church, with burial of George Strawbridge on 2 October 1862.

235   Pennsylvania and New Jersey, Church and Town Records, 1669–2013, online database at ancestry.com, citing Historical Society of Pennsylvania, Philadelphia, Historic Pennsylvania Church and Town Records, Reel 1078; record shows page of marriages register of Grace Church Episcopal Chapel in Philadelphia, with marriage of George Strawbridge and Jane V. West of Philadelphia on 23 June 1842.

236   U.S. Passport Applications, 1795–1925, online database at ancestry.com, citing NARA, Washington, D.C., Roll 226, 1 Sep 1878–31 Dec 1878; application by Jane V. Strawbridge on 3 October 1878 says she was born in Philadelphia on 12 September 1820 and is now 58 years of age. Philadelphia, Death Certificates Index, 1803–1915, online database at ancestry.com, citing Death Records housed at Philadelphia City Archives, FHL film number 1011822; record shows Jane B. [sic] Strawbridge, born about 1820, died in Philadelphia on 14 July 1894, age 74. Death notice, *The Philadelphia Inquirer*, 17 July 1894, reporting death of Jane V. Strawbridge on 13 July.

22.   i. JOHN[5] STRAWBRIDGE was born in Philadelphia in about 1843[237] and died in Philadelphia on 23 April 1873.[238]

+ 23.   ii. GEORGE STRAWBRIDGE was born in Philadelphia on 18 October 1844 and died in Philadelphia on 28 June 1914.

24.   iii. ANNIE WEST STRAWBRIDGE was born in Philadelphia on 13 February 1847[239] and died in Philadelphia on 26 January 1925.[240] She never married, but she was quite involved in the lives of her family members, and was a favorite with the children in the family.

Figure 54. Annie West Strawbridge

237   1850 U.S. Federal Census, Spring Garden Ward 1, Philadelphia, Roll M432_818, Page 360A, shows household of George and Jane Strawbridge with John, age 7, and others. 1860 U.S. Federal Census, District 1, Ward 22, Philadelphia, Roll M653_1173, Page 248, shows household of George and Jane Strawbridge with John, age 17, and others. 1870 U.S. Federal Census, District 72, Ward 22, Philadelphia, Roll M593_1408, Page 95B, shows John Strawbridge, age 26, listed as farmer, living with Jane as only other member of household.

238   Philadelphia, Death Certificates Index, 1803–1915, online database at ancestry.com, citing Death Records housed at Philadelphia City Archives, FHL film number 2021793; record shows John Straubridge [sic], born about 1843, died in Philadelphia on 23 April 1873. Pennsylvania and New Jersey, Church and Town Records, 1669–2013, online database at ancestry.com, citing Historical Society of Pennsylvania, Philadelphia, Historic Pennsylvania Church and Town Records, Reel 196; record shows page of burials register of St. Luke's Church, with burial of John Strawbridge on 28 April 1873, date of death 23 April, burial in St. Luke's churchyard, cause of death not listed. Death notice, *The Philadelphia Inquirer*, 26 April 1873, p. 4, reporting death of John Strawbridge, son of the late George Strawbridge, on 23 April.

239   U.S. Passport Applications, 1795–1925, online database at ancestry.com, citing NARA, Washington, D.C., Roll 684, 16 Jun 1905–25 Jun 1905; application by Annie West Strawbridge on 19 June 1905 says she was born in Philadelphia on 13 February 1847. 1850 U.S. Federal Census, Spring Garden Ward 1, Philadelphia, Roll M432_818, Page 360A, shows household of George and Jane Strawbridge with Annie, age 3, and others.

240   Pennsylvania, Death Certificates, 1906–1966, online database at ancestry.com, citing Pennsylvania Historic and Museum Commission, Death Certificates, 1906–1965, certificate number range 3001–6000; certificate no. 3155 shows Annie West Strawbridge, born in Pennsylvania, age 77 years, single, father George Strawbridge, mother Jane V. West, died 26 January 1925, burial 28 January 1925 at St. Luke's Church.

The Fifth Generation

23. GEORGE[5] STRAWBRIDGE (*George*[4], *John*[3], *John*[2], *John*[1]) was born in Philadelphia on 18 October 1844 and died in Philadelphia on 28 June 1914.[241] He married, in Philadelphia on 5 June 1873,[242] ALICE WELSH, who was born in Philadelphia on 24 July 1848 and died in Camden, Knox County, Maine, on 29 July 1925, daughter of John Welsh and Mary Lowber.[243]

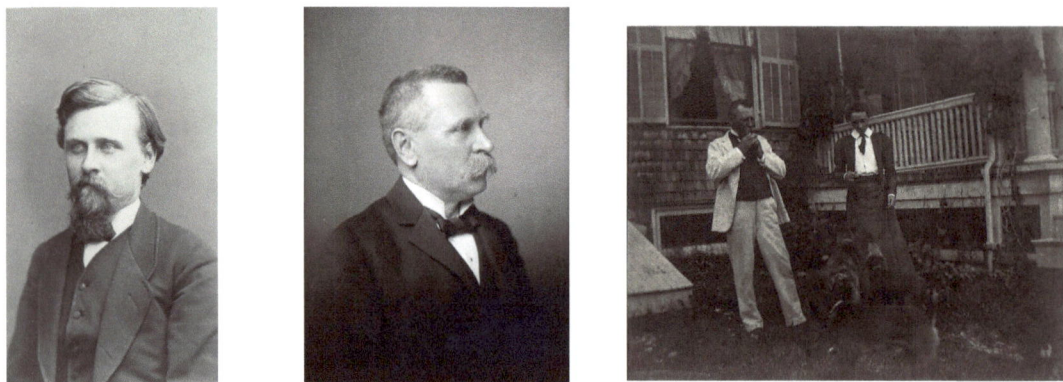

Figure 55. George Strawbridge. Right: With his Daughter, Anne West Strawbridge, Early 1900s

After George Strawbridge died in 1914, a professional medical association of which he was a member paid tribute to him in a detailed summary of his career:

> By the death, on June 28, 1914, of Dr. George Strawbridge, the American Ophthalmological Society has lost one of its early and most distinguished members, and the Wills Eye Hospital has been deprived of an Emeritus Surgeon who, in his day, was one of the most brilliant of the active surgical staff that helped to establish the world-wide reputation of that institution during the early seventies and the decade following.

> Dr. Strawbridge was born in Philadelphia on October 18, 1844. He was the son of George Strawbridge and Jane B. West. He acquired his preliminary education at the Germantown Academy, Philadelphia, and was graduated from the University of Pennsylvania in 1863 with the degree of Bachelor of Arts.

---

241   Pennsylvania, Death Certificates, 1906–1966, online database at ancestry.com, citing Pennsylvania Historic and Museum Commission, Death Certificates, 1906–1965, certificate number range 64481–67800; certificate no. 65095 shows George Strawbridge, born in Pennsylvania on 18 October 1844, age 70 years, married, father George Strawbridge, mother Jane A. [sic] West, died in Philadelphia on 28 June 1914, burial 30 June 1914 at St. Thomas churchyard. Certificate signed by Joseph Sailer, M.D.

242   Wedding announcement, *The Philadelphia Inquirer*, 6 June 1873, p. 5, reporting wedding at St. Peter's Church on 5 June.

243   1850 U.S. Federal Census, Roxborough, Philadelphia, Roll M432_820, Page 262A, shows household of John Welsh, with Alice, age 2, and others. Online image at findagrave.com/memorial/105706760, photo of gravestone shows Alice Welsh Strawbridge, 24 July 1848–29 July 1925. Death notice, *The Philadelphia Inquirer*, 1 August 1925, p. 9, reports death of Alice Welsh Strawbridge, widow of Dr. George Strawbridge, in Camden, Maine, on 29 July.

In 1866 he graduated from the Medical Department of the same institution, and was made a Doctor of Medicine. He was then elected a Resident Physician to the Episcopal Hospital, where he remained for one year. He was one of the first of a small coterie of American physicians to go abroad for the avowed study of ophthalmology, which at that time was just beginning to be differentiated as a special field of medicine, and was being developed in the great hospitals of Europe. He also planned to include otology in his field of study.

Having made up his mind to go abroad, he naturally explained his plans to his preceptor, Professor Joseph Carson, who promptly retorted, "A fool and his money are soon parted." In relating this incident he naively added, "With this encouragement I sailed for Europe the next day." He went abroad in May, 1867, and spent three years in study under the brilliant masters of that time. In Vienna he associated himself with Arlt, Jaeger, and Stellwag, and was thus enabled to observe many of the interesting cases which they afterward placed on record. He was especially fortunate in being able to study, at first hand, many of the ophthalmoscopic pictures which have been immortalized by Jaeger in his "Atlas." He studied for some time with von Graefe in Berlin, and often related to his friends the interesting experiences which he enjoyed while there. Later he took a course with Donders and Snellen in Utrecht, and with Helmholtz in Heidelberg. He also spent several months with Bowman and Critchett in London. He was thus imbibing his knowledge at the very fountain-head of modern ophthalmology.

He returned home in 1870, and at once associated himself with the Philadelphia Dispensary, establishing an eye dispensary on Seventh Street, which attracted 700 new patients during the first year. During the same year he was appointed Clinical Lecturer on Diseases of the Eye and Ear at the University of Pennsylvania, which position he held until the division of those specialties into two chairs, in 1873, when he was made Clinical Professor of Diseases of the Ear, the professorship of Diseases of the Eye falling to the lot of his associate, Dr. William F. Norris. He held that position from that time until he resigned in 1890. He was always a forceful and interesting lecturer, and every student in his ward class carried away with him some impressive and practical point in otology.

In 1872 he was elected Ophthalmic Surgeon to the Presbyterian Hospital, which position he held until he retired in 1913, when he was made Consulting Ophthalmic Surgeon.

In 1873 there was a reorganization of the Surgical Staff of the Wills Eye Hospital and he was elected an Attending Surgeon. Owing to failing health he resigned this position in 1890, and was elected Emeritus Surgeon. This brilliant service, therefore, covered a period of seventeen years.

Notwithstanding his many other professional activities he founded, in 1875, the Pennsylvania Eye and Ear Infirmary, which he maintained as a private free dispensary at Thirteenth and Chestnut Streets, Philadelphia, up to the day of his death. He carried this work on much as he had seen it done under similar auspices during his sojourn in Europe.

Dr. Strawbridge was married on June 5, 1873, to Miss Alice Welsh, daughter of John Welsh, a well-known banker of his time. She proved to be a good helpmeet, and bore him four children, two sons and two daughters, all of whom survive him.

Dr. Strawbridge had one of the largest and most lucrative practices of his day. He was a good business man, and accumulated a large fortune through judicious real-estate investments. He was always kind to those around him, and most generous in all his dealings. Although he sometimes spoke cynically of human affairs as he saw them, he was a true optimist at heart. He was always genial and often jovial. He invariably inspired hope and confidence in his patients. He never lost his temper or even became rattled under the most trying circumstances. If the patient lost his nerve under the stress of operation, he never gave sharp orders. He simply patted him on the back and encouraged him by saying "you are doing fine," when he was possibly squeezing out the lens and part of the vitreous. It is related that in the pre-cocain days, when eyes were trained for operation by daily tapping the cornea, he allowed an excited patient to jump out of bed and run around the ward with the knife sticking through the eye, after which performance he calmly asked the patient to lie down again if he had finished with his exercise.

The writer was House Surgeon at the Wills Eye Hospital for two years, from 1887 to 1889, during which period cocaine was first being used and antiseptic surgery was in its infancy; he can, therefore, speak of many things from the standpoint of personal association. Dr. Strawbridge was a great operator, a good clinician, and an expert in the use of the ophthalmoscope. He was not wholly a therapeutic nihilist, but he had no great faith in drugs, although pleased and happy when his therapy proved successful. He seldom used mydriatics, and even persisted in " non-mydriatic refraction,"as he called it. His expert use of the ophthalmoscope enabled him to secure a fairly accurate refraction. In a series of cases requiring refraction that he referred to the writer he wagered that both methods would give the same result. It was demonstrated, however, that the so-called "Philadelphia Method" of refraction, under a cycloplegic, was the more accurate. He accepted antisepsis reluctantly, but finally became an enthusiastic supporter of the method. He first used mercury biniodid in Panas' solution, but this produced in several cases a persistent and puzzling quiet iritis, which led him to adopt other measures of a less irritating character.

He was essentially a surgeon, and performed more operations than his colleagues, chiefly because of his personal following and because of the large number of cases referred to him by his private infirmary. He was a rapid and accurate operator. His record in cataract operations was excellent. He made the high corneal incision, which was a counterpart of the more modern so-called Smith-Indian incision. He used the narrow Graefe knife, and turned the blade-edge sharply forward at a right angle with the cornea as he emerged, thus leaving a square-edged shoulder. As his points of puncture and counterpuncture were outside the limbus, there was more gaping of the wound than was customary with the incisions of other operators. Occasionally a small fragment of tissue which had lodged in the angle of the wound, or a rubbing together of the square-shouldered wound edges, would cause delayed union. When such a condition became evident to him, he removed all the bandages and allowed the lid friction to stimulate the healing process. This was usually followed by prompt union of the wound.

His plastic work was excellent and usually successful. During the final year of the writer's service as House Surgeon all his efforts and ingenuity were directed toward devising a successful method for making an artificial pupil. He tried von Graefe's knife A la Cheselden, he used Hays' knife in many ways, he performed de Wecker's iritoectomy, he devised a pair of very small scissors for puncturing and incising the iritic membrane, and finally, in 1888, he began the use of von Hippel's trephine, which he employed to transplant the cornea, to trephine the occluding iritic membrane, and to trephine the sclera. He usually covered the scleral wound by replacing the conjunctiva, in order that it might become a transparent visual membrane. He also performed scleral trephining for glaucoma, and in one instance for retinal detachment, some of which cases were reported by him. He should, therefore, receive credit for being a pioneer in this work, even though his technic was not the same as at present employed. The Transactions of this Society contain the most of his papers describing his various operations. His many attempts to secure a successful artificial pupil inspired the writer to similar efforts, and led to the discovery of the V-shaped iridotomy, which at a later date was practised on one of the same patients.

During the latter part of the year 1899 Dr. Strawbridge noticed that his judgment as to the counterpuncture in cataract incisions was not good, since his knife sometimes emerged too far in the sclera. A consultation with Drs. Heyl, Harlan, and Knapp revealed a doubtful elanosarcoma of the choroid in the left eye. An early enucleation was performed. A microscopic examination by Dr. Knapp showed a fibrous character that led to a favorable prognosis of non-malignancy. This prognosis proved correct, as he lived for a quarter of a century, but he never quite recovered his normal poise, and his activities were considerably limited for many years. He resigned from the Wills Eye Hospital, from the University of Pennsylvania, and from most of his medical societies in 1890. He continued to serve his own dispensary and to maintain a limited office practice up to the time of his death.

He finally succumbed to what appeared to be a recurrence of the original trouble, which brought hepatic involvement and metastases to other parts of the body. His hopeful mental attitude persisted to the very end of a life that was active, honorable, and most useful to mankind.[244]

Dr. Strawbridge also was an astute real estate investor. He acquired a property at the northeast corner of Thirteenth and Chestnut Streets in Philadelphia for $36,200 in the 1870s, which was eventually sold by his widow, Alice, in 1925 for $600,000, an enormous amount of money at that time.[245]

Dr. Strawbridge's wife, Alice Welsh Strawbridge, was the daughter of John Welsh, considered one of the most influential Philadelphians of his time. In 1876, he served as one of the leaders of the Centennial Commission, which produced the ambitious Centennial Exhibition in Philadelphia. In that capacity, he was able to extend invitations to members of his family, including one that was designated for his grandchild, Mary Lowber Strawbridge, who was born in 1875. The invitation to the one-year-old was never used, and remains with the family papers.

---

244   S. Lewis Ziegler, M.D., "Dr. George Strawbridge," *Transactions of the American Ophthalmological Society, 1915*, page 4, available online at https://www.ncbi.nlm.nih.gov/pmc/articles/PMC1318015/?page=1.

245   "Chestnut Street Landmark Conveyed to New Ownership," *The Philadelphia Inquirer*, 1 February 1925, p. 72.

Figure 56. Invitation for Mary Lower Strawbridge to the Philadelphia Centennial, 1876

In 1877, John Welsh was appointed by President Hayes to be the Minister to England, a position he held for two years.

As the daughter of a prominent and wealthy family, Alice led a privileged existence. In 1870, she traveled through Europe on a grand tour, visiting England, Italy, Egypt, Constantinople, and Berlin over a period of more than one year. She wrote home in a series of letters, including the following letter from Berlin, written to her half-sister Anna Maria Welsh, who was eighteen years older than Alice and was married to James Somers Smith; they had a son also named Somers. The letter also mentions Alice's sister, Ellen, who was traveling with her, and who later married Thomas Stokes:

Berlin

June 4th, 1871

My dear Sister Anna,

Many thanks for your letter of May 20th. It reached me on the first of this month, only eleven days, which we thought quite fast travelling. I was quite frightened, at first, about Somers. Father was out (his letter came at the same time as mine) and I could not tell what had been the matter, but when I heard I was somewhat relieved, thinking that he must be very much better or you would not have allowed him to go out. I hope he is all right now.

The other day your Pa and I went to visit Harmon's sister, taking an interpreter with us for she cannot talk English. She seemed very much pleased to see us. Her two sons, aged twenty-two and sixteen, have not yet returned from France. They have been in a great many battles, but fortunately have never been wounded. They have both received the Iron Cross, given for bravery, and the youngest has been made an officer. Tell Harmon about them. His sister has been ill but has quite recovered.

Ellen suffered very much for a day and night during the past week from toothache. Upon going to the dentist, she found the pain was caused by an abscess as the root of an old tooth which had been of no use to her for several years. The dentist advised her to have it taken out, which she did, but it was a very painful operation for it broke in half and altogether was very difficult to extract. But she is very glad to have had it done as she has had scarcely any pain since.

I suppose you are probably all out of town by this time. I hope you have not such a disagreeable day as we are having today for it would be dreary indeed for your first country Sunday. All day the rain has been falling fast and it is cold and windy. Indeed we have had miserable weather ever since we have been here. I think we shall probably leave here on Tuesday for Hamburg. I was much surprised to hear that Miss M. Coles is coming abroad so soon again, particularly as last Spring Mrs. Coles seemed so anxious to get home, and so tired of travelling.

Yesterday I saw the Emperor, and indeed had a capital view of him, he was standing at one of the windows of his palace, laughing and talking to someone in the room with him. He is remarkably fine looking, handsomer, I think, than any photograph that I have seen of him.

The days are very long here, last night when we were coming home at about ten o'clock it was still so light that the stars could not be seen, although the sky was quite clear. And it is light in the morning before three. I must now say Good Night. With much love to Mr. Smith, kisses to Somers and love to everyone at home, including Big Jon.

Your loving sister

A.W.

Please remember me to the men and girls.[246]

---

246   Letter from Alice Welsh to Anna Maria Smith, 4 June 1871, original in possession of the author; text available online at https://strawbridgefamily.net/letter-from-alice-welsh-to-her-sister-anna-maria-welsh-from-berlin-june-4-1871/.

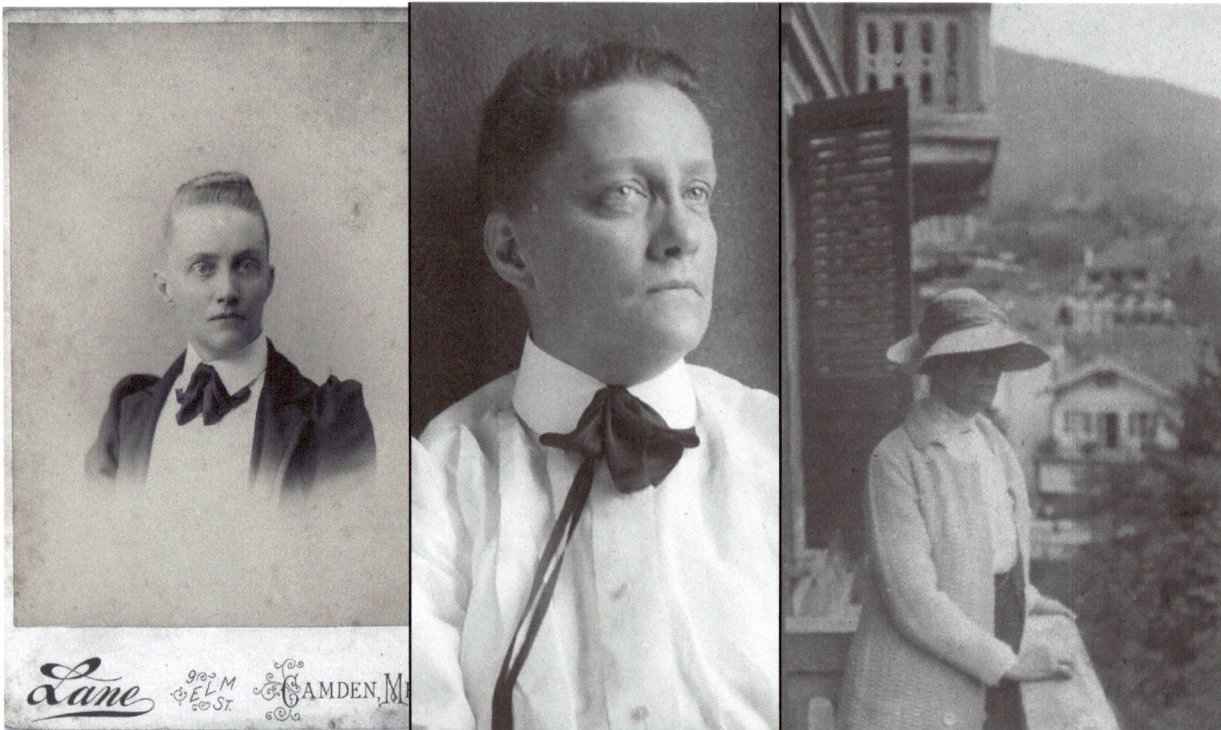

Figure 57. Alice Welsh Strawbridge. Right: In Zermatt, Switzerland

Alice married George Strawbridge in 1873 and settled down to a quiet life, managing the household and raising their four children who survived infancy. At first, they lived in downtown Philadelphia. In later years, they moved to an area closer to Mt. Airy and Chestnut Hill that in those days was considered the "country." Alice's father, John Welsh, had a property called Spring Bank on Wissahickon Avenue. Across from Spring Bank he had houses built for three of his children: Alice Welsh Strawbridge, Elizabeth "Lilly" Welsh Young, and Ellen Welsh Stokes. The house built for the Strawbridges was called "The Wilderness."[247] Alice's granddaughter, Mary Lowber (Sailer) (White) Knight, wrote about her impressions on visiting the house as a child:

> My grandmother and grandfather lived in a large Swiss Chalet style house. It had been built for her by her father on about 12 acres of land. On either side of this house he had built comparable houses for her two sisters, Aunt Lilly Young and Aunt Ellen Stokes. But these houses were of different styles. My grandmother's house had a large hallway that went from the front door straight back to a door that opened onto the orchard, not the back door. On one side of this hall were three parlors. The front parlor was for my Aunt's exclusive use. The other 2 parlors were for anyone who wanted a private place to sit or visit. Then there was the large billiard room, so called because of the billiard table in the center. But this was where the family sat. It had a large fireplace and various comfortable chairs and sofas. It had a great many windows, by one of which my grandmother had a knitting machine. I remember watching her knit socks on it during World War I. She also had her desk in a corner by a window. There were bookcases full of books that lined the back wall and above this there was a very large model of a sailing ship. All in all it was a room to enjoy and have companionship, though my aunt more often sat in her private parlor. Upstairs were the bedrooms, but the bathrooms, two that were side by side, were in a separate wing. To reach them you had to go down a short

---

247   Jackie Strawbridge Hunsicker, *The Strawbridge Family in America* (Privately printed 2013) 151.

flight of stairs, and beyond them was a large room known as the sewing room. Here Jane Weir held sway. She sewed continually and made all the clothes my Grandmother and Aunt wore—always the same pattern and, of course, always white or black. This was also a playroom for us when we were children.[248]

Figure 58. "The Wilderness," Home of George and Alice Welsh Strawbridge

After using The Wilderness as a summer home for a few years, the Strawbridges gave up their house in the city and moved to The Wilderness permanently. In 1891, they purchased a property in Camden, Maine, called Rockledge, on the ocean, for use in the summertime.[249]

Figure 59. "Rockledge," Summer Home of George Strawbridge and Family in Camden, Maine

Mary L. Knight described her grandparents' property in Maine this way:

[W]hen my mother was about 16 her parents decided to have a summer place in Camden, Maine. In those days you could pick and choose your spot. Mountain or shore properties were available in choice and varied locations. My grandfather chose a beach front property about three miles out of town on the Belfast road. It had a beautiful beach, though more stones than sand, and a series of large rocks going out to sea making a

---

248   Mary L. Knight, "The Wilderness," recollections of childhood and family history, date unknown, available online at https://strawbridgefamily.net/documents/the-wilderness-philadelphia-home-of-george-and-alice-welsh-strawbridge/.

249   Jackie Strawbridge Hunsicker, *The Strawbridge Family in America* 147.

small breakwater for the beach. Along these rocks was built a wooden walk, at the end of which were steps leading down to a dock, and beyond that was moored their sailing boat "The Sunbeam." On the property they built a large house, the outside of which was grey wooden shingles. It had a huge veranda that went across the front and one side of the house. From the time I was about three or four until I was around eight years old our whole family went there while my grandparents and Aunt travelled to Europe, generally staying several weeks in Switzerland.[250]

Figure 60. Postcard Sent by Alice Strawbridge from Zermatt to her Grandson Joseph Sailer Jr. in 1910

Margaret Strawbridge, the wife of Alice's son, Welsh, described Alice as she knew her at the Wilderness:

> She was a little austere. And I remember they didn't have air conditioning in those days, and she used to have an enormous piece of ice, maybe fifty or a hundred pound block of ice, and a fan right by it, in her bedroom. And I can see that great block of ice and the fan. . . . She entertained Welsh and me every Sunday night.[251]

After George Strawbridge died in 1914, Alice moved to an address on Crefeld Street in Chestnut Hill, where she lived until her death in 1925.[252]

Children of George[5] Strawbridge and Alice (Welsh) Strawbridge:

25. i. JOHN[6] STRAWBRIDGE was born in Philadelphia on 7 May 1874 and died there on 18 February 1963.[253] He married, first, in Philadelphia on 26 April 1902,[254] LOUISA STELWAGON WEIGHTMAN, who was born on 1 September 1880 and died on 24 March 1921, daughter of William Weightman and Sabine d'Invilliers.[255] He

250   Mary L. Knight, "The Wilderness."

251   "Now It Is All In Memory and I Shall Treasure It Always": Recollections of Margaret Marshall Strawbridge, transcript of interviews with Margaret Strawbridge (The Friends of Graeme Park, 1989) 107; copy in possession of the author.

252   Jackie Strawbridge Hunsicker, *The Strawbridge Family in America* 155.

253   Pennsylvania, WWI Veterans Service and Compensation Files, 1917–1919, 1934–1948, online database at ancestry.com; record for John Strawbridge shows he was born in Philadelphia on 7 May 1874 and served overseas from 19 May 1918 to 4 April 1919. 1900 U.S. Federal Census, District 505, Ward 22, Philadelphia, FHL film no. 1241464, showing John Strawbridge, age 26, in household of George Strawbridge. Pennsylvania, Death Certificates, 1906–1966, online database at ancestry.com, citing Pennsylvania Historic and Museum Commission, Death Certificates, 1906–1965, certificate number range 19951–22800; certificate no. 20857 showing John Strawbridge, born in Pennsylvania on 7 May 1874, age 88 years, father George Strawbridge, mother Alice Welsh, died in Philadelphia on 18 February 1963, burial 20 February 1963 at St. Thomas churchyard.

254   Pennsylvania Marriages, 1852–1968, online database at ancestry.com, shows marriage in Philadelphia on 26 April 1902. "Notable Wedding at Holy Trinity," *The Philadelphia Inquirer*, 27 April 1902, p. 6, reporting wedding on 26 April.

255   U.S. Passport Applications, 1795–1925, online database at ancestry.com, citing NARA, Washington, D.C., Roll 1043, certificates 161376–161749, 20 Jan 1920–21 Jan 1920; application by Louisa W. Strawbridge on 14 January 1920 says she was born in Philadelphia on 1 September 1880; sworn statement in application by her mother gives same birth date. Pennsylvania, Death Certificates, 1906–1966, online database at ancestry.com, citing Pennsylvania Historic and Museum Commission, Death Certificates, 1906–1965, certificate

married, second, in Laverock, Montgomery County, Pennsylvania, on 1 February 1950,[256] MARY TROTTER WHITE STARR, who was born in Philadelphia on 27 August 1876 and died in Laverock on 3 May 1952,[257] daughter of Floyd Hall White and Emily Trotter, and widow of Isaac Tatnall Starr.

John attended the University of Pennsylvania for one year, then transferred to Trinity College in Hartford, Connecticut, where he was a star athlete in baseball and football, with some boxing on the side. He graduated in 1895, having taken one course taught by Samuel Clemens (Mark Twain). In 1897, he worked as a stockbroker for a while, then joined the army, where he served as a captain. He participated in three wars or skirmishes: The Spanish-American War of 1898, the Pancho Villa Expedition in Mexico in 1916, and World War I, in which John was stationed in France.

Figure 61. Left: John Strawbridge at Right with Welsh, Mary, Anne West, and Alice, About 1885; Center: Louisa Stelwagon Weightman Strawbridge with Daughter Louise, About 1906; Right: John Strawbridge

After the war, he resumed his career as a stockbroker. He loved horseback riding and was an enthusiastic participant in the Whitemarsh Hunt Club for many years.[258]

---

number range 23501–26500; certificate no. 23678 shows Louisa W. Strawbridge, born in Pennsylvania on 1 September 1881, died in Springfield, Montgomery County, Pennsylvania, on 24 March 1921, burial at St. Thomas Churchyard on 24 March, parents John Weightman and Sabine Danvalliers.

256   "Along the Social Way," *The Philadelphia Inquirer*, 2 February 1950, p. 16, announcing marriage of Mrs. Isaac Tatnall Starr and Mr. John Strawbridge at Laverock, Pennsylvania, on 1 February.

257   Pennsylvania and New Jersey, Church and Town Records, 1669–2013, online database at ancestry.com, citing Historical Society of Pennsylvania, Philadelphia, Historic Pennsylvania Church and Town Records, Reel 1018; record shows page of baptisms register of Holy Trinity Episcopal Church, Philadelphia, with baptism on 20 May 1897 of Mary Trotter White, born on 27 August 1876. Pennsylvania, Death Certificates, 1906–1966, online database at ancestry.com, citing Pennsylvania Historic and Museum Commission, Death Certificates, 1906–1965, certificate number range 42901–45450; certificate no. 45059 shows Mary Trotter White Strawbridge, born in Philadelphia on 27 August 1876, died in Laverock, Pennsylvania, on 3 May 1952, daughter of Floyd H. White and Emily Trotter.

258   This account of the life of John Strawbridge is taken from Jackie Strawbridge Hunsicker, *The Strawbridge Family in America* 173–190.

26. ii. MARY LOWBER STRAWBRIDGE was born in Philadelphia on 4 July 1875 and died in Philadelphia on 26 July, 1963.[259] She married, at Philadelphia on 5 February, 1901,[260] JOSEPH SAILER.[261]

Mary was the second child of her parents, and the only girl to survive infancy until her sister Anne West, who was not born until 1883, eight years after Mary. In this largely male environment, Mary learned to be independent and self-reliant. Her daughter Mary described the situation years later in her recollections:

> My mother was 8 years old when Aunt was born, so she was the only girl for eight years [except for the sister who died young], in an almost private world of 2 brothers and 6 boy cousins. One of her bitterest childhood memories is the fact all these male relatives scorned her as a girl. The phrase "She's only a girl" rankled with her all her life. She had no coquettish ways or feminine wiles but tried to meet these boys on equal ground. Her hair was cut like a boy's and she tried her best to play with them as an equal. To no avail—"She's only a girl" put her at the bottom of that particular totem pole. She greatly admired her oldest brother, Jack, but he in no way returned this admiration. He, when he became a young man, was a great beau and much admired by the ladies. But my mother was never his type at all. At parties he was outgoing and jovial, quite the life of any gathering of friends but the opposite in his boyhood family.[262]

At another point, Mary's daughter said, "My mother had beautiful golden hair and very blue eyes. She was forthright and determined with none of the wistful haunting quality of my aunt [Anne West Strawbridge]."[263]

259   1880 U.S. Federal Census, District 149, Philadelphia, Roll 1171, Page 470A, showing George W. Strawbridge, age 35, Alice, age 30, Mary, age 4, and others; 1900 U.S. Federal Census, Ward 22, Philadelphia, shows George Strawbridge, age 55, Alice, age 51, Mary, age 24, and others; Pennsylvania, Death Certificates, 1906–1966, online database at ancestry.com, citing Pennsylvania Historic and Museum Commission, Pennsylvania Death Certificates, 1906–1965, certificate number range 71551–74400, certificate no. 74374 shows death of Mary Lowber Sailer in Philadelphia on 26 July 1963, shows her birth date as 4 July 1875.

260   Pennsylvania and New Jersey, Church and Town Records, 1669–2013, online database at ancestry.com, citing Historical Society of Pennsylvania, Philadelphia, Historic Pennsylvania Church and Town Records, Reel 196; register of St. Luke's Episcopal Church, shows wedding of Joseph Sailer, M.D., and Mary Lowber Strawbridge on 5 February 1901.

261   The facts for Dr. Joseph Sailer and the children of his marriage to Mary Lowber Strawbridge were set forth in Part A of this book, in connection with the history of the Sailers.

262   Mary L. Knight, "The Wilderness."

263   Mary L. Knight, "The Wilderness."

Figure 62. Mary Lowber Strawbridge (Later Sailer). Left: 1893 with Sister Anne West on the Left; Center: 1901

Although Mary was home-schooled until she was twelve years old, when she finally attended school she enjoyed it greatly.[264] She later went on to study chemistry at Drexel University in Philadelphia, and then taught for a while.[265]

Then she met Joseph Sailer, eight years her senior, who was already practicing medicine. In one letter that she wrote to him from her home at "The Wilderness," she said:

> My dear Dr. Sailer
>
> Did you get my telegram in time? I was in hopes that I would feel better and so held off sending it until the last moment. I am so much disappointed when I think of the good time I am going to miss.
>
> Won't you come out on Wednesday and take supper, for the next best thing to going would be to hear all about it, and if you can get off in time to make the 4.25 train from Broad St. Station "Headlight" [a horse that pulled her carriage?] and I will meet you at Upsal [train station], and we can take a drive.
>
> Hoping to see you on Wednesday,
>
> I remain,
>
> Very Sincerely Yours,
>
> Mary L. Strawbridge.

Friday, June 8th [year not stated, but must have been 1900 according to calendar and context][266]

A couple of months later, she wrote:

---

264   Mary L. Knight, "The Wilderness."
265   Interview of Mary L. Knight by Alexander S. White, 1992.
266   Letter from Mary L. Strawbridge to Joseph Sailer, 8 June 1900, original in possession of the author.

My dear Dr. Sailer

Such delicious candy never before has been tasted, of that I am quite sure, no matter what Headlight says about his sugar being even better, I know it is not possible, we both send a <u>great</u> many thanks. I was so glad that he was not here when his letter came yesterday, for if he had been perhaps he would not have let me open it up for him, he does have such silly ideas about liking to open his own letters, especially if it is one that I want to see very much myself.

I quite agreed with Headlight that this particular letter was a very nice one, excepting what wire pullers you both seem to be about some mysterious something. I remember now that you were both in Washington at the same time, two and two makes four I'm afraid, although I can almost hear you say, "I'd like to hear you prove it," but they <u>do</u> you know.

It was horrid of you both not to ask me to be a middle aged friend too I think, would not three be just as good a number as two. I don't see why not.

There aren't any girls with red hats up here, they don't know what's pretty, do they? Just wait until next Winter.

Very Sincerely,

Mary L. Strawbridge

Aug. 19th [1900][267]

After she and Joseph were married on February 5, 1901, Mary sent a letter to her mother, dated February 11, from the Windsor Hotel in Montreal, Canada. In the letter, she uses the nicknames Nan for her sister, Anne West, and Mamie for herself; Van Sciver was a furniture dealer. An image of the first page is shown below, followed by the full text of the letter.

267   Letter from Mary L. Strawbridge to Joseph Sailer, 19 August 1900, original in possession of the author.

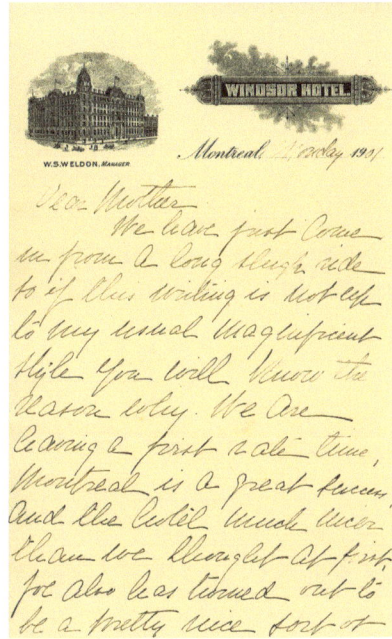

Figure 63. First Page of Letter from Mary L. Sailer to her Mother, Alice Welsh Strawbridge, 11 February 1901

Dear Mother

We have just come in from a long sleigh ride so if this writing is not up to my usual magnificent style you will know the reason why. We are having a first rate time, Montreal is a great success and the hotel much nicer than we thought at first. Joe also has turned out to be a pretty nice sort of a boy although I know that is pretty hard to believe.

Every thing is on runners here, even the fire engines and baby coaches. Ever since leaving Albany we have seen nothing but sleighs. We have been sleighing every day, I have never seen more perfect roads for it and we are so bundled up with rugs that I haven't felt cold at all. We expect to leave here for New York to-morrow morning, and reach home either on Wednesday or Thursday. What news from the house?

Your letters told all the news we wanted most to hear, thank you very much Mother dear. A letter from Mr. Sailer a day or two ago said that he did not think the house would be ready for a week, in that case on account of Joe's office, we think we will go right to 330 So. 16th St first, so ask Nan if she will either write or telephone to Van Sciver to send the brass bed there with the springs etc. And telephone to Miss O'Brian that it is coming and that Dr. Sailer would like his own bed taken down. (She can stand it in his front second story room), and the new one put up in its place.)

A very nice letter from Marjorie to-day telling all about the wedding etc. I have never seen a more terrible throwing of rice in all my life before, have you?

      With love to Father and lots to you.

          Lovingly,   Mamie[268]

---

268   Letter from Mary L. Sailer to Alice Strawbridge, 11 February 1901, original in possession of the author.

During most of their married lives, the Sailers lived at 1718 Spruce Street in downtown Philadelphia. They had a large house with four floors, and several servants. The children often played in Rittenhouse Square, and interacted with the organ grinder and his monkey.[269]

In 1918 and 1919, during and immediately after World War I, Dr. Sailer served in the U.S. Army Medical Corps, part of the time in France. During this period, Mary and Joseph corresponded regularly. Following is one sample out of the many she wrote. She numbered it in the upper left corner; perhaps she used the number so her husband would know what sequence the letters were in, and whether he had missed one:

Jan. 23rd [1919]

No 52

Dearest Boy,

Fine news: yesterday the cablegram came saying "orders received, stop writing." Isn't it splendid that the orders for home leave really came, even if you do not get off for some time. Now that we know you are really coming it is not half so hard to wait.

Dr. Packhard arrived yesterday. Dr. Carnett has not started yet, at least Mrs. Carnett had a cablegram from him almost four days ago saying he hoped to get off soon, it must have been at least six weeks since he first received his orders for leave, so in case yours might be the same way I am going to continue writing for a few days more.

Dr. Riesman and Dr. De Corta have been in bed for the last day or two with the grippe, I hope it will be all over by the time you get back again.

Miss Biddle is thrilled by the idea of your return, poor soul she is so kind hearted always doing things for people and still so queer.

Alice's dinner takes place to-morrow night, there are to be thirty-two children, fifteen girls and seventeen boys, she is looking forward to it with much pleasure.

I have just had the back roof painted, the fourth story roof was beginning to leak and Oteeper said they all needed paint, so I let them go ahead.

Dick expects to go west to see about his oil lands next week. I have not done any thing about investing in it yet.

All well with love from every one and oceans from me, I can hardly wait.

Mary[270]

In 1934, she wrote to her daughter, Mary White, in Philadelphia, from Camden, Maine, in an undated letter, sent in an envelope postmarked 20 June 1934:

Dear Mary,

The great wedding took place yesterday. The bride was dressed in Miss Robbins' wedding dress. It had a very long train and beautiful old lace, and she looked quite lovely.

269   Letter from Priscilla Kelley to David Churchman, approximately 1993; copy in possession of the author.
270   Letter from Mary L. Sailer to Major Joseph Sailer, 23 January 1919, original in possession of the author.

She is very small and dark and the groom tall & fair. The Navy officers stayed with Parker & Andy and could just about manage to get through the wedding, excepting the Commander (Walker) who was best man, & seemed to keep in very good condition.

I saw them all having their photographs taken, on the lawn of the Robbins cottage. They certainly had a time when they crossed swords to let the bride & groom walk under, as they had done in the church.

Wally McNeel, Ike, the two older Lees and Andy and also Joe Janney are here now, so that Betty has plenty of company. She is going to the McNeels to lunch to-day.

The Richards cottage is rented to the Taylors (Johnnie etc), for the summer. I guess Mrs. Richards thinks it safer for Arthur.

Mr. Forman is not going to be here, did I tell you. Ike thinks he is going to England for a month or two as he told Ike his nerves are in bad shape.

The Bibbs cottage is for sale; the old father & mother are still in it, but it seems as though the Bibbs' income is cut, and he does not want so much expense.

I visited Mr. & Mrs. Merrill yesterday. Mr. does not look nearly as well as he did last summer, he seemed quite sick to me but Mrs. Merrill seemed cheerful, and said he was trying some new vaccine, and they thought he could soon be much better.

Mrs. Kelley did not say much when we saw her, excepting that the baby is lovely, much more like Stillman than the older one, and that she had decided to remain in her own cottage for the summer, and not join Stillman and Kay in the big house, as she thought it would make it much too complicated.

Andy says that Bee Borland's husband, Mr. Plimpton, is one of the outstanding men of intelligence in the country, but he could not tell us what his line of work was or where he lives.

I will write a line to the Lloyds and inquire for Cousin William. How did Dr. Fife think little Bill was progressing. Does he still have to wear his band, and did you arrange about having Dr. Jones? (I guess not.)

Nancy Hooper & her fiancé are now in Camden. The fiancé only speaks French. They are to be married up here in August. Lots of love to you & Wilson.

Mother[271]

In 1945, Mary accepted an invitation to travel to the Sperry Gyroscope Company to watch the motion picture produced by that company in remembrance of the mission undertaken by her late son, Joseph Jr., in transporting the company's secret bomb sight to England in 1940. She wrote about the trip to Sperry in a letter to her daughter, Mary:

Feb. 20th [1945]

Dear Mary,

---

271   Letter from Mary L. Sailer to Mary L. White, postmarked 20 June 1934, original in possession of the author. Some of the names may be transcribed incorrectly because of difficulty in reading the handwriting.

On Saturday Alice & Lawrence, Betty, John and I went to Great Neck, Long Island and saw the moving pictures that Fred Vose took on the trip to England. Bill Harcum arranged every thing for us, and we could not have had a more cordial reception. We were met at the station by the Sperry Co.'s car, and driven to the new plant, about a mile and a half from the station. It is an enormous building, and very streamlined. Joe would have loved working there. They have given up the old building, in Brooklyn, where Joe did work.

Bill Harcum and three others, all friends of Joe's, met us when we came in. A man named Paul Cullen, the executive for the president of Sperry, seemed to be in charge. He took us to the camera room, and their camera man ran the movie for us. Fred Vose talked all through the picture, and explained what every thing was. He sounded just as he did when we met him at that dinner in New York. The picture was all in color, and parts were very beautiful. Joe came in it quite often. A great many of the pictures were of the air ports in England, the big bombers going off on their missions over Germany, and one or two of London, and the wreckage caused by the German bombs. The pictures of Joe were very characteristic, especially in one when he is smiling, and bowing to a man to whom he has just been introduced.

I kept wishing all the time you, and Priscilla Deaver, could have been there. After the movie was over, it took about forty minutes, Bill Harcum had them run a cut from the long film. It had not the sound attachment, he had just put together duplicate parts, from the film, that had Joe in them. Bill then gave me the duplicate cuts to take home with me, so that you will see them some day.

Afterwards they gave us lunch at the guest house. Mr. Lea, the one that arranged for Joe to come to Sperry, he is the vice president of the company, was our host, and they had every thing beautifully arranged. Mr. Lea, Paul Cullen, Bill Harcum and our family, eight in all. I thought their attention to us was a great tribute to Joe. Every thing was done in the most perfect way possible. It would have pleased Joe very much, I know.

John Nutter received your letter yesterday. I talked to Mrs. Goursley to-day. She said he was delighted to get it, and very much pleased with the part about Welfie, and how much he missed John. Also he was greatly interested in hearing that the furniture had arrived.

Lt. Moredock drove over, with B. Pelfield, and took Vickie home. Bobby told Betty that they were going to take Viking down, last Thursday, to see John. I asked Mrs. Goursley if they had been there, but she did not think they had. John still feels very weak, and has not been off the second floor.

The walking is very slippery still. Yesterday Aunt Daisy and I went over to see Aunt Nancy, in the train. Hildreth met us at the station. Aunt Nancy looked about the same. She has had some trouble with her eye lately, but seemed bright and interested in every thing.

Neither Lawrence's one female, or Laynor, took any prize at the show in New York. Never send Welfie and Bill on a trip together. Jennie, Grace, Hattie, and I all find Welfie perfection unless Bill is there. They do not do well together.

Priscilla L. is having a nice time at N. Conway.

Lots of love to all of you.

Mother[272]

Figure 64. Visit to Sperry Headquarters, February 1945. From Left: Sperry Executive, Elizabeth Churchman, Lawrence Litchfield, Alice Litchfield, John Sailer, Mary Lowber Sailer, Sperry Executive

Mary continued going to Camden every summer through 1962. She had varying groups of her children and grandchildren staying with her in the "Forecastle," the Sailer "cottage" at the top of Chestnut Street. She often sat on a ledge down at the beach, overlooking the grandchildren at play in the mornings, and sat in her lake cottage overlooking water play at the lake in the afternoons.

Figure 65. Mary Lowber Sailer, Probably in the 1950s, at Left, with her Friend, Mrs. Huntington, at the Beach, Camden, Maine

For most of those years, she drove her prized Moon automobile, which she and her husband purchased in 1923 for use in Camden. She continued to drive it there in the summers until she was in her eighties, even though it had no power steering or brakes and could be difficult to start and maneuver.

---

272   Letter from Mary L. Sailer to Mary L. White, 20 February 1945, original in possession of the author. The reference to Fred Vose's talking meant that Vose's voice was on the film's sound track; Vose was killed in a plane crash in 1942.

Figure 66. Moon Automobile Driven by Mary Lowber Sailer for Many Years in Camden, Maine

After she died, the car went to her grandson Joseph Sailer Churchman, who, over a period of years, painstakingly restored it to its original condition.

In her long period of widowhood, Mary was occupied with family matters as well as community activities, including playing bridge and breeding prize-winning miniature schnauzers and serving at one time as president of the Schnauzer Club of America.[273]

After her husband died at the end of 1928, Mary moved to a house on Crefeld Street in Chestnut Hill. Then, in the late 1940s, she moved to a house on Lynnebrook Lane, still in Chestnut Hill, adjoining the property of her daughter, Mary White, and her family. She remained there until her death in July 1963.

27.   iii. GEORGE STRAWBRIDGE was born in Philadelphia in April 1877 and died on 8 May 1877.[274]

28.   iv. WELSH STRAWBRIDGE was born in Philadelphia on 24 June 1878 and died in Hatboro, Pennsylvania, on 21 June 1969.[275] He married, first, in Dresden, Saxony, Germany, on 16 August 1916,[276] IRENE ANNA THOMASS, who was born in Haynau, Germany, on 9 August 1891 and died in Lake Saranac, New York,

---

273   "Mrs. J. Sailer, Dog Breeder," obituary, *The Philadelphia Inquirer*, 27 July 1963, p. 11.

274   Philadelphia, Death Certificates Index, 1803–1915, online database at ancestry.com, citing Death Records housed at Philadelphia City Archives, FHL film number 1003703; record shows George Strawbridge, born in Philadelphia about 1877, died in Philadelphia on 8 May 1877 at age three weeks, to be buried at St. Luke's Church. Pennsylvania and New Jersey, Church and Town Records, 1669–2013, online database at ancestry.com, citing Historical Society of Pennsylvania, Philadelphia, Historic Pennsylvania Church and Town Records, Reel 196; record shows page of burials register of St. Luke's Church, with burial of George, infant son of George and Alice Strawbridge, died on 8 May 1877 of jaundice, buried on 9 May at St. Luke's Churchyard.

275   1880 U.S. Federal Census, District 149, Philadelphia, Roll 1171, Page 470A, shows Welsh Strawbridge, age 2, in household of George Strawbridge. U.S., World War II Draft Registration Cards, 1942, online database at ancestry.com, citing NARA at St. Louis, Missouri, World War II draft cards for the State of Pennsylvania, Records of the Selective Service System, 1926–1975, Record Group 147, Series number M1951; original record shows Welsh Strawbridge, farmer, living in Horsham, Pennsylvania, was born in Philadelphia on 24 June 1878. "W. Strawbridge Dies, Prominent Horse Breeder," *The Philadelphia Inquirer*, 22 June 1969, p. 16, reporting death of Welsh Strawbridge at his home in Hatboro on 21 June.

276   U.S. Consular Reports of Marriages, 1910–1949, online database at ancestry.com, citing NARA, Washington, D.C., Marriage Reports in State Department Decimal Files, 1910–1949, Record Group 59, General Records of the Department of State, 1763–2002, Series ARC ID: 2555709, Series MLR Number: A1; original record is Certificate of Marriage of Welsh Strawbridge and Irene A. Thomass at the American Church of St. John in Dresden, Saxony, Germany, on 16 August 1916, signed by Consul-General of the United States.

on 31 December 1916.[277] He married, second, in Philadelphia on 4 January 1922,[278] MARGARET ELY MARSHALL, who was born in Philadelphia on 24 April 1898 and died in Horsham, Pennsylvania, on 16 November 1996, daughter of George Morley Marshall and Harriet Putnam Ely.[279]

Figure 67. Welsh Strawbridge. Left: Age 16; Center: Age 35; Right: With his Wife, Margaret

Welsh lived with his parents at their homes in downtown Philadelphia and then "The Wilderness." When he was about seventeen years old, he contracted diphtheria, which left him slightly deaf. His deafness increased in later years, and he left college after one year because of his increasing problem with hearing.[280]

---

277   U.S. Passport Applications, 1795–1925, online database at ancestry.com, citing NARA, Washington, D.C., Roll 262, certificates 5501–5900, 13 August 1915–19 August 1915; application by Irene A. Thomass on 15 January 1915 states she was born in Haynau, Silesia, Kingdom of Prussia, on 9 August 1891, and that she was a U.S. citizen temporarily residing in Dresden, intending to return to the United States. Pennsylvania and New Jersey, Church and Town Records, 1669–2013, online database at ancestry.com, citing Historical Society of Pennsylvania, Philadelphia, Historic Pennsylvania Church and Town Records; record shows information card of undertakers for funeral of Irene Anna Strawbridge, who died on 31 December 1916 at Saranac Lake, New York, burial date 2 January 1917 at St. Thomas' Churchyard, Whitemarsh, Pennsylvania; cause of death tuberculosis; place of birth Germany.

278   "Miss Marshall Bride of Mr. Welsh Strawbridge," *Evening Public Ledger* (Philadelphia), 4 January 1922, p. 9, reporting wedding earlier that day at Calvary Presbyterian Church, 21st and Walnut Streets.

279   Florida, Passenger Lists, 1898–1963, online database at ancestry.com, citing NARA, Washington, D.C., U.S. Citizen Passenger Lists of Vessels Arriving at Miami, Florida, NAI number 2774842, Records of the Immigration and Naturalization Service, 1787–2004; passenger list for S.S. Seneca, arriving from Havana, Cuba, at Miami, Florida, on 9 February 1927, shows Margaret Strawbridge, born in Philadelphia on 24 April, 1898. 1910 U.S. Federal Census, District 47, Solebury, Bucks County, Pennsylvania, Roll T624_1320, Page 19A, shows household of George Marshall, physician, with Margaret, age 12, born in Pennsylvania, and others. U.S., Social Security Death Index, 1935–2014, online database at ancestry.com, shows death of Margaret M. Strawbridge of Horsham, Montgomery County, Pennsylvania, on 16 November 1996; date of birth 24 April 1898.

280   "Now It Is All In Memory and I Shall Treasure It Always": Recollections of Margaret Marshall Strawbridge, transcript of interviews with Margaret Strawbridge (The Friends of Graeme Park, 1989) 45–46; copy in possession of the author.

Figure 68. Welsh Strawbridge, Left, and Anne West Strawbridge, Riding as Children

Welsh Strawbridge grew up around horses and was considered to be an excellent steeplechase rider in his youth. For a number of years, he served as master of the hounds at the Whitemarsh Valley Hunt Club, of which he was a founder. He was employed for a while as a stockbroker in Philadelphia, but eventually moved to an historic farm in Hatboro, Pennsylvania, "Graeme Park," which included a house built in the 1720s by the colonial governor of Pennsylvania, Sir William Keith. Welsh and his wife, Margaret, occupied another historic house dating back to about 1810. In 1957, the Strawbridges gave to the state the governor's house, which was maintained as a state park, but they continued to occupy their historic farmhouse.

In 1916, Welsh embarked on a journey that must have been quite challenging, and had a sad ending. According to one account, he had met a young German woman on a ship when he was traveling to Europe, and became engaged to her.[281] In 1916, in the middle of World War I (though before the United States had entered the war), Welsh applied for a passport to travel to Germany. The application was accompanied by a letter from a court official stating that Mr. Strawbridge "advises me that the object of his visit to Germany is to bring home an American lady to whom he is engaged to be married, and who is now sojourning in Germany."[282]

---

281   Mary L. Knight, "The Wilderness."
282   U.S. Passport Applications, 1795–1925, online database at ancestry.com, citing NARA, Washington, D.C., Roll 312, certificates 27501–28100, 24 Jun 1916–01 July 1916; application by Welsh Strawbridge on 29 June 1916.

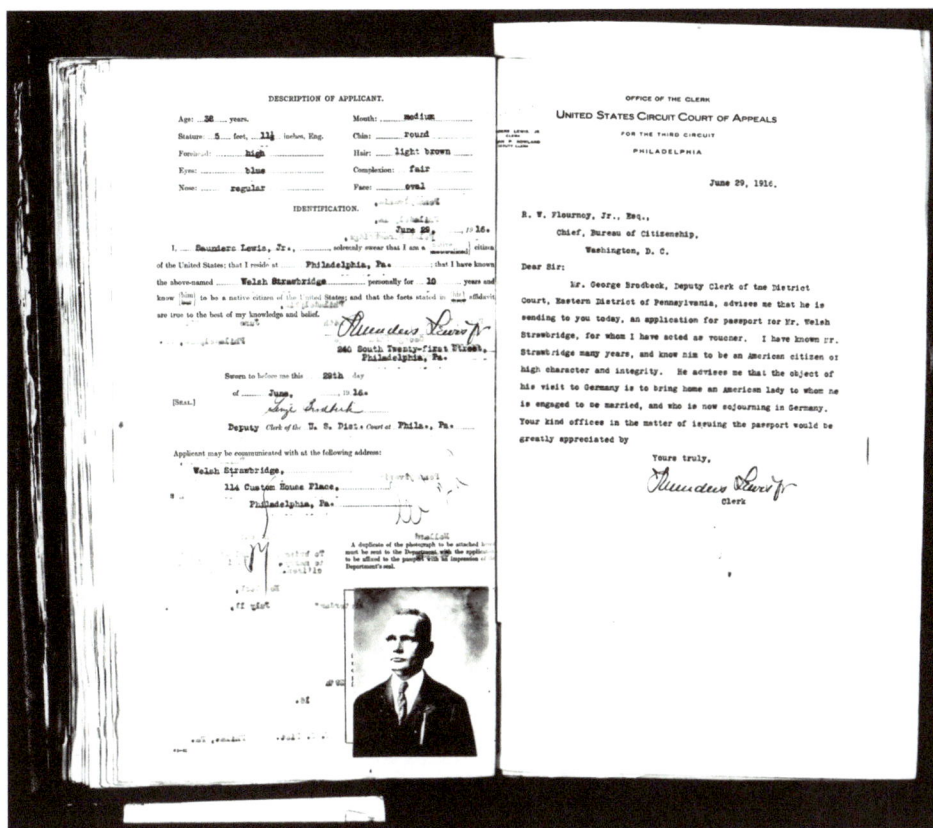

Figure 69. Part of Welsh Strawbridge Passport Application, 1916

On 16 August 1916, at an American church in Germany, Welsh married Irene Thomass, whose passport photograph is shown below.[283]

Figure 70. Irene Thomass Shortly Before Her Marriage to Welsh Strawbridge

They traveled back to the United States, apparently going directly to Lake Saranac, New York, the site of a well-known treatment facility for tuberculosis. Sadly, Irene succumbed to the disease on 31 December 1916.

283   U.S. Passport Applications, 1795–1925, online database at ancestry.com, citing NARA, Washington, D.C., Roll 262, certificates 5501–5900, 13 Aug 1915–19 Aug 1915; application by Irene Thomass on 15 June 1915.

In 1922, Welsh married Margaret Ely Marshall, with whom he had a long and stable life at their historic farm in Hatboro. Margaret always displayed her sunny disposition, which was somewhat of a contrast to the taciturn demeanor of Welsh, who was extremely deaf in his later years and difficult to communicate with.[284] Margaret was heavily involved in activities of her church, and was remembered as "one of the Philadelphia Orchestra's most loyal followers," attending virtually all of the orchestra's Friday afternoon performances.[285]

Figure 71. Margaret Strawbridge. Left, with Great-Nephew Welsh White in 1983; Center, at Her Farm; Right, at her Farm with Niece Mary L. Knight

29.   v. ALICE WELSH STRAWBRIDGE was born in Philadelphia about 1881 and died in Philadelphia on 7 August 1882.[286]

30.   vi. ANNE WEST STRAWBRIDGE was born in Philadelphia on 20 March 1883 and died in Abington, Montgomery County, Pennsylvania, on 9 September 1941.[287]

As the youngest of the four Strawbridge children who survived past early childhood, Anne West was given special treatment. This special treatment also was a consequence in part of the fact that another child, Alice Welsh Strawbridge, died at the age of about one year old just six months before Anne West was born. According to her niece, Mary Sailer:

> Consequently her parents, and especially her mother left, as they thought, no stone
> unturned to guard her against harm or sickness, or in fact any kind of distress. If she
> was taken outside even in fairly pleasant weather, she was bundled up in layers of

---

284   Personal knowledge of author.

285   "Margaret M. Strawbridge, Orchestra Lover, 98," *The Philadelphia Inquirer*, 19 Nov. 1996, p. B6.

286   Philadelphia, Death Certificates Index, 1803–1915, online database at ancestry.com, citing Death Records housed at Philadelphia City Archives, FHL film number 2057283; record shows Alice Strawbridge, age ten months, died in Philadelphia on 7 August 1882.

287   1900 U.S. Federal Census, District 505, Ward 22, Philadelphia, FHL film no. 1241464, showing Anne W. Strawbridge, age 17, in household of George Strawbridge. 1920 U.S. Federal Census, District 620, Ward 22, Philadelphia, Roll T625_1624, Page 4B, shows Ann Strawbridge, age 36, in household of Alice Strawbridge. U.S. Passport Applications, 1795–1925, online database at ancestry. com, citing NARA, Washington, D.C., Roll 684, 16 Jun 1905–25 Jan 1905; application by Anne West Strawbridge on 19 June 1905 says she was born in Philadelphia on 20 March 1883. Pennsylvania, Death Certificates, 1906–1966, online database at ancestry.com, citing Pennsylvania Historic and Museum Commission, Death Certificates, 1906–1965, certificate number range 83501–86350; certificate no. 83922 shows Anne West Strawbridge, born in Philadelphia in March 1883, died in Abington, Montgomery County, Pennsylvania, on 9 September 1941, daughter of George Strawbridge and Alice Welsh; certificate signed by Dr. J. M. Deaver. Online image at findagrave.com/ memorial/107182101, photo of gravestone shows Anne W. Strawbridge, 20 March 1883–9 September 1941.

blankets to guard against any possibility of catching cold. It is a wonder that in her baby helplessness she did not suffer heat prostration. But she was always pale and delicate.

When she was old enough to understand, she was repeatedly warned against touching anything that might be crawling with germs. She was a timid, shy and apprehensive child. The idea that germs were everywhere, to be invisibly lurking on anything she might touch was terrifying. When she grew older the fear of germs obsessed her, and she did many strange things to avoid them. She could not touch a newspaper, so John Nutter, the man who did all the work on her place—and made for her beautiful vegetable and flower gardens—held the newspaper up to the window and my aunt could in this way read it, telling him when to turn the pages. However, all of that happened after her parents died and she lived in her own small house alone with 2 maids. When my aunt was a child (her name was Anne West but we always called her Aunt) she was sent to school, but she did not like it. It was all strange, and she was very shy, so she was allowed to stay at home. My mother had not gone to school till she was twelve, but being a very different temperament from my aunt, and of course being more strictly brought up, she had loved it. But my aunt never went more than a day or two, so it is hard to say if she would have ever liked it or not. Certainly she could not have reigned the supreme princess as she did in her home.[288]

Figure 72. Anne West Strawbridge. At Right, with her Autogiro

Later in life, Anne West indulged in a variety of pastimes involving art, literature, and adventure:

As my aunt grew older she showed a marked talent as an artist, so she took the great step of enrolling as a pupil in The [Pennsylvania] Academy of [the] Fine Arts. This was a new and fascinating life for her. She made close friendships—Miss Alice Stoddard, who later became a well-known artist and portrait painter, was one, and Miss Beatrice Fenton, who became a most famous sculptress, was another. There was Elizabeth Bishop, considered at that time the most talented of all, but she had very little money and consequently often not enough to eat, so she died very young, probably due to malnutrition. But Miss Stoddard (who later married Mr. Pearson, also an artist) and

Miss Fenton were lifelong friends. To further her art career, my aunt was given her own studio built on the place. This was a brick building the size of one very large room, the north side having windows that covered the top half of the wall. It was kept locked! I remember our great desire was to see inside—Never! But occasionally we would boldly climb high enough to look through the bottom of those high windows. Not that we ever saw much, but the excitement was intense.

My aunt was also a marvelous storyteller. When we were young, my sister Alice and I often went to "Granny's" for the week-end. We came and went by train, getting off at Upsal Station and walking a good bit of the way across "Wilderness" fields. In the back field were my Aunt's ponies. These were quite small ponies and she bred them. I don't know exactly why except that she loved horses and ponies, and anything she wanted she could have if her mother could give it to her. So she had a field of ponies and made numerous paintings of various ones and just enjoyed having them. In the evening after we were in bed she would come up and sitting at the foot of the bed she told us stories. They were wonderful stories about little magic people and exciting situations. Samantha was the little girl in the stories and later my Aunt wrote a book with her as the heroine, but of course, although clever, the stories had lost the appeal of being told while we all sat in that dimly lit room, my aunt perched at the foot of the bed and her questions, "Oh, dear, what could she do?" or "What do you think happened next?" asked in a voice that heightened our suspense. We were totally agog with apprehension and curiosity.

Her niece described further adventures by her intriguing aunt:

From the time I was about three or four until I was around eight years old, our whole family went there while my grandparents and Aunt travelled to Europe, generally staying several weeks in Switzerland, where my Aunt became a renowned mountain climber. In those days few women went in for dangerous sports, but she did—climbing to the top of the Matterhorn with her two guides Gabriel and Joseph, one of the first women to accomplish such a feat.[289] As my Aunt was beautiful with large dark grey eyes and dark brown hair, quite a few young men who were also climbing the mountains in Zermatt paid her attention, though it was stilted and reserved compared to what would be considered attention today. She fell in love with one of them, Mr. Dwight. He never materialized beyond a name, as far as I was concerned. Perhaps he visited her at the "Wilderness." I know she occasionally went to spend a day with him in New York. But it all came to nothing, except that my Aunt now had an unfulfilled love affair in her background, as was all too often the case in those days when women had to be "protected." It was not considered suitable for a lady to stand on her own two feet. Aunt now considered herself the heroine of a "Grand Passion." Mr. Dwight had married a widow when he had seemed on the verge of proposing to Aunt. Why? Perhaps it was just so much easier. He and the widow both lived in New York. She was readily available and maybe, too, his courage deserted him at the thought of living up to such a romantic role as was expected of him.

---

289   It is somewhat of an exaggeration to say that Anne West was "one of the first women" to climb the Matterhorn, a feat that was actually first accomplished in 1871 by Lucy Walker. "First Ladies: The First Women to Climb the Matterhorn," online article at https://www.zermatt.ch/en/Media/Zermatt-inside-stories/focus-women-alpinists. However, Anne West reportedly did reach the mountain's summit in the summer of 1911, according to a society page item in the newspaper. "Jolly Main Line Astir with News Notes Now," *The Philadelphia Inquirer*, 1 October 1911, p. 9.

However, Aunt had several love affairs after Mr. Dwight and oddly enough, even she and Mr. Dwight kept in touch with each other. She phoned him every summer before she went away, and then again when she came back. Once, years later when she was deeply unhappy due to the death of a man she was then very much in love with, he wrote desperate notes proving the power of mental telepathy. Apparently he sensed she was greatly troubled and needed help. He wrote "She has been in my mind continually all day. Pull getting very strong" ... Next, "No sleep. Pull getting from strong to terrific—most since the 'Rock' yet different. It seems now as if I might help her instead of getting help from her. This makes it worse."

There is more. The dates of these notes exactly coincided with the death of Mr. Mitten, who Aunt considered the love of her life, a man who for many reasons she found totally fascinating. He seems to have been equally charmed by her and for several years they had an exciting and exhilarating love affair. Why? Part of the charm lay in the fact they were so totally different in their upbringing, family background and the life each had led. I can't remember why he originally came to visit her, but I do know that on that first visit she told him to put on her galoshes, and sat down and stuck out each foot in turn while he struggled with a task totally new to him. He was intrigued. Miss Strawbridge was a real lady. Perhaps he had been used to less aristocratic women. She fell for him hook, line, and sinker. A dynamic self-made man, successful and powerful in her city of Philadelphia. He consulted her on many of his projects, and often called her late at night. Sometimes Aunt would drive up to visit him at his place in the Poconos. She would go and return the same day but while she was there they had a lovely time together. One day he took her rowing. She offered to row, but he said, "No. My life is too valuable to risk having you at the oars." A few days later he was rowing alone. The boat tipped over, and he was drowned. At the time his affairs at the PRT were under fire. He was being investigated. There was a suspicion he had tipped over the boat on purpose. But my aunt was sure this was not the case. She quoted his remarks about her not rowing to prove it. At his funeral she rode in the carriage with his son and the son's wife. She was mentioned in the papers as the mysterious lady in black.[290]

Aunt was devastated. Never again was she to fall so deeply in love. But Jennie Walker's symbol of the strong fist rising above despair still described her. She now decided to write a book. She also decided to take up flying, and bought herself a helicopter and took lessons at Wings Field. Soon she was enjoying life again. She said she found flying the best possible substitute for climbing, now that she was too old for the mountains, but tragedy gave her flying a bad setback. One day she urged one of the pilots there — they all loved her—to go up in a trial spin. He resisted. She said, "Oh, go ahead," urging him on gaily. At last he did, but for some unexplainable reason he hit some wires and was killed. It was an unreasonable and unexplainable tragedy. Something unexpected had gone wrong.[291]

Anne West's sister-in-law, Margaret Strawbridge, gave her recollections of Anne West in an interview:

---

[290]   Thomas E. Mitten, the president of the Philadelphia Rapid Transit Company, was born in 1864 and died in October 1929. For more information, see https://www.facebook.com/oldimagesofphiladelphia/posts/thomas-e-mitten-was-president-of-the-philadelphia-rapid-transit-company-prt-he-w/1772125682850362/.

[291]   The incident mentioned by Anne West's niece evidently happened in 1935. "Pilot Killed in 'Giro Crash at Hatboro," *The Philadelphia Inquirer*, 11 August 1935, p. 25.

She had her own [autogiro], but she didn't know how to drive an automobile, but she did learn that. And she was also an artist, and painted pictures. And she was very good at painting horses. . . . [S]he'd land [her autogiro] right here at the field [at the Welsh Strawbridge property in Hatboro], and then she came right over here. And I remember, her first time up, she came over and had lunch with us, which was very unusual, because all that family never liked to be invited in unexpectedly to a—you know, they would say, "Oh, no, thank you." They wouldn't think anything on the spur of the moment—you have to have a more formal invitation. But this was unusual, and she was so on the crest that she was willing to sit down and have lunch with us. And I remember it made a great impression on me, that she would do that.[292]

As her niece, Mary, mentioned in her recollections, Anne West Strawbridge had a strong interest in creating stories. This literary impulse resulted in the publication of five works of fiction: *Dawn After Danger*, a novel, published by Coward-McCann in 1934; *The Black Swan*, a novel, published by Coward-Mc Cann in 1935; *Above the Rainbow*, a novel, published by Stackpole Sons in 1938; *Jane's*, a novel, privately printed in 1940, and *Samantha*, an illustrated children's book, published by Dorrance & Company in 1951.

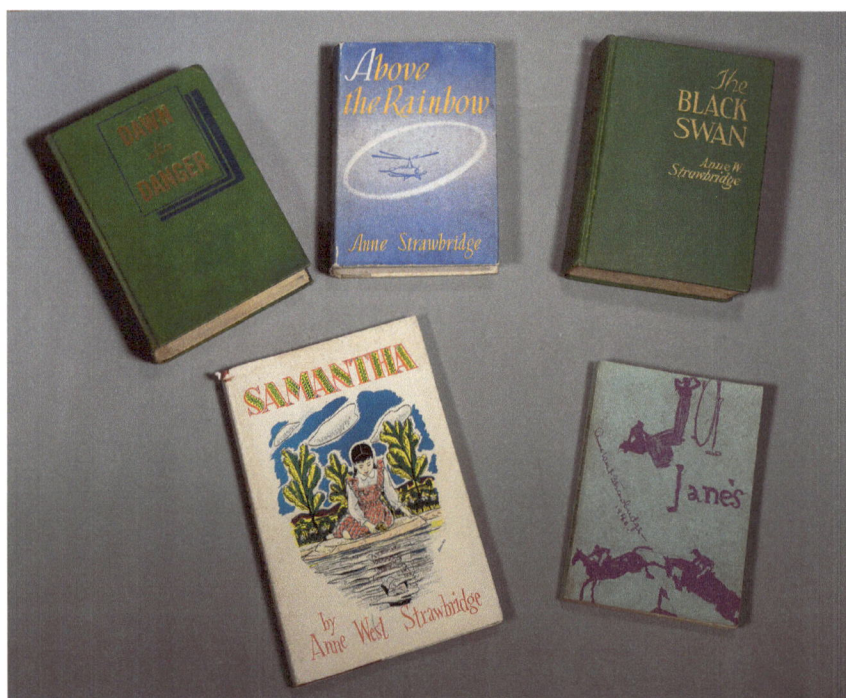

Figure 73. Books by Anne West Strawbridge

These books did not move reviewers to excesses of enthusiasm. Of *The Black Swan*, the reviewer for the Philadelphia Inquirer concluded with the following summary:

As a romance, this novel has many good points. Technically it is well-handled, its characters are extremely personable, its descriptive passages charming, and its progress smooth and direct. But it is entirely unreal. There is little in the story with which to quarrel,—and it leaves us utterly untouched and unmoved.[293]

---

292   "Now It Is All In Memory and I Shall Treasure It Always": Recollections of Margaret Marshall Strawbridge, transcript of interviews with Margaret Strawbridge (The Friends of Graeme Park, 1989) 108; copy in possession of the author.

293   "'The Black Swan,' an Experiment with Romance," *The Philadelphia Inquirer*, 19 October 1935, p. 9.

Above the Rainbow, a novel about the experiences of a woman as aviator and mountain climber, did not fare much better with reviews. Its review, *The New York Times* concluded with this statement:

> The book contains one entertaining bit of folklore, the tale of the little black cat sometimes seen crouching on the bridge, but for the most part it is evidently intended for those who take a very great interest in mountain climbing. Others are likely to find it repetitious, a trifle muddled and somewhat dull.[294]

Samantha undoubtedly found some satisfied readers, but it was an uphill battle to sell the book. A local bookstore owner tactfully explained the situation to Anne West's older sister, Mary Lowber Sailer, who diligently tried to market the books after the author's death in 1941:

June 20, 1949

Dear Mrs. Sailer:

I have read "SAMANTHA" with great pleasure and think that the episodes have a great deal more charm and humor than many books we sell from day to day.

However, I must honestly say that we have tried very hard to sell the book, saying how much we enjoyed it, and so far have had no success. People are so conditioned to the regular type of book that it seems on the whole impossible to overcome this barrier.

I, therefore, would not recommend running off any more copies as I do not think you would sell them. I am very sorry to have to say this as I loved Miss Strawbridge dearly and nothing would give me more fun than selling her book, but I don't seem to be able to do it.

Please forgive my slowness in answering but we felt that we should not only all read and give thought before answering but also try to sell so that as to be fair in every way.

I hope that you have a lovely time this summer. Thank you for the thoroughly pleasant evening I had with you and Mary.

Sincerely yours,

Mary F. Brinley

In September 1941, Anne West, who had been flying her autogiro within the past few weeks, fell ill while looking for a place to store the craft for the winter. She walked to the hospital, where her condition worsened and she died on September 9.[295]

The back cover of her novel *Jane's* featured a portrait drawn by her former art teacher, the prominent portraitist Alice Kent Stoddard, which appears to have captured the beauty and the wistful yearning for romance that was characteristic of Anne West Strawbridge.

---

294   "Mountain Climber: *Above the Rainbow*," *The New York Times*, 13 February 1938, p. 23.
295   "Anne Strawbridge, Authoress, Is Dead," *The Philadelphia Inquirer*, 10 September 1941, p. 6.

Figure 74. Drawing of Anne West Strawbridge by Alice Kent Stoddard

Index